The Child's Secret
of Learning

The Child's Secret of Learning

Gerald van Koeverden

iUniverse, Inc.

New York Lincoln Shanghai

The Child's Secret of Learning

iUniverse books may be ordered through booksellers or by contacting:

iUniverse
2021 Pine Lake Road, Suite 100
Lincoln, NE 68512
www.iuniverse.com
1-800-Authors (1-800-288-4677)

ISBN-13: 978-0-595-34615-8 (pbk)
ISBN-13: 978-0-595-79361-7 (ebk)
ISBN-10: 0-595-34615-4 (pbk)
ISBN-10: 0-595-79361-4 (ebk)

Printed in the United States of America

"But the Emperor has nothing on at all!" cried a little child.
  (Hans Christian Andersen)

That…depends…upon our sense of time; or, if you prefer, upon our sense of eternity; or, if you insist, upon our sense of the present moment. For when we have succeeded in giving ourselves to the present moment we are as near to eternity as we shall ever get. Eternity is not a lot of time; it is no time at all, and so is this moment that passes before we know it has come—except that we do know some moments when they come, and it is these and only these from which we learn.
  (Mark Van Doren)[1]

Contents

C: The Quartet

"Whose speech Truth knows not from her thought."

"…I saw that everything, all paths I had been following…were leading back to a single point—namely, to the mid-point."

"…by dark gropings, by feelings not wholly understood, by catching at hints and fumbling for explanations."

D: Dancing

"…mediating the chasm."

"And the end of all our exploring/Will be to arrive where we started."

E: Science

"For nothing can be sole or whole/That has not been rent."

"How wonderful that we have met with paradox."

"Life is not a problem to be solved."

"If God does not play dice…"

"…we must inevitably see the universe from a centre lying within ourselves."

F: Literature

G: Two Conclusions

Introduction: An Obsession with a Question

Have you ever experienced an obsession with something you could not let go, or maybe that would not let you go? You gradually discovered yourself trapped in the eye of a whirlwind of focus. By the time it fully dawned on you, you just accepted it was your center. There must be a good reason why you were drawn into it at all, and why you were now spending most of your waking hours attending to it. Besides, was life worth living without it?

I suspect this phenomenon is much more common than we are led to believe by the outward appearance of the humdrum of people's lives. People like to keep their obsessions secret to share with only a few close friends. Most of us are not so foolish as to let them "get out" and bore our less intimate friends and neighbors to death. We mask them through the mechanical performance of everyday routine and act like everybody else—the normal everyday folk who might not really exist at all. And in fact to the extent they have no interest in burning with us in our magnificent obsession, they do not exist for us. But it is essential to keep up normal appearances to maintain the complex weave of mutual support necessary for physical survival, even while mesmerized by the fires within.

But more than that, in our constant interactions with the others, we discover essential clues to the puzzle of that in which we are really interested. We pick up one clue here and another there, while not having the faintest idea how they will eventually all fit together. Intuitively we gamble on which one is more important than the other. We ransack our memories for clues that stand out within the massive volume of accumulated experiences over time and combine them in various ways with the new ones, looking for parallels, analogies, and correspondences. Like the facets of a diamond, each clue shines clearest and brightest from only one particular angle. What is the whole shape and energy of this diamond flashing?

Whether our obsession with something lasts ten days, or ten years as mine did, we eventually reach some point in time at which we can no longer afford it, are just sick and tired of the chase, realize the ridiculousness of the idea, or, in the best of results, reach a calm wherein it has merged with the rest of what we know and has become part and parcel of our everyday life.

How Do We Learn?

I became obsessed with the question "How do we learn?" I had gone back to school to learn about learning after twenty years of working at learning in the "real" world, half of it in the West and half in the East, while marrying into a tonal language, an oriental culture, and raising kids. In proud middle age I had entered graduate school to read a hundred books and listen to hundreds of hours of lectures, until I was so confused I could make no sense of any of it. I had discovered many different ways of understanding how we learn, but totally failed to put them together into one whole.

Why even try to put them all together? Why not just choose my "favorite" one, and join into the exhilaration and excitement of the many academic battles fighting for victory for one particular "side"? I had lost all heart in being on this or that side of any argument. I could see the validity of them all, depending on what was assumed and believed. I had become lost in the dead center of the academic storm, of being a confused, no-label nothing. I had no identity of belonging to any school of thought. I had become a nonentity inside the amorphous mass trapped between the clashing and slashing of this extreme and that. What did I believe about learning? Where did I take my stand? After investing a pile of money and two years of life in study I was more confused than when I had started. I was mad!

Rooting for Memories of the Phoenix

In a pique of chagrin, I started writing through memories of my own everyday experiences with learning: driving a car, typing, teaching Jane to read, doing speed math with Anne, understanding scientific concepts with Paul, appreciating poetry, learning basic astronomy, playing bingo, going to the theater, growing apples, and learning a fourth language. I hoped to explicate those examples real to me from my own experiences in concrete images to discover the fulcrum through which I could philosophically reinterpret what all those academic voices were talking and writing about.

It is devilishly difficult to know how we learn. What we all do know is that at one point we become aware of knowing or knowing how to do something that before we did not or could not. For example, in learning a second language there comes a point in time at which we discover we are no longer translating between it and our native language, but when we are thinking directly in the new one. In learning to drive a car, there comes a time when we can do it while daydreaming about something else entirely. We say we are skillful at something when we can do it smoothly without thinking about it, without continually going back and forth between a self-conscious knowledge of it and our action of doing it. In order to become really good at anything, it appears we must forget we are doing it.

How do we jump from not being able to do something into doing it? As adults we often fool ourselves into thinking that if only we can understand something first, we can then do it. But many of us experience the nonsense of this idea while reading the instruction manual in order to play our first video game or set up the VCR to record automatically. We give up and turn to our children to figure it out, which they do very well with very little help from the manual, as though accidentally-on-purpose.[2] But we do learn to type, to drive a car, and to become fluent in a second language. It is as though driven by caring about a subject we are led to inventing questions and discovering answers through our actions. Understanding and skill emerge like the phoenix out of the heat and smoke of our struggles in an organic fusion between our sensory perceptions and emotions, while moving back and forth between questions and answers. We really understand only after we have learned to do it.

We can discover a general pattern in the process of learning. Watch a student seriously committed to learning to type. Mary's whole body squirms and twists every which way as though forcing all her emotional energy into the contortions of her fingers over the keyboard. Some of the time she appears puzzled, as though she cannot determine the best way of getting it. Some of the time she just appears intense as she practices some newly acquired aspect over and over to nail it down. The increase in typing speed is not gradual. It comes in leaps and bounds, plateauing for periods of about a week at a time. In the period immediately after each jump to a higher speed, a great deal of effort must be used to maintain it. The amount of effort required is gradually reduced as the new increment in skill at that speed becomes entrenched, until Mary is ready for the next jump in a do-or-die effort. Each jump is an intuitive leap of which she has no prior knowledge, an accidentally-on-purpose act. Yet, curiously, all successful typing students, regardless of whether they are tutored, travel the same path from the initial pecking style through the same steps until they finally attain a speedy rhythm of accomplished typing.

The Child's Secret

The most incredible learning achievement is language. From not having even the foggiest idea of what language is, every child learns to speak. And every child, though he or she might stumble over different aspects of learning, discovers the same path as every other child in developing her grasp of the fundamentals of language skills. Furthermore, any child just out of diapers and being raised in English, if transplanted into a Chinese, Thai, French, or Spanish setting, learns the second language without any formalized teaching in grammar in several months' time. But for most adults, especially those who already explicitly comprehend the workings of grammar, foreign language learning is a much slower, tedious, and painful struggle requiring years of formalized study to attain only partial fluency.

What is the child's secret? The majority of linguists are so dumbstruck by the enormity of the task of learning one's first language that they have virtually washed their hands of the question and passed it on to the biologists! They assert that it must be innate. Already, geneticists are working on the idea that language originates in the genes, as though humans are programmed with the right genetic "software" at conception and just need time to mature and ripen with age.

Is learning then only the gradual actualization of this software? What about all our other skills like driving a car, writing poetry, or using a computer? How did we learn them? Since the linguists have failed to discover the origin of language in consciousness, it is up to the philosopher to at least ask the right questions before abandoning the idea altogether. Through exploring the basic structure and dynamics of language, can we rediscover it as the resolution of a creative synthesis? Can it be shown that learning our first language, like any other skill, is a personal work of art emerging from the integration of mind and brain, in making one "common sense" of the world?

Since we can't converse with infants about their secret in learning their first language, we are limited to speculating about how we lost it. For the learner-in-diapers, all parts of his world are pieces of just one puzzle. The baby deals with all his ways of knowing together before he grows into more mature teenage and especially adult conventions of sorting his or her overall consciousness of reality out into separate boxes of self-consciousness.[3] The university is the ideal place to start studying the extremes of this adult "boxing" phenomenon.

John Newman defines a university as "a school of knowledge of every kind, consisting of teachers and learners from every quarter…a place for the communication and circulation of thought by means of personal intercourse."[4] But since the teachers have so many different ways of looking at even the same thing, they have to be divided up into faculties of study, and then even further into departments, to save the university from chaos and maintain some semblance of order.

The two biggest boxes at any university are named Arts and Science. The first is reserved for the artists and idealists of the emotional world and the second for the theorists and empiricists of the physical world. It struck me these four types of characters are exemplary of different modes of knowing. As children, had they learned naturally through all four modes at once, albeit un-self-consciously, in a continuous cycling through them, spiraling out into wider and wider circles of increasing self-consciousness? As adults, perhaps they developed strong personal biases especially for only one or two of those modes, effectively stunting the development of the others—at least in how they allowed themselves to be self-conscious of their particular subject matter?

It is obvious the die-hard purists in both the arts and science camps have little or no idea of what is going on in the other. They are too preoccupied bustling about exploring their own to care about what's going on "over there." Besides having confined their hard thinking to the box of their own specialty, they cannot really make much sense of the other. I thought if only I could tear down the walls of the boxes separating the purists and get them to interact dynamically as one person, then I would have a template for the fundamental "operating system" to explicate learning!

A Roundabout Step-by-Step Process

It is the philosopher's job to facilitate understanding and sharing between the arts and science camps so that they can creatively catalyze each other's work. But this is a difficult and dangerous road to travel. The purists in both camps have spent many long years cultivating their specialized take on reality. The philosopher has to not only get one group of purists interested enough to get a solid grasp on something the other purists already know as common sense, but also do it without insulting their incredibly learned intelligence. Consequently, instead of taking a direct hit on the subject, I evolved a roundabout step-by-step process.

In **Part A**, we begin by exploring our personal experience of everyday skills like driving a car, singing a song, and doing arithmetic, before going on to the dynamics of insight in playing bingo and the art of racing dune buggies. Then we can incorporate both emotions and physics into our understanding of learning to type. This leads naturally into the first chapter of **Part B** on some reflections about the nature of language as garnered through learning a second one, and then two chapters on how a child even develops his or her first language.

With these basic images down, the reader can move into **Part C**—the theoretical part describing the functioning of our "operating system." I have rooted this quarrelsome quartet squarely in both the emotional and thinking centers of the brain to catch all the inputs from the sensory organs as well as enable it to motor into action. The artist is the "antenna" of the system, reveling in the whole kaleidoscope of perceived and felt sensation. The theorist processes the artist's raw perceptions originating ideas, which in turn allows the empiricist to be able to conceive the world and all the things in it. Finally, it is up to the idealist—the "transmitter"—to choose the right purpose to bring them all together and do something. Instead of there being only one type of creativity, we have "four-into-one."

But having dissected the person into four parts of a cycle, it is then difficult to see how all four can be active in one person at once. That is why I developed a metaphor earlier in **Part B** on language. The basic sentence provides us with an ideal framework. The artist's spontaneous emotion fits the felt energy of the "verb." The theorist—our deep thinker—perceives the ideas for the "subject" in which the empiricist can dwell to conceive and study her "objects." To complete it, the idealist provides the right intentions for the "subject" as the agent of the action to motivate her to fulfillment in the right aspirations for her "objective." (For the sake of literary convenience, I have made the artist and theorist male, and the empiricist and idealist female throughout the book.) This basic structure and dynamics of the sentence is very flexible. As young children, we invented it through struggling to make one common sense out of the quartet of our operating system. As adults, we use it as a template to accommodate all four characters separately, in various combinations, or all four at once!

Part D describes how we can dance to both poetry and physics. There is a natural "to-fro-and-around" movement both in appreciating the classic examples of short poems discussed, as well as the physics of the sun and earth going around each other. We can only get the complete cycle when we can harmonize the quartet.

Part E bears the brunt of my efforts to apply the quartet to scientific knowledge and explicitly incorporate the dynamics of emotion into the scientists' dualistic view. This could help them transcend the blinders of their theoretical and empirical boxes in the physics of light, psychology, and even the biology of evolution. In earlier parts, it will already become apparent I have a few bones to pick with certain doyens of the academic universe—Chomsky, Piaget, Skinner, Dawkins, Gould, and Wilson. In this part, I tackle them head-on. What is genetically inculcated and what is environmentally effected in "I—the learner"? What is the full breadth and depth of creativity?

For the arts in **Part F,** I apply the model of the quartet to interpret the characters of famous figures of literature like Othello and Don Quixote who, in addition to their obvious idealism, also have strong empirical and theoretical sides. That leads us into a discussion of the nature of belief and religion—how we attempt to put all the pieces of the puzzle together into one for purposeful and satisfying action.

Part G has only two chapters. The first, "Paradise Lost," is an interpretation of the bliss and battle of the sexes living with children. The second chapter takes a step back to the initial germ of this book in summarizing the paradox of our attempts to digest and synthesize the metaphors and facts of the arts and sciences, as well as sharing my recipe for how I cooked up the idea of the quartet in the first place.

A Workbook of Intuitions

This journey through understanding learning is obviously not a textbook of quick answers to easy questions. It is about framing questions in a new way to explore the nature of how we function, how we learn skills to perform everyday activities, and how we understand some basic ideas in science and literature. It is not so ambitious as to lay claim to bagging the shy elusive moment of creative intelligence in learning. Who can catch the wind? These writings merely strive to finger its comings and goings and offer some clues as to where it likes to happen.

Please accept this book as a gift from an older child's imagination. Do you care enough to throw in with a graying dilettante pounding the keys of a rickety word processor armed only with creative spirit in this fight to establish a fresh inquiry into the art of learning? I hope you will enjoy wrestling with it as much as I did in teasing my intuitions into self-consciousness.

A: Doing

1

An Anatomy of Skill in Driving, Math, and Teaching

"Education is what survives when what has been learned has been forgotten."
B. F. Skinner [5]

How do we function during the action of a well-developed skill? Whether we examine ourselves while driving, doing arithmetic, typing, or even teaching, we find it is as though we are in an "automatic pilot" mode. The pilot is guided on the one hand by bits and bytes of sensory perceptions and is sustained on the other through emotional rhythms that modulate speed and style.

Oddly enough, while the body is in this automatic pilot phase, the mind can be preoccupied with other things, like dreaming about winning the lottery or trying to figure out what to get for a child's next birthday. Of course, the mind can successfully give general instructions to the body, but the functioning of the skill virtually collapses if the mind takes direct control over any one essential element of the coordinated activities.

The Effortless Skill of Driving

My father stumbled onto the idea of how to separate his skill of driving and his thoughts out of a peculiar necessity at the age of seventy-eight. He loved driving and making the rounds of his friends' homes on all the country roads. But in the early stages of dementia (Alzheimer's?) he found he could no longer remember where they lived. I first found out about it when he asked me to draw him a map to his best friend's house. A week later I realized he could not make heads or tails of my map, but he was still making regular rounds in his car. Finally I worked up the nerve to ask him how he managed. He said if he thought about it he could not remember even how to get home anymore. But he had discovered that if he just told himself "Go home" or "Go to Joe's," and trusted his body to do it, he

11

would get there. And this is how he made his rounds in the following several months, by avoiding any self-conscious interference with his driving, letting his old habits take him wherever he commanded.[6]

Have you ever driven to work, and upon arrival suddenly realized you had been so absorbed in your thoughts you had no memory of anything that happened between home and work? This happens to me all the time. It is frightening when I think about it. It means that for periods of time, while I am inside an upholstered tin can dodging other tin cans, all moving at high speeds, I completely hand over responsibility for my life and death to a sort of automatic functioning of the body, as my father did, while I focus my thoughts on something entirely different.

Let us look closer at the nature of the action in the skill mode. A perfected skill such as driving a car functions as an organic whole. All the required organs and limbs work together in coordination. The eyes, hands, and feet function as a set integrated with those rules of the road we have accepted. If we are very careful, while we are driving we can monitor, for example, the movements of our hands on the steering wheel without interfering in their activity. We notice that our hands are making adjustments every few seconds to the steering wheel without us feeling any effort.

Traveling on today's expressways, we can drive for hours without tiring or even realizing what our hands and feet are doing, even though our eyes are constantly scanning the road, our hands making their adjustments, our right foot controlling the throttle in response to changing traffic patterns and road conditions.

Only once in a while are we drawn from our thoughts and called to pay close attention to some detail that is puzzling our "driving robot." For instance, when traveling in a foreign city our attention might be drawn to a strange sign. It is as though our robot had pasted a question mark over it for us to address. In response we run through our memories to look for correspondences with it. Once the most plausible solution is settled on, we can return to our daydreaming or pondering.

But if someone were to suddenly cover our eyes, this whole organic integration would collapse. Suddenly we would not be driving anymore; we would lose control and our hands instead of steering would merely be grasping the wheel, our foot instead of controlling the throttle would merely be pushing against it.

What control did I have over the car in the first place? For instance, I tell myself to drive to Thamesville. My body is driving very well by itself while my mind is daydreaming. What if suddenly I notice a garage sale just off to the left on a side road and decide to slip down there to check it out? I can tell my body to turn left. But it does not respond immediately. It will do it on its own time according to information from the eyes and in accordance with the rules of the road unless I override the integration of driving. In other words, a skill is like an automatic pilot directly controlling the car. I just supervise the pilot, giving it a purpose or objective in general instructions as in, "Make a left turn up ahead and stop at that house." This is the mark of a well-established skill or integration.

The nature of our control over the action of driving is very different from that of our body controlling the car. When my body steers the car left, the car turns left. But when I tell the body to turn left, it does so on its own timing, in coordination with all the other parts of the body required to make it go smoothly. There is a pervading rhythm tying all these actions together as though in a dance, whether one of aggression or placidity. The body "controls" the car, but we only "have control" over our bodies, a very remote and indirect control.

Have you ever watched yourself driving, not watched as in a video replay, but as in watching yourself out of the corner of your eye, so to speak, without taking the focus of your eyes off the roadway ahead? This technique reminds me of how I learned to hunt rabbits as a teenager. If I actively tried to spot a sitting rabbit camouflaged within its environment by focusing my gaze here and there, it would escape before I had time to aim. Rather I just scanned the forest like the driver of a car scans the roadway, not focusing on anything in particular, but rather using an "inner eye" to detect any suspicious motion within that whole screen of vision. Only such motion triggers the eyes to focus on any point in particular. As drivers we do not want to take our eyes off the road to focus on the phenomenon of our hands constantly making micro-adjustments in steering without self-conscious control, so we have to work like the rabbit hunter on not taking direct control of our eyes when doing this. Once you get really good at hunting, you can even "watch" your eyes constantly scanning the roadway ahead while driving.

To summarize then, we have noticed how the body drives the car with no direct instructions from the thoughtful mind. It is as though the movements of our eyes, hands, and right foot are woven together, smoothly functioning in coordination with their interpretation of the traffic rules and the road situation. Let us name this phenomenon "skill," or using Polanyi's[7] terminology, "integration."

Idea Fused with Emotion

A skill is a fusion of idea and emotion. You can check this by studying how you act differently even while applying the same skill but under different emotional conditions. For example, I have noticed that while listening to rock and roll music, I tend to drive about five km/hr faster than normal. But I drive slower by about the same speed when listening to classical music. If I am very nervous or worried about something my driving speed becomes irregular, as though the emotional half of my automatic pilot is synchronizing with my emotions of the moment. Skill cannot operate smoothly without a sustained emotional rhythm.

On the one hand our driving integration is very tough and resilient, as well as extremely efficient. In nice weather, we can drive hundreds of miles on an expressway and feel very little fatigue upon arriving at our destination. After learning an integration such as driving a car or riding a bicycle, we can stop performing it for twenty years, yet within a few minutes of practice are able to do it as well again, presuming we are still as physically fit. On the other hand, it is very tenuous in nature. If we interfere with even one element of the whole integration while we are doing it, for instance if a sheet of paper suddenly flies off the dash to cover our eyes, that is if we become self-conscious and take control of one or another element of it, the integration collapses immediately and we no longer have control over our skill of driving. Then we no longer "know" driving because we have changed our attention to one subsidiary of the overall integration, and the body loses its seemingly effortless control over the car.

Up to now I have avoided talking about the intentional part of the action. It has happened to me several times when driving that I suddenly realized I did not know where I was going. I had been so preoccupied with other things that the intention slipped out. Sometimes I find out only after I have arrived in the wrong place. The "automatic pilot" needs a minimum of purposeful direction. If our attention is so completely drawn to something else, like an involved conversation on a cell phone, we start driving blindly.

The need to occasionally arouse ourselves to a self-consciousness of driving is important, especially in familiar territory. Because we know our home area so well, we have all occasionally been surprised to discover we have just made a maneuver without paying any attention to any ongoing sense perceptions. In this way in broad daylight, parents in their driveways and farmers in their barnyards have driven over their own children. They were driving completely in their memory, oblivious to sensory perception in the present moment.

A Warning to Experimenters

This is an appropriate place for a word of caution. Playing around with integrations is not without danger, especially when engaged in an activity like driving. We are tampering with the basic mental structures that we have built up within our cultural patterns over our lifetimes. They are responsible for an ease of communication with others around us and for our ability to do everything we do well with a tremendous economy of effort, for our pleasure and safety.

As a practical example, one incident that scared the life (nearly) out of me was suddenly realizing I had no control over my truck at over 100 km/hr on a highway. This was the direct result of playing games with my consciousness of the driving integration. I had focused fully on mentally acting out the part of myself swinging a bat. And even though my hands stayed on the steering wheel, this mental activity took control of my hands away from involvement in the driving integration, leading to its collapse. Of course, if I had merely been daydreaming of being a baseball star hitting home runs in the bottom of the ninth, it would have had no effect. But I had apprehended the actual swinging of a bat.

Though I quickly recovered after experiencing this total surprising breakdown in having control, I had misgivings about my driving skills for some time thereafter. I had to work to "rebury" the integration by avoiding any self-consciousness of driving by focusing on an emotional awareness of its sensual aspects.

At this time, it was fortunate I had just discovered Thich Nhat Hanh's treatise on how to wash dishes in *The Miracle of Mindfulness.*[8] Most of us just wash them to get them done. We are focused only on the objective of this activity, having no interest or awareness of what is happening because we consider it a menial task. But by opening our awareness to the various physical sensations of touch, sound, and sight experienced while washing the dishes, we can thoroughly enjoy it. Feel the heat of the water, the slipperiness of the soap, the smoothness of the plate; listen to the sound of water splashing, water gurgling into a glass; see the foam, the colors. Be aware of all these sensations happening at once. By similarly so working to "touch the inside" of the driving skill, I quickly became more comfortable with driving again.

Louis MacNiece loses himself in the total awareness of sensation in the first two stanzas of "Snow":

> The room was suddenly rich and the great bay-window was
> Spawning snow and pink roses against it
> Soundlessly collateral and incompatible:
> World is suddener than we fancy it.
>
> World is crazier and more of it than we think,
> Incorrigibly plural. I peel and portion
> A tangerine and spit the pips and feel
> The drunkenness of things being various.

The poet's vantage—submersed within feeling the action—is the opposite of the empirical watcher of the skill in action. How can the watcher of the skill of driving be observing his body's actions? He does not seem to be using his physical senses of perception to do so, because those senses are already fully preoccupied in facilitating direct control by the body of the car at 100 km/hr. How is the watcher—the mind's eye—riding on their coattails? What is this mirage of self-consciousness—this quiet observer remote from the action—which theoretically has control over the body driving car, but inadvertently and apparently inevitably only destroys the intricacy and fluidity of the integration of this skill when it interferes and takes direct control?

> The water beetle here shall teach
> A sermon from beyond your reach
> He flabbergasts the human race
> By gliding on the water's face
> With ease, celerity and grace.
> But if he ever stopped to think
> Of how he did it, he would sink.
> ("The Water Beetle" by Hillaire Belloc)

During the observance and comprehension of a skill in action, we keep this mind's eye through which we know the action separate from the sensory and emotional activity of the skill, to allow the latter to function without misfiring. It was only in the original development of that skill that the mind was fully involved with the body.

Mad Minutes of Math

"Arithmetic is where numbers fly like pigeons in and out of your head."
(From the poem "Arithmetic," by Carl Sandburg)

At some point I realized it should be as normal for a person with good arithmetical skills to be able to do arithmetical calculations without thinking about them as for one who is very experienced in driving to be able to drive long distances while daydreaming. And, in fact, after a few evenings of practice with some "mad minutes"[9] from a daughter's fourth grade class, I could easily obtain ninety-nine to one hundred percent accuracy, even while carrying on a casual conversation with another daughter.

I pointedly ignored thinking about the numbers to get the answers to just come out of the end of my pencil, completely bypassing any mental calculation or self-conscious effort. I figured that at the age of almost fifty I had already done all these calculations thousands of times as well as written them enough, the body should be ready to do both skills together without my interference, just like driving a car. So I ordered myself to do it and just waited for the pencil to start moving. The point is I did not want to waste time calculating the answers and rushing to write them down. I wanted the whole process of reading the question, calculating the answer, and then writing it down to be autonomous of self-conscious thought, like the skill of driving. At first it was a little tentative, but gradually it sped up. After awhile I was kept busy concentrating on writing fast enough to keep up. After the third evening of practice it became an automatic skill, and I could do it while carrying on that conversation.

After the first shock of popping out the answers, a very strange memory surfaced. I suddenly recalled experiencing this same phenomenon as a child. I remembered a moment at which I became self-conscious of answers popping into my head upon just looking at arithmetical problems. The discovery was followed immediately by fear. The experience so disturbed and frightened me as a child that I suppressed my self-consciousness of it until my mad minutes experiment, maybe thirty-five or forty years later. It was strange to learn that for all those years I had hidden from the awareness of how to solve arithmetical answers without self-conscious calculation.

What is behind this popping thing anyway? Changing over from the self-conscious calculating method of doing these operations to popping the answers feels identical to the transformation in style of speaking Thai or Dutch while translating from English-language thoughts to being able to think directly in those languages. It is the same difference as between trying to control a car and having control of it.

The difference feels the same as that between calculating the speed of a train as a bystander by timing the train along a measured length of track and that of merely checking the speedometer on board the train. There is no calculation involved in using a speedometer. There is no abstract point of view, as in calculating the distance traveled divided by time formula. A speedometer situates us as though we were at the interface of the two frameworks—the train and track.

Typing without Crutches

In these days of the word processor and e-mail, most of us require some basic typing skills to survive. In the early stages of writing this work I realized that although I had been typing off and on for some years, I still looked at the keys. It occurred to me my fingers certainly must already know where each key sits. After all, there are not all that many of them. And if I could drive my car, which is a much more complicated and dangerous affair, without thinking about it, and if I could pop arithmetical calculations, why did I have to pay this particular attention to typing individual letters? I was struck by the thought that my looking at the keys was no different than forgetting to take the training wheels off a bicycle, or dropping the crutches after a broken leg has healed.

.Putting my fingers on the keyboard, and without looking at the keys, I instructed them to type whatever I put into mind. At first nothing happened. But I refused to relent since I was convinced of my theory! I was amazed to feel them start moving. At first their movements were very tentative. They typed just a few letters at a time. I resisted the temptation to look at the keys, and even to think about where the keys were. I stuck with reinstructing the fingers to type whenever they stopped and putting words in mind for them to set down. The interruptions became fewer and fewer as they started to type whole words. After a while my fingers started working as though possessed of a life of their own.

For the first time I could wholly focus my mind on thoughts, as my fingers took care of the rest. Of course, I do not type enough to build the solid skills of a professional typist. Perhaps my old habits are too fossilized to change completely in my graying years. But at least I am much faster now, especially in those moments of totally absorbed inspiration when thoughts fly in.

Learning to Sing

Consider Joanna Field's experience mastering the trick of how to get herself into the skill mode in order to set up the conditions for focusing purely on the melody, the emotion, and bursting out into song:

> As a child I had been teased for singing out of tune, so all my life I had felt thwarted, ashamed to burst out into song whenever I felt like it, and deeply envious of those who could. I could always hear when other people were out of tune but seemed incapable of producing true notes myself. Then one day I happened to start humming without thinking about it, for there was no one close enough to overhear, and I suddenly listened to my own voice and heard that it was in tune. I was so interested that I went on listening, and as long as I listened, so long did I stay in tune. But as soon as my attention slipped back to the problem of trying to sing, then my voice wandered off the note. It seemed that I had always to keep in tune by attending to the muscles in my throat which felt as if they controlled the sound, just as I had tried to play tennis by the deliberate placing of my limbs. After this I found

that I could keep in tune whenever I chose, so long as I thought only of the melody and forgot my throat existed.[10]

Teachers Forgetting the Questions

I remember a professor once boasting how little attention he needed to pay to what he was teaching. Because of his long experience he could literally be thinking about something completely different from what he was lecturing about. At first this surprised me, because by all objective standards he was an excellent teacher: smoothly organized delivery punctuated by appropriate anecdotes and stories, student participation, and timely breaks. How could he do this without having to work at it? But at the same time I realized how bored we students were in this excellent class.

The professor had perfected a polished product he was not paying any real attention to presenting, so we the students did not pay any real attention to listening. Instead of working to answer a question he was pondering at that particular instant, he was merely orchestrating the presentation of information. Not having much of a clue as what questions his materials were addressing, we the students could not get excited about listening to the answers. Instead, we listened mechanically recording what we figured were the highlights, while we pondered whether the graduate lounge would ever start carrying Belgium Trappiste beer.

I speculate that the primary occupational hazard of the teaching profession lies in forgetting the questions to the answers being taught. Having lost touch with the meaning of these questions to which the answers make sense in the back of his mind, the teacher is reduced to getting students to memorize his hierarchy of facts or ideals. In fact we could go further and speculate that the root cause of poor quality teaching is the nature of the teacher's experience as a pupil. Maybe his teachers did not help him frame those questions, depending instead on the incredible power of his child's memory to literally absorb the material and regurgitate it at exam time.

Even if the teacher as a student really understood what was being taught in a particular lesson or only understood it later when the right question occurred to him, through the repetition of those answers over the years in a classroom, those answers became detached from their questions. Remember as a child repeating a word over and over again very fast until it sounded like nonsense? At that final point the word has become detached from its meaning or action. Similarly, through repetition over the years, the answers become so familiar that teachers can repeat them mechanically, with only the faintest shadow of any consciousness of their relationship to questions. He is like the experienced driver in his own backyard, driving without sensing what is around him in present time. Of course the students end up being the casualties, until the teacher wakes up to this fact and works to revive his existential connection with the subject as well as to develop a stronger awareness for keeping track of what is happening "out there" in the classroom.

Teachers are not alone in losing touch with the core or the magic of the art of their professions. Persons of all professions face the same challenge in both work and personal lives. A sense of meaninglessness in just going through the motions, the hollow kiss, the empty prayer, the vacant expression, the feeling when we sense we should feel something but do not, are all symptoms of being out of touch, of acting mindlessly and carelessly when we have forgotten the questions and aspirations that made particular answers meaningful.

2

Danger and Delight in Insight

"Work without hope draws nectar in a sieve,
and hope without an object cannot live."
Coleridge

The Study of Vacuum Cleaners

I remember sitting on the floor as a young boy surrounded by the hundred pieces of our old vacuum cleaner. When my mother had finally thrown it out, I had attacked it with a screwdriver and pliers to find out what made it work. Of course what I discovered inside were all these weirdly shaped pieces. I could not find the magic secret of the appliance's working energy. Furthermore, I had had so much fun taking it apart, I had not paid any attention to the order in which I had dismantled it. So I could not reconstruct it. I was lost and bewildered. No matter how hard I tried, I could not put it back together again. Gradually I realized that having taken it apart I had no way of formulating a theory of how it worked since I could not watch the patterns of how its inner parts moved together nor the flow of materials through it to establish what it could and could not do.

Nowadays, as fixer of my wife's vacuum cleaner, I am smarter. Before I take anything apart I direct my energies in two ways. First I study its form. I try to remember from the previous times how the mechanism of the machine works by peering into its guts, tweaking a belt here and twiddling a cog there to jog my memory and further develop my idea of it in action. Then, as an experimenter, I look for what its energy can still do, how much is it still sucking under what conditions, and compare that with what I know it could do before. The task of putting both aspects together as one comes next, in order to get insight into the problem to solve it.

If I try to solve the problem too quickly and fail, it usually means I did not spend enough time to get a deep enough grasp on its workings or a clear enough feeling of its effects on dust and dirt. Then I have to go back through each of these again separately to strengthen my idea of how it works with the motional facts, before I try again to put it all together to intuit an answer to my question.

The practical handywoman—the Shirley Holmes of vacuum cleaners—uses such an involved procedure only as a last resort. It is much quicker to work backward. She has already abstracted a whole series of lessons out of her many experiences and has stored them in memory. By conceptualizing the symptoms of the problem, she can quickly zero in on the one or two most likely causes and focus all her efforts there. Only if she fails to identify the dysfunction does she have to start over and go through the same process I like to take—the Inspector Maigret[11] approach. Of course, when I am in a hurry working on a piece of farm equipment of whose workings I have only the vaguest idea, I mimic the technique of the handywoman by turning to the troubleshooting section of the instruction manual to help me out. This is usually the most practical and efficient approach to solving the problem. Diving into a storehouse of organized facts—whether my own or others'—I can work quickly toward deducing the most likely answer to the question. But this method is not nearly as much fun and exciting as starting at the beginning with the basics and fighting intuitively toward insight.

In the insight method, I can both enjoy the rush of delight in the insight of discovering the answer and get satisfaction in using it to accomplish the initial purpose—fixing the vacuum cleaner. The handywoman's shortcut method provides only the self-satisfaction of being able to draw on a body of knowledge to find the right solution to accomplish that initial purpose. One problem with the insight method is that the delight in getting it can be so powerful in itself, there are some intuitives who no longer feel even the slightest interest or desire to go further and actually fix the vacuum cleaner! We have literally forgotten why we tackled the problem in the first place. All the motivation of the initial tension in the problem is dissipated in a theoretical resolution.

These contrasting methods of problem resolution lead to different understandings of how we learn. If you lean more toward the practical shortcut bias of the technician to "get the job done," you probably also lean toward the filing-cabinet conception of the mind of the cognitivist and the button-pushing emotional stimuli of the behaviorist. You lean toward both an understanding of mind as a system to be better able to use its contents and to an understanding of emotional drives, and you work to figure out how to fuse the two to get the work done most quickly and efficiently. However, if you lean more toward gaining new insights into things, you will probably lean more toward the intuitive model of isolating between theorizing and grasping the evidence of energy, of fighting it out between the "nouns" and "verbs" of learning to understand how we built up that knowledge base in the first place, through child-like play.

This book focuses more on elucidating the bias of the second, of the impractical playful human. There are already more than enough self-help books published for the earnestly practical. What about one for us, the intuitive players: a book for those who just love working through the problem and forget about fixing the machine? If you are one of those super-practical technicians interested only in getting the vacuum cleaner to work, this book might be totally bewildering. You, the pragmatist, want to explore "ends" while I want to focus on the "means." The practical human enjoys the cool calculation of comprehension in deducing from his storehouse of established knowledge to get results. The dreamer who revels in the hot tensions of apprehension prefers to navigate through a foggy maze of intuitions toward insight.

The Goose in Learning

We learn from the day we are born, or actually even before—in the womb—without any idea of what we are doing. Of course as adults we are self-conscious of the great effort and energy we must put into it, even more if we dislike the subject. But after we have insight into something, we rarely reflect on how we got there. We just "know" it and want to get on using it for something, whether to make money, achieve honors on a test, or explore some odd personal interest. What makes understanding learning itself so difficult is that we can never go back to not knowing the things we know. What was a mystery before is now so clear and obvious. We cannot erase it and start over to watch ourselves getting it for the first time.

Being unself-conscious of how we learn might be a natural safeguard. Maybe we should take a lesson from X.J. Kennedy's goose in his poem *"Ars Poetica"*:

> The goose that laid the golden egg
> Died looking up its crotch
> To find out how its sphincter worked.
>
> Would you lay well? Don't watch.

In one way, this is very good advice. When we become self-conscious while in the act of doing something creative, we lose the rhythm and flow. We start to stumble and lose the drift of what we were saying, writing, painting, or fixing. Yet at the same time we know the more attention we pay to what we are doing, the better it will come out.

We cannot both be watching ourselves doing something and doing it creatively at the same time. Of course, we can mechanically do something at which we are very skilled while watching ourselves. For example while driving, we can watch or be aware of the back and forth movements of our hands controlling the steering wheel. While watching ourselves we can gain certain insight into those skills, but we cannot get insight into insight itself.

The only way to get around this limitation is to learn to re-create the sequence of mental events that took place to get there immediately after we catch ourselves learning something new. We can only study insight in retrospect. If it happens when reading a book, we could immediately reread the part that led to it and focus on all those emotions, ideas, and facts aroused to interact with the words that sparked the "aha!" It is not easy. It is like trying to catch a feather while skating on a quarter inch of ice on a lake in a snowstorm.

There is one useful tool to help in exploring insight: adrenaline.[12] Have you experienced any rushes of adrenaline in reading this book up to now? If you have not, it means you already know the things you have read here or it has not made any sense to you because you aren't interested in the same questions about it. Or maybe you are newly getting it, but have not noticed because you haven't been watching for the rushes? The best way to get at it is to delineate a few examples of insight, one in solving the sock problem and the other in Archimedes' solution for the counterfeiting of gold.

The Sock Problem

In your bedroom, the sock drawer contains four green, six purple, and ten red socks, all singles. Early morning before sunrise, during a power blackout in pitch darkness, you reach into the drawer to get some socks. How many socks do you have to pull out before you can be certain of having enough to make one pair of the same color?

I hope you will stop here for a few minutes and solve it. And after you get the answer, try to remember how you got it, and how you felt when you did.

Did you find that if you tried strictly to intellectualize the problem it was very difficult and confusing? But it is very simple to solve if you first change the problem into a question and then watch yourself act it through.

The problem becomes: *How many socks can I pull out before the last one is necessarily of the same color as one previously drawn?* Now, while holding this problem in your mind, just imagine yourself doing it. Start drawing socks of each color out of the drawer until you cannot get a new color. In this process you are dwelling in the problem while observing the action you have contrived in your imagination. And suddenly during the enactment you see clear as a bell that the fourth sock has to match one of the previous draws. Once you have the problem in mind, or "*in de gaat*" as the Dutch say, and the enactment is properly set up, you play it out and the answer becomes apparent. In fact it just pops out without any effort at calculation.

Archimedes' Bath Study

Let us visit the communal bathhouses of Greece in the time before a bathtub sat in every house. Can you see Archimedes sitting alone over there in the corner of the bath? He is obviously not enjoying it today. He is more quiet than usual. Perhaps he is angry with his wife for nagging him into coming more often. A bath once a week is certainly enough for any man! Perhaps he is unwell…He is most unsociably engrossed in his own thoughts…

Your friend next to you, noticing your concern for him, whispers that the king has put pressure on the great mathematician to find a solution to the recent rash of counterfeiting. Goldsmiths are adulterating gold with silver and passing off items made from the amalgam as pure gold. The only way the king can be sure the crown he just purchased is made from pure gold is by smelting it down. He has asked Archimedes instead to find him a technique of determining the purity of the gold content in the crown without destroying it. Let us enter into this bather's head and see what he has worked out so far…

"A cube of gold weighs more than a cube of the same size of silver. The more weight per unit of volume an element has, the 'denser' it is. From having weighed identically-sized cubes of gold and silver, not only can I say that gold is denser than silver, I also have an exact numerical value for the densities of both. If I could only measure the volume of metal in the crown, I could get a value for its density too, and compare it with the densities for pure gold and pure silver. If the density I get for the crown is not the same as that of pure gold, I can deduce it is not made of pure gold. But how to calculate its volume seems impossible without melting it down into a cube…"

Hey, the local Olympic wrestling team is coming in for a bath after their practice. As each player gets into the communal bath, the water level rises higher. While Archimedes is holding the question of how to calculate the volume of the crown in the front of his mind, he is simultaneously apprehending in amazement something he has probably seen a thousand times before without realizing it until now, when he is looking for it. As the first wrestler enters the bath and submerges, the water level rises, and with each body, it rises somewhat more…if all those bodies get in the bath, the water will overflow…there appears to be a direct relationship between addition of the volume of the athletes' bodies and the apparent increase in the volume of the body of water…perhaps the volume of water displaced by a body is equal to this apparent increase…

He has his solution! He has discovered the link between his known facts of density and his perceiving of objects displacing water. Just submerge the king's crown in a container absolutely full of water, while catching the entire overflow. This overflow could then be measured for its volume in a graduated cylinder, which when divided into the crown's weight will provide the value of its density.

Next thing we know, Archimedes is flashing the populace of Syracuse yelling, "Eureka! Eureka!" Talk about an adrenaline rush…or is it ecstasy?

Adrenaline is like an exclamation mark at the moment of insight: "Bingo!" The more important the insight to us, the bigger is the shot. But unfortunately there is no certain correlation with "truth." It is not like there is a miniature "teacher" inside us that gives us a little shot of adrenaline every time we get something "right." The insight is only "right" within the context and limitations of the knowledge and experiences we apply to resolving the issue. And because that knowledge and experience is limited, the insight might be right or wrong, straight or crooked, safe or dangerous in the long run for our life. But usually for that moment we go with it because it is the best resolution for what we know and feel, or at least for what we allow ourselves to know and feel at that point in time.

The Art and Rush of Bingo

The game of bingo is characterized by a mental state of continuous anticipation punctuated by a haphazard series of insights. As ridiculous as it may sound, bingo, as played by serious professionals, has all the earmarks of an art form.

Perhaps you too have spent many hours walking up and down the alleys between the rows of tables in local bingo halls selling cards to the players to raise money for your community service group, and wondering how people get addicted to playing the game. It is easy to forget that as small children many of us were excited to play it at home or school: the waiting in anticipation for the new number, hunting through our cards to find the corresponding ones, and with each mark (kernel of corn, penned "x," daub) comes another little thrill, another tiny shot of adrenaline with every new discovery and the realization we have moved another number closer to bingo. But many years later most of us fail to understand why other adults are not bored to death playing it.

There are a number of bingo players out there who appear to play the game for the excitement of the sport. While the average player plays twelve to fifteen cards at a time, the super player I once observed, Jeanie, one of the Wayne Gretzkys and Michael Jordans of bingo, can do fifty cards simultaneously without breaking a sweat. In fact she looks perfectly calm. There is this serene expression of imperturbable equanimity on her face as she smoothly and efficiently daubs her way through all her cards with each number called. At the same time, like any super athlete, she is totally loose and totally focused on playing the game.

For the period of any sport the athlete tries to avoid thinking about it; he does not want to consider the possibility of losing for fear it will prejudice his efforts. He does not want to change his focus from the overall game to just one part of it for fear he will lose his overall rhythm and focus. To think about the game in an objective frame of reference is the job of the referee. He must ensure the rules are being followed and check the validity of any score claims, just as in bingo it is the job of the caller and his helpers. Like the committed athlete, the dedicated bingo player wants to lose herself in the total action and concentration of playing and dare to win in the face of enormous odds.

The Drama of Organized Play

Once we observe bingo players close up, we know for the most part they are not there to have a relaxed pleasant time socializing. Bingo playing is tense business. Upon walking into a bingo hall or any gambling casino we immediately notice the forced gaiety of smiles and jokes. Underneath the public face, few are relaxed and at ease. They are psyched up, full of wants and anxious anticipations. They are there for an exciting time. The gambler is focused on winning. Jeanie desperately hopes to win.

Objectively she should know the odds are stacked against her, and she is much more likely to lose money than make it. But this is going to be her lucky day! Of course, she is not going to tell anybody about it. That would jinx her luck. Just wait until she wins and can show them Lady Fortune is smiling on her. Throughout the evening Jeanie is looking for signs of her luck and building up her expectations. Here and there she comes very close to winning something, perhaps even ten or twenty dollars on one of the games. Maybe she has not won anything at all, but then maybe that is just Lady Luck's way of teasing her—it is all a buildup to the climax, the final game of the evening for the jackpot.

How is it possible for her to keep going all evening with most of her expectations riding on the final game of the night? Each game is another act in the overall drama. Each game is broken into scenes entitled "first line," "H's," "full house." Thus the playing of each game becomes a mini-drama in itself which can be described scene by scene the next day during the coffee klatch, with details like the good luck charm going missing, running out of ink, the smearing of a card with ketchup stains, the coffee spilled, running out of smokes, using the last fiver to buy more cards, and getting that last lucky card from the seller who reminded her of Omar Sharif.

But I suspect that the real secret of bingo is that it is designed to let Jeanie win something every several seconds. The player is continually moving toward winning during every minute of the game. For every number called, the player has an even chance of being able to daub some ink on one number for every three cards she is playing. Thus, the average person playing on the order of twelve to fifteen cards simultaneously is able to make an average of four to five hits for every number called; yet all of them are surprises, new insights; none can be predicted. Each new discovery of another correspondence between the number called and the numbers on her cards is a micro-hit of adrenaline to the system. She avoids thinking that the odds of winning are against her, so she can build up her hopes of winning the jackpot. Instead of seeing an average of four hits per number called as her due in view of the laws of probability, she follows their random sporadic arrival with the interest of any bookworm collecting an accumulation of clues in a murder mystery, or the psychic reading the latest pattern in her tea leaves.

The game starts out low key. But as each "scene" is consummated, tension mounts and the hits are more highly anticipated and thus more powerful. Of course, at any particular act's mini-climax, as she discovers she has lost yet another game, a slight wave of depression is experienced, culminating eventually in the biggest one on failing to win the jackpot, as everyone except the winner picks up and hurries out the door in veiled disappointment.

The jackpot round located at the very end is the climax of the evening, in the same way Othello's murder of Desdemona is the climax of Shakespeare's *Othello*. Desdemona's strangulated cry of shock is similar to that of the bingo winner. Those who have never worked a bingo hall might assume the winner's cry of "Bingo!" would have a joyful, triumphant ring and be followed by generous applause. It does not sound like that at all, and it is not followed by cheering. The cry generally sounds more like that of a shipwrecked sailor, who after drifting alone without food and water for several days has just spotted a passing ship. Her first cry is not that of hope somebody will spot her, but in terror nobody will.

In the same instant of this poignant cry, all the other players realize they have daubed their last number of the night and become the audience. There is no sound of cheering for the winner. As with the audience at the moment of the murder of Desdemona, there is an unearthly silence as everyone works to absorb the significance of what has happened. The bingo-player audience, with one exception, is busy learning they have all lost again tonight. For both the Shakespearean audience and the bingo customers, the climax marks the low point of the drama.

Fortunately for the theater audience, Shakespeare follows up with an anticlimax. When Othello discovers what a horrendous act he has been beguiled into carrying out and realizes his own culpability for it, he seeks atonement. In this way, Othello is brought full circle, from action into reflection on and realization of what he has done. Othello finds closure with a final act of suicide. The theater audience walks out of the show with a whole story to mull over in reflection on their own lives.

Unfortunately for the bingo players, the business end of organizing bingos ensures they do not get any psychological closure. The number caller does not stand up after the final jackpot round and explain to them how minuscule were their chances of winning and how foolish they were to assume otherwise. Instead, the players shuffle out of the hall with the memory of that shipwrecked voice crying "Bingo" echoing in their minds, and the ghost of a feeling of what it would have been like to have won, along with all the leftovers from all those micro-hits of adrenaline. Of course, they have their stories of close encounters with Lady Luck, and their retellings in the following days with Jeanie at the coffee klatch. These bingo stories provide content for their social lives that the playing of the game does not. This and their personal need for those shots of adrenaline and being in that groove "in the zone" between the called numbers and their cards will bring them back again another night.

Fool's Gold

Most of us learn early in life to be careful not to want something too much, because if we do not get it, the letdown is a kick in the teeth. So we modify our anticipation, whether about gifts from friends or marks in school, to suit what we figure we can realistically expect. Then when we get more than we expected, when we get a bigger shot of adrenaline than we had anticipated, we are delighted in realizing we can now adjust our hopes higher in that regard for the next time. If we get less, we are disappointed and accordingly lower the level of anticipation for the next time.

We can think of the setting of these varying levels of anticipation as a way of setting expectations based on our tacit knowledge. After something has been done we realize right away through our adrenaline system whether our guesses, premonitions, intuitions, or predictions were right or wrong. For instance, it might occur to us we feel a little disappointed by something someone did. This immediately cues us to check our premises and emotional expectations in that situation. Just as often, the emotion we felt could have been of delight, shock, laughter, sadness, or a hundred other emotions, or some mixture of them. But whenever an emotion arises that is unexpected or comes in a dose larger or smaller than expected, it sticks out like a red flag and is our cue to trace the discrepancy back to its origins, so that we can adjust our sense of reality in that regard, or to figure out how to change our strategy to achieve our hopes.

Can we escape being trapped between expectations and results on a roller coaster of emotions? While in prison awaiting his execution, did the innocent Boethius learn well enough from his nurse, Philosophy, to enable him to transcend it all?

> Let men compose themselves and live in peace,
> Set haughty fate beneath their feet
> And look unmoved on fortune good and bad,
> And keep unchanging countenance:
>
> ...
>
> If first you rid yourself of hope and fear
> You have disarmed the tyrant's wrath[13]

Or are we forever squeezed between, as Folly—Erasmus's muse—boasts?

"Without me, the world cannot exist for a moment. For is not all that is done at all among mortals, full of folly; is it not performed by fools and for fools?"[14]

Hope springs eternal it seems. This to-and-fro between hoping and action followed by realization is a basic pattern. But the bingo player, like any other gambling addict, video game nerd, or workaholic, has subverted this natural system by ignoring the red flags and becoming obsessed with an activity to artificially attain meaningless insights to produce an internal drug.

Remember the suicidal rat in Psych 101? Psychologists planted electrodes into the pleasure centers of its brain. It could then get quick shots of its pleasure hormones merely by alternately pressing and releasing a lever. The rat metaphorically masturbates itself to death. Thomas Merton wrote a follow-up poem about the experimenter himself:

> After warning the rat
> He worked his own button to death
> Back went the fires of ecstasy
> And blew the rat sky-high.[15]

Of course, socially acceptable addictions like playing bingo and video games, or smoking and drinking, or even working in moderation, are much milder forms of this phenomenon. One of these days we will all be perfect and not need such social crutches and reality "enhancers," won't we?

Contrast the bingo hall addicts' scenario with that of a group of children playing during recess in the schoolyard. Active children appear to be fully charged with adrenaline. They are continually learning. As just one tiny sample, consider that a child learns an average of ten new words per day over ten years. As parents we know this is definitely not through their deductive efforts in studying dictionary definitions of words. They learn words startlingly quickly and efficiently, intuitively, through the confused hurly-burly of everyday communication.[16] But the emotional atmosphere of that spontaneous and delightful interaction we sense among children is totally different from that among gamblers. With the children we sense an excitement and joy, in fact a whole gamut of lively emotions both positive and negative. In contrast, the gambler is isolated within a cocoon of self-absorbed concentration. The nature of the addict's compulsive activity feels intense but is in fact very boring and limited in range and expression. The addict's emotional gamut has been reduced to vacillating between artificial stimulations of hope and fatalistic acceptances of fate's decrees, sprinkled with occasional bursts of excitement in near-triumph, and the very rare occasion of triumph in winning the jackpot.

In the gambler, the role of adrenaline is in punctuating and maintaining the drive toward incidental and trivial discoveries within a known set of variables. In effect, the production and enjoyment of the adrenaline rush becomes the underlying motivation. In contrast, in the child adrenaline is functional in encouraging and enabling his efforts to continually grow further into a wider and deeper mastery and consciousness of a huge, wonderful, and mysterious world. The addicted gambler, already bored with the wonder and magic of living in the real world, uses the pursuit of trivial discoveries in order get a rush. The gambler has learned how to subvert nature's means of punctuating and maintaining the creative process.

Emotions for Sale

The commercial advertiser also knows how to utilize Folly's mischievous nature. His job is to associate desirable feelings with commercial products so consumers will then want to buy them in order to "acquire" that feeling. At first glance, what feelings we associate with an inanimate object might not seem to be of much importance. But emotions give an object meaning over time. In fact, without emotions we would not have even a feeling of time.

Research into advertising shows the emotional value the advertiser persuades us to accept in association with his product is a much more important determinant in consumer decision-making than any intellectual idea consumers might have about the product. It is the basis for how we so easily and quickly make many thousands of decisions throughout every day.

Consider the ease of the communication of images from the advertisers through televisions into our homes and hearts. As viewers, already enjoyably relaxed in empathy with the main characters of a sitcom, hearing a favorite tune woven into a commercial, we welcome those images and their energy into the privacy of our inner world. Later through purchasing the advertised products, we can then "rightfully" own the emotions with which the advertiser aroused and teased us in the commercial. "Eureka! Look at the new me!"

Adrenaline and Frameworks

Solving the sock problem and that of determining the volume of the crown are examples of single insight. But the playing of high-speed bingo is one of maintaining a rhythm of continuous insight. In single insight, adrenaline punctuates the discovery of an apparent resolution. In a continuous series of insights, whether in playing bingo or in creative writing, adrenaline not only punctuates particular insight, but more importantly facilitates the continuous juxtaposition of opposite frameworks required in the maintenance of that groove or zone of the professional player. Think of it as a drug that enables us to be conscious through opposite frameworks—both perceptive and emotional—simultaneously for an extended period of time. We will need it to break through from understanding the nature of the skill of driving to that of appreciating the art of dune buggy racing.

3

The Art of Dune Buggy Racing and Video Gaming

There's no secret. You just press the accelerator to the floor and steer left.
(Bill Vukovich, after winning the Indy 500)

We now have an idea of what the skill of driving both looks and feels like. We also have some idea of insight and adrenaline. It is time we bite the bullet and risk going deeper to appreciate the inner dynamics of apprehending and comprehending simultaneously the art of racing a dune buggy in present time.

Art is the doing of a skill with our full attention. When we drive to work while daydreaming about a girlfriend or planning our day, driving has become merely an automatic skill. If Jacques Villeneuve drove his Formula A car in the Monaco Grand Prix the same way we drive our old bus to work, he would not survive two seconds. He treats driving as an art he is carrying out in the present moment. The difference between the mere execution of a skill and the performance of art does not lie in the characteristics of the activity itself—whether painting, racing, embroidering, or conversing—but in how we are totally physically and emotionally involved in doing it.

Though we ordinary drivers usually drive absentmindedly, most of us have had our special creative moments. We have all experienced emergency situations in a car. For example, it happened to me once that while driving at high speed I came to a very sharp curve in the road. It was too late to brake normally. Instead, I put the car instantly into a reverse slide. Since I had never done one before, I knew this did not happen as a reflex action. A few months before, however, I had read an excellent article about the technique taught to chauffeurs of the rich and famous of reverse skids to elude kidnappers. But my being able to learn it and do it all in the same instant meant everything happened together in total harmony, even if just for an instant. For that instant, it was as though time slowed to a crawl and I could think and act all at once with complete ease.

This task to understand the "art" of doing will be much more difficult than understanding a mere skill. We could watch our own skill in action. But in the art of dune buggy racing—whether on a real track or a computer simulation—there is no room at all for self-consciousness of the actual act, so we have to tackle it in a roundabout way. So before we get into racing, let us first make sure you and I both know what I mean by dwelling in different frameworks.

Learning to Fly

One of the first times I was a passenger on an airplane, I found myself sitting alone by a window near the wing on a clear summer's day. We were flying over the hills and valleys of New Brunswick's forests. In my imagination I reached out as though with a giant hand and caressed the hills and valleys, feeling the shapes of the rolling contours and even the prickly tips of the spruce trees tickling the skin of the palm of my hand.

I noticed the tiny cars and trucks wending their way on the highway. I pretended I was one of those drivers on the curvaceous road through the beautiful forests. I imagined what the trees, shrubs, flowers, hills, and valleys looked like from a car driving on that road. By chance, I looked up and saw us in the plane above.

Suddenly, I was a plane passenger again. It was astonishing to realize how high up we were—a mass of metal, motors, and fuel containing several score of human bodies, buoyed up by nothing more substantial than air. I noticed the airplane wing was trembling. It seemed the rivets holding the sheets of metal together were coming loose and would pop out at any minute. I started to panic. My eyes searched the plane to find the airhostess to warn her.

Then I was struck by the fact nobody else on the plane was in the least concerned. They were laughing and talking, or just sitting quietly absorbed in a newspaper or their thoughts. I considered the idea that they were "right" and I was just "imagining things." I decided to be them, and relax.

But I did not relax entirely. I was still apprehensive about looking out that window again. I wanted to look, but I was afraid. Suddenly it struck me that if only it was a television screen, not a window, I would be okay. Then I could just sit back, stretch out my legs a little, and watch the show. So that is what I did. I leaned the seat backward to enjoy the rest of the trip, being careful this time to restrict myself to merely observing the scenery on the "screen."

Opposite Frames of Reference

When we are sitting on a veranda by the railroad tracks and enjoying the landscape, we see the train flashing by. But when we are riding on that train and casually glance out the window, the earth and buildings beside the train appear to be flashing by us. In fact, as long as the train is rolling perfectly straight at a steady speed on a very smooth track, we cannot get over the sense that it is everything else moving, not us. Of course when the conductor tells us our speed is 100 km/hr, we believe her. But we have no more sense of that speed than we do of the fact the planet on which we are a full-time passenger is itself revolving at 100,000 km/hr around the sun. If now we draw the curtains on our rail car, we cannot see any evidence that we ourselves might be moving at all. When we look in a full-length mirror at ourselves standing on the floor of this moving train, we feel even more assured that we are quite stationary.

We cannot sense absolute motion or its energy. We can only be self-consciously aware of *relative* motion through our senses. We will encounter this in a later chapter while discussing our understanding of gravity.

But let us sit down on the moving train and open the curtains on the car windows again and abandon ourselves to enjoying the scenery. At some point after we have succeeded in doing this, we will be startled to suddenly apprehend our train as moving away from the scenery outside. Suddenly we feel ourselves being pulled along by the rush of the train on its tracks. Inadvertently we have transferred our framework of motionlessness from the train to that of the scenery outside, whereas our senses were still working from their pinpoint sources on our body from the train. Embarrassed at this discrepancy, we quickly readjust our motionless framework back to the train to reintegrate it with that of our sensory feelings. Now again it is the scenery that is moving and the train that is still.

All drivers periodically experience this misplacing of the motionless framework at stoplights. For example, Helen is at a stoplight and holds the brake with her foot to keep the car from moving. While waiting for the green she gets absorbed in admiring the car beside her, or maybe its driver, forgetting all about the traffic light. Suddenly she gets the sense she is moving backward. But on checking this out, she discovers her foot is still on the brake. Immediately she realizes it is the car beside her that is starting to move, not she.

In the above situations we find ourselves seesawing between dwelling in our own framework within the train or car and that of what we are contemplating. We have just switched between the one we used as a subject and the one as the object of our thoughts. In the creative act, however, we dwell actively in both simultaneously while being absorbed in how all the sensual perceptions and emotions relate the two frameworks to each other. In the creative act, both frameworks become subjects while the still point is in the tenuous balancing act, in how we relate them together through our actions—the verb.

The Dune Buggy Racer and the Video Game Player

Let us trade our train and landscape in for some dune buggies, a fast track, and a racing event. Of course, our television spectators are all ensconced in the framework of their couches. They see their favorite driver in his buggy bouncing up and over hills and slewing around curves. But the expert driver engrossed in driving his buggy does not see himself as moving about at all. He knows he is in a race vehicle moving around a track, but his focus is to remain as in the still eye of a hurricane, in what appears to all the spectators as a mad haphazard motion. If the driver starts to see himself as the couch potato does, as a tiny body being continually flung about violently in every which direction, he loses his orientation and thus control of the car at those very high speeds. On the other hand, if he forgets he is moving wildly around the track, he loses the edge he needs to maintain control. He needs a double framework that includes both views as the references through which he can operate.

Having studied the track well before entering the race, he is completely motionless within his dream image of a 3-D track. He is strapped so tightly into his buggy, it is one with him. He is racing as quickly as possible while dwelling in his motionless 3-D track and relating it all to sensory cues from a multitude of individual perceptions—visual, auditory, olfactory, and tactile—from particular points of place at particular instants of time to steer left or right and accelerate or decelerate. While racing, he feels simultaneously motionless within his buggy and in motion around the track, totally absorbed in how all his various sense perceptions are relating the two frameworks to each other. In fact, his frameworks are positioned analogously to both the one in which we have lost ourselves in contemplation of the scenery while on the moving train and the initial one in which we saw the scenery from the train. In the original case when we are on the train and we lose ourselves in contemplation, we correct ourselves as soon as we become aware of it. But the racer must be careful *not* to "correct" himself in order to avoid losing control. He needs to keep active in the opposite frameworks simultaneously.

Just imagine giving our television couch potato a remote control box with which he could control one of the dune buggies by watching a huge screen showing the whole track. He would not be able to reach high speeds without crashing.

It is very awkward to steer a moving car from merely visualizing the framework of a stationary track. When video car racing games first came out, the player was presented that scenario, with a screen showing the whole track. In one example, there were four dune buggies racing around this track over and around obstacles. The player controlled only one of these with his joystick and tried to beat the others to the finish line. Their speeds were very slow.

Speeds could be increased only when computer games called simulations were introduced. In these, the video screen is divided into two parts: across the bottom third the player sees his cockpit controls showing his speed, steering wheel, and gas gauge, and across the top two-thirds is the track. In simulations, the player is placed stationary relative to his car, and it is the track that moves. In all the latest Nintendo and Sega games, this simulator orientation, though usually without the lower control panel, is standard. Whether the player is driving a racing car or riding a water ski, the vehicle stays stationary in the middle of the bottom of the screen. It leaves this position only when the player loses control and takes a tumble. The gamer is actually steering the moving track to keep it under his vehicle.

We experience the parking lot as the still framework for steering and maneuvering our cars to get them into the right slot without hitting anybody else. But as we accelerate on the road we switch into the opposite framework in which we are the still point, and then like the video gamer it is as though we are actually steering the road to keep it under the car. But, the professional racer has to work in both frameworks simultaneously to stay in control. Otherwise he would not have the presence of mind to be able to deal with the tangible feelings of his body's resistance to acceleration and deceleration.

The video gamer's sense of inertia is still within the actual world in which he is functioning, in the hardness and the motionlessness of the chair in which he is sitting. He just has to completely block out self-consciousness of these tangible sensations of sitting in a chair in order to forget he is actually motionless. In the excitement and exhilaration of full play and racing, both racer and player feel they have pulled up their "anchors." Both are like the high-wire acrobat who has released her hold on the swing and is tumbling in midair toward an imaginary point at which she hopes to meet with a swing arching in from the opposite direction. Luckily for the video game player he is already sitting in his own safety net. But the racer's consists of only that provided by the thickness of his skull and the cushion of his helmet, and the structural design of his safety harness and the buggy's chassis.

Both the video game player and dune buggy racer invest much emotion—both fear and hope—into playing. Of course the video game player's investment is less than the racer's. He does not have the menace of possible fatal injury and economic loss staring him in the face. He can crash without injury and get another car at the press of a button. But neither does he have a chance at the financial rewards nor the adulation of thousands of fans. He merely gets to a higher level within the game for his reward. He is in the calm center of the tenuous balance between the fear of not making the next level and his hopes that he will. Of course, the true complexity of the various professional and personal tensions pulling and pushing both racer and player to drive slower or faster, more carefully or more recklessly, more intently or more indifferently, is far beyond what we are ready to explore here.

The driver can feel his emotions working in the moment-by-moment activity of steering, changing gears, and throttling. At this busy level of all those ongoing actions, he is trying to find the right rhythm and tempo, the optimum roller coaster of emotions to guide his integration through the twists and turns for each orbit around the real track. At the dream level, the object of both racer and player is to find a deep still point in the middle of all the major tensions, to be in the zone in which they are most ideally balanced to give them that edge in being able to as fully exploit their physical and emotional talent as possible and drive their best race.

Putting them all together into one "driving" motivating force is the trickiest part. What should the dune buggy racer dwell on to make it all happen smoothly? Thinking about the prize money he needs to pay his mortgage, he speeds up. Remembering his hopes of playing with his children that night, he slows down. Desiring the adulation of the fans, he speeds up. Fearing death, he slows down. Wanting to maintain the image of himself as a great driver in the history of racing, he speeds up. Thinking about his mother's warnings, he slows down. Waffling between hopes and fears can make for sensitive poetry, but it spells certain defeat in competitive racing. The racer has to struggle through all his conflicting purposes to bring them together into one unified steadfast purpose to win.

Learning to "Zone" in Reading

While I was reading Milne's *Winnie-the-Pooh* aloud, my youngest, who had learned the basic alphabet and some phonetics, started to interrupt me. She would stop me every once in a while and insist on reading small parts of it herself. At first I was quite relaxed and casual about it, just keeping quiet and letting her ramble through her parts as well as she could. But after awhile I felt I should be doing something more constructive, more useful than just listening. Besides, I was afraid that by letting her make all those mistakes over and over they would become entrenched.

I started to interrupt her to correct all the mistakes she was making that I had ignored at the beginning. Immediately her overall pace and rhythm of reading changed. Whereas at first she had merrily charged through the page, mistakes and all, now she became hesitant. Her pace slowed considerably. I suddenly realized that my beginning to correct her had made her so self-conscious of her efforts and of her mistakes she was losing her confidence and the groove through which she was trying to flow. After I stopped correcting her she started to pick up the pace and was soon again merrily charging through it. After that I no longer worried about correcting her, but waited for her to choose the times during her reading when she wanted my advice.

About every tenth mistake she would stop and ask for help. I wonder why? Was she just taking little breaks from the effort of trying to get the hang of this skill and using those opportunities to get the assurance and moral support implicit in the response from me? After all, it must have been very tiring to tackle such a difficult task in its early stages. Or did she become aware of only certain mistakes? Maybe she had the idea that learning to read was something learned just by doing it, like walking or riding a bicycle, that she did not need any more knowledge to do it, just time and practice until she got the hang of it? Perhaps she thought it was better for her to ignore her mistakes in general, assuming as soon as she got the action of reading right, she would not be making any more?

Becoming the Song

I cherish those rare times when I am carried away in singing a hymn, when the song sings me, when I cannot tell where the song starts and I end, when my body seems totally possessed by the song, when I am the song.

4

Learning to Type and Talk

How the Hell Did I Do That?
(Kilgore Trout) [17]

In the last chapter, we got an overall taste of the jump we have to take to move from understanding how we function within a well-learned skill to how we developed that skill in the first place. In this chapter we will start by reviewing a scientific paper on the details of the suspenseful series of jumps in learning to type.

On the one hand all students of typing progress through the same series of steps regardless of whether they are provided formal instruction or not. But on the other they all feel as though they are continually groping about in the dark, grasping at tenuous straws to discover the next step. Their progress as measured by increase in speed occurs in leaps and bounds, plateauing for stretches in between as they practice the latest innovation before searching for the next. In this chapter we will examine this phenomenon and compare it to a few examples of what Gallwey, Edwards, and Goldberg—the most widely read authors in their particular fields—write about learning to play tennis, draw, and write.

Could this same process explain how we learn our first language? Some linguists would have us believe we learn to speak our native language through genetically inherited software, as though it were an instinctual or mechanical activity. But nobody would argue we learn to type through instinctual mechanisms. We learn it jumping from step to step, with a great deal of practice in between, through a roller coaster of emotion.

For learning to type, we will use the thesis *The Psychology of Skill with Special Reference to Its Acquisition in Typewriting*, as researched and written in 1908 by W. F. Book. It was republished in 1973 as one of the *Classics of Psychology*. [18]

The most intriguing aspect of Book's experimental methodology is that he attempts to integrate both objective and subjective data as recorded by both machines and the participants. Besides having the machines record typing speeds at discrete intervals of clock-time, he had other machines tracking the pulse rates of the student typists during their practice sessions. Immediately after each typing session he had the students write a stream-of-conscious summary of their efforts. He wanted raw subjective ideas arising spontaneously and fresh from the flush of their efforts, before they had time to self-consciously edit and make sense of it in the light of what they already explicitly knew.

Unfortunately, Book never came up with one grand interpretation of all his data that made much sense to me. His idea of consciousness is very limited, as we will discuss. But he did come up with many fascinating insights into how typing develops. I have culled a portion of them to help us get some general idea. (Note: all bracketed insertions within quotes from Book are mine.)

A Progression of Purposive Accidents

To the casual observer, learning physical skills is merely the learning of a series of steps, and then just getting faster and smoother at doing those steps until the muscular speed limits are reached. But it is not quite like that. Typing *does* start out as a series of five steps, some of which are abandoned once the student realizes they are redundant, while others are gradually combined into fewer and fewer shortcuts until finally the latter are all merged into one skill or integration that the skilled typist ends up supervising in the same way a driver drives.

The increase in typing speed is not gradual. It increases in leaps and bounds, plateauing out for periods of about a week at a time. In the period immediately after each jump to a higher speed, a great deal of effort must be used to maintain that new speed. The amount of effort required is gradually reduced as the new increment in skill at that speed becomes entrenched, until he is ready for the next jump in a do-or-die effort.

At first the novice typist, Wayne, follows a series of five steps he has figured out for himself: one, getting a copy—for example of the letter *j*—into memory; two, spelling it; three, mentally locating the corresponding key on the keyboard; four, reaching for the key with appropriate finger; and five, initiating the finger movement. A few other steps creep in on their own. For example, after the last step, he automatically starts to check whether he did it right or wrong.

The first gain in typing speed comes from just getting faster and faster at going through these steps. But at some early point a limit is reached. And as long as Wayne is focused on just going through the steps, he can never get any faster. He has to learn to lose himself in the action of doing it, to be totally absorbed in it. One of Book's students writes, "'By far the major portion of attention in this stage goes to the feeling of touch and movement…I can avoid errors much better by attending strictly to the feel of the fingers and keeping constantly in mind where the fingers are.'"[19] Book directed his students into focusing all their attention on the present moment of typing and going at it hard.

Working in this state, the steps gradually merge into each other. The second step merges with the third and the fourth with the fifth. Some steps are adapted. For instance, the reflex step of checking to see whether the letter typed is right or wrong is abbreviated to becoming aware of a mistake only when it occurs.

Gradually…the four steps fuse into one continuous process which came to be attended to as a whole.[20] All adaptations and shortcuts in method were unconsciously [unself-consciously?] made, that is, fallen into by the learners quite unintentionally on the good days while practicing under strain.[21] Only in moments of extreme effort am I able to make innovations or lay hold of higher and better ways of doing the work[22] "It takes intense effort on my part," wrote Z in his earlier notes, "to bring about the wished for coordinations." In fact the strain is so great that a beginner literally works his whole body when trying to write.[23]

All the forward progress of shortcuts learned by Book's student guinea pigs appears accidental. Yet an enormous amount of purposive effort is expended for this accidental progress. We are back to the paradox of "accidentally-on-purpose" to describe even the learning of typing.

Remember the Goose?

For successful learning, what we choose to avoid is just as important as that on which we focus! Whether we read Gallwey on sports,[24] Edwards on drawing,[25] Goldberg on writing,[26] or Book on typing, we find the learner must avoid self-conscious thought as much as possible. Once we start thinking about how to control the parts of our body, or how well or badly we are doing, we lose the flow of doing it. But we have to pay our overall work the closest attention.

In teaching typing, Book went so far as to keep all scores away from his students. He saw scores as just so much more interfering mental baggage that would need to be excised later on. Gallwey makes a similar point in *The Inner Game of Tennis:*

> The next time your opponent is having a hot streak, simply ask him as you switch courts, "Say George, what are you doing so differently that's making your forehand so good today?" If he takes the bait—and 95 percent will—and begins to think about how he's swinging, telling you how he's really meeting the ball in front, keeping his wrist firm and following through better, his streak invariably will end. He will lose his timing and fluidity as he tries to repeat what he has just told you he was doing so well.[27]

Ongoing evaluations or judgments cripple a person's ability to perform smoothly in the groove. The mental habit of critically viewing oneself inadvertently forces the student to step outside himself and his mental focus, breaking off the continuum of action.[28] The student is advised to leave that to the referee—the teacher.

Book had his students describe their experiences immediately after finishing a session, before reflecting on it. A "well-known difficulty encountered in getting reliable introspective data is to keep consciousness [self-consciousness?] from concerning itself with the observing act. This was met in the present experiment by having each learner take care to write at a maximum rate and without thinking of how the work was done or how attention was working."[29] This is the same philosophy espoused by Goldberg for creative writing! We can get a grip on what we truly have experienced only if we write it out before we have a chance to censor it, edit it, or rephrase it in conventional ways.

To help the art student get around this thinking habit, Edwards, in her book *Drawing on the Right Side of the Brain,* directs him to draw copies of pictures held upside down so he cannot tell what he is drawing to keep the mind from thinking about what is being drawn. She tries to keep the student from being self-conscious of the figure being drawn. I think she would agree for drawing with what Book writes about learning to type: "It is strenuous effort carefully applied to the details of the work when all conditions are favorable and when the learner is thoroughly warmed up and has the right psychosis for making a leap that results in new adaptations and lifts the learner out of his habitual ruts onto the higher planes of work."[30]

Intuitions and the Right Questions

It is more difficult to nail down exactly what these teachers want us to focus on than what to avoid. There is a general theme of meditating on questions. Remember Socrates' statement? "But do you suppose that he would ever have enquired into or learned what he fancied that he knew, though he was really ignorant of it, until he had *fallen into perplexity* under the idea that he did not know, and had desired to know?" (For our purposes we can easily substitute the idea "able to do" for "know" in this passage.) If we do not know how or what or why or who, questions are the logical place to start. The problem is in being able to formulate a question both focused enough to give direction and yet open enough not to constrain the ability to answer freely. The best questions do not have any words, but how can I give examples of them?

When the typist says, "Only in moments of extreme effort am I able to make innovations or lay hold of higher and better ways of doing the work," he is implying that he is formulating very particular questions about what he is seeking at that stage of learning. Edwards, in teaching her students to develop skills by copying a drawing, tells them to ask such things as "Where does that curve start?" "How deep is that curve?" "What is that angle relative to the edge of the paper?"[31] as they are drawing. Gallwey and Kiegel use a similar questioning technique in getting skiing students to focus on the physical awareness of what they are doing at the moment of doing it, and away from thinking about or reflecting upon it.[32] Their goal is to get the student to integrate awareness of the action with the action of doing it as opposed to the split model of a mind observing and directing the body's actions.

Book emphasizes only two essential roles for the teacher. Both occur at what he calls the "'critical stages': (1) to encourage the faint-hearted learner; and (2) to see that he attends to all details until they are mastered."[33] In effect, he puts the teacher's role essentially as that of cheerleader for the discouraged student, and that of disciplinarian to keep the overeager student from trying to progress too quickly before she has sufficiently mastered the particular step most recently discovered. This is his application of positive and negative reinforcement. Though Book was aware of the student's constant internal questioning in creating faster and more accurate artifacts, he apparently did not see the need to help in that aspect. But it *is* apparent the aspect of questioning is crucial even in learning a simple skill like typing. How else can we explain Wayne's feelings of surprise in discovering new innovations? If he had not had a question in mind, he would not even have noticed the answer.

Book doesn't address the novice typists' self-motivation either. The initial stimulation for learning to type came from him. He needed some guinea pigs to test his hypothesis about learning to type. What kept them in the experiment? What purposes did those students harness together through their will to keep slogging through all those hours of tedious and repetitive drill? When they were tired, frustrated, and confused, what purposes did they draw on to keep on trying to master this skill?

As an artist, the novice typist attends "strictly to the feel of the keys." As a theorist, he is forming questions for the empiricist to try out. As an empiricist, she patiently tries out a myriad of different ways to answer those questions, until she finds the ones that work at each level and then practices the successful ones until the whole skill "sets." The idealist provided and unified the purposes to keep herself focused on the objective until it was achieved. After having achieved the final level, the typist has reached a similar level of skill to the commuter driving to work: "Learning typing is something like mowing a field. The farmer takes out his machine to cut the grass. All he [the typist] can do is keep his machine [body] in perfect condition and properly and vigorously applied to the work."[34] At this point Wayne learned to trust his body completely to perform the details of typing. All the steps have melded into one integration, and his mind is free of the task of having to work to think about what he is doing. Wayne can now merely watch what he is doing or just daydream some nonsense to get through a boring day while mindlessly copying the boss's scribbles.

But all skilled professionals are at times asked to deal with an extraordinary situation, as the typist is by an urgent report or a typing contest. Wayne is now skilled enough to freely abandon himself to the interplay of skill with full apprehension to attain peak performance in the art of typing, just like the driver of the dune buggy in the chase for the gold cup trophy.

Conscious, Self-Conscious, Unconscious, or Unself-Conscious?

The one major stumbling block I came up against in understanding Book's thesis was his use of the words "unconscious" and "conscious." The only way I could make sense of them in their contexts was to replace "unconscious" with the meaning of "unself-conscious" or even its opposite "conscious," and his use of "conscious" with the meaning of "self-conscious."

What can he mean in saying his subjects in learning did something "unconsciously"? Obviously they were not in a coma; nor were they "sleep-typing." Being totally—both cognitively and emotionally—engrossed in their typing exercises they had to be totally awake, that is totally conscious in pursuing them. He could not have expected them to write introspective comments on what they had done "unconsciously." Book's use of the word "conscious" parallels that restricted meaning as implied in Descartes' statement, "I think, therefore I am," in the sense that they both consider reflection as full consciousness itself. And thus Book is forced to erroneously label the very lively "unself-conscious" or "conscious" state we experience in the heat of action as "unconscious."

Take his statements: "A fact worthy of special emphasis is that our learners, who were left without the guidance of a teacher, worked out unconsciously a method of dealing with the special difficulties encountered in typewriting, which had the same result in the end,"[35] and an earlier quote, "all adaptations and shortcuts in method were unconsciously made, that is, fallen into by the learners quite unintentionally on the good days while practicing under strain."

Does it not seem contradictory to describe our state during the most intense moments of learning as being "unconscious"? At those moments when we exert ourselves to the utmost, we feel more intensely aware and alive than at any other times in our lives. An artist, Robert Henri, wrote, "The object, which is back of every true work of art, is the attainment of a state of being, a state of high functioning, a more than ordinary moment of existence…We make our discoveries while in the state because then we are clear-sighted."[36] As Book describes it, learning even the simple skill of typing is a series of intuitive leaps. In those leap moments we are not self-conscious of what we are doing. In those moments we are feeling, thinking, observing, and doing altogether at once. The spontaneous act of learning in itself is "unself-conscious." Just as we cannot watch ourselves getting an insight, we cannot watch ourselves in the actual moment of learning a skill. We only become self-conscious, that is "conscious of" what we are learning as the realization of acquiring the new skill or knowledge gradually dawns on us.

The Progressive Emergence of Skill

What is fascinating about the progress of Book's typing learners is that despite the fact they were not guided by a teacher, they all progressed through the same steps in the same order, from starting out following the same five steps in typing a letter to where they ended up. Just as I did not try to explain to my daughter how to learn to read, Book did not tell his experimental subjects the skill on which to focus next at each stage in their development. He merely observed the progress of how they learned to type by their own efforts, encouraging them to keep trying when discouraged and slowing them down through difficult stages. "The learners suddenly noticed that they were doing certain parts of the work in a new and better way, then purposely adopted it in the future."[37] He found that the most critical time in learning is the later stages of entrenching any particular new shortcut. "…habits are perfected or sink to the realm of the unconscious [mechanical skill?] very gradually. If we might speak of their final perfection or dropping out of consciousness [self-consciousness?] as dying, they die hard."[38]

The students' experiences were somewhat different in where they had most problems and how fast they progressed, but essentially it was as though they were all on the same track, a series of leaps to ever more efficient plateaus of performance that were never explicitly defined for them and of which they become aware only after they had passed through each particular stage. It is as though, flying blind like bats, students have a subconscious radar system in place to find their way.

There is a similar phenomenon in the universal progression in the infant's development of grammatical skill in native language learning, as elucidated by the "formalists" or "Chomskyists."

Trask writes:

> Now consider how children learn negation. All children do this in exactly the same way. First, they stick a negative word (usually 'no') at the front of the sentence: 'No I want a juice.' After a while, that negative word is moved to the front of the verb: 'I no want juice.' Finally, the rather complicated English negative auxiliaries appear: 'I don't want juice.' And here's the crunch: parents, if they like, can correct the child until they're blue in the face, but she will continue to use her current pattern for making negatives until she's ready for the next stage. Even if they do not correct her (and most parents do not), she will still move through the same stages until she settles on the adult form.
>
> What is she doing? Once again, she is clearly formulating rules for making negatives, and she's trying different rules until she finds one that gives her the adult forms. But look: she's not just trying out any old rules. Every child tries the same rules in the same order! Moreover, children learning other languages do exactly the same thing—though a child learning, say Spanish can stop at the second stage, because the 'I no want juice' pattern is exactly the way negative sentences are constructed in Spanish.[39]

Not only do children not learn language structure from their parents, it has been proven children are the leading innovators in developing new languages. For example, in a situation in which adults of different linguistic groups are thrown together, for example, in Hawaii (through immigration), in Haiti (through slavery), and more recently Papua New Guinea (through improved communications), "pidgin" is the first result. These pidgins are differentiated from languages, because they are basically a heterogeneous mixture of different pieces from different languages; simply they are a "language mix." But the children of the people speaking pidgin turn it into a real homogenous language, with, for example, a fixed word order, or a general rule for forming plurals. This new language is called a "creole."[40]

Children are a language's creative grammarians! Think about that the next time you find yourself correcting a child's grammar: Did the child make a mistake or is he or she beginning to create a new language?

Gene-Actualization or Creativity?

In the face of this evidence, the Chomskyist's argument that universal grammar is innate and as such genetically based appears irrefutable. It would seem children have a universal language grammar instilled into them from birth and are merely actualizing or "real-izing" it through their prepuberty period of development. Of course, I hasten to add that nobody has ever been able to even tenuously prove this through an actual genetic experiment. But at first glance, it seems a perfect answer to the riddle.

The discovery of how children learn their native language while seemingly ignoring their parents' efforts puts the behavioral empiricist at a severe disadvantage in the nature-versus-nurture debate. But at least she can argue the child cannot have invented language in a vacuum. Proof is in past experiences with the rare infant children lost in the wild who, grown up past puberty without any interaction with humans, can never become fluent in any language. Furthermore, the learning of native language is not only triggered by social interaction, it also builds on the particular sounds, whole words, expressions, and grammatical peculiarities employed by parents, siblings, and friends. Children in the care of English parents learn English, not Chinese. Success in language learning is just as tightly tied to doing it in particular times and places as that of typing is to the tedious and repetitive task of practicing long hours on a keyboard.

But neither the innate theorist nor the behavioral empiricist would argue that since we all progress through exactly the same path of learning the skill of typing, we must have a genetic blueprint for it. We have not lived and evolved with typewriters nearly long enough to even remotely give credibility to the suggestion that typing has become 'instinctual.' But learning the skill of typing and the invention of grammar are similar phenomena in this aspect of their development.

Could it be that the universality of the basic structure of language merely reflects the basic dynamics of how we learn anything? If these dynamics could be broken up into components, then maybe we could eventually understand the order of progression in language learning as no more mysterious than a child learning to control his thigh muscles before learning to crawl, and learning to crawl before balancing on his legs, and learning to run only after walking.

Furthermore, linguistic researchers have no idea as to why children, who supposedly are so good at actualizing their genetic code for the basic linguistic structure while following their parents' example for the basic sounds, keep inventing new languages—completely new sounds and new variations of the thousands of grammar rules. What is the impetus behind the evolution of languages? For example in Papua New Guinea over 700 distinct languages arose! That these linguistic communities were isolated from each other in an extremely rugged mountainous island allowed it to happen. But why and how did the children keep reinventing their language? These bursts of linguistic diversity, like the variations on any art form, must be the work of strong creative impulses. The invention and constant reinvention of language is our original and most basic art form.

Instincts or Emotions?

The only things we can definitively label as instinctual in humans are the newborn's searching for and suckling his mother's breast, and later on, sex. Even in the sexual drive, how much is inherited and how much is learned? Whereas animals are limited to sexual activity during only one point of the estrus cycle of a nonpregnant female, the frequency and variety of our desire and expression is significantly greater. In fact, sex—this bottomless yearning for intense physical-emotional union with others—is obviously a much stronger drive in humans than in animals. It permeates our whole personality. But at the same time humans seem to have much more freedom and flexibility in how, if rightfully channeled through the best ideas and ideals, it can reach culmination in acts of love, whether directly or in how it is sublimated. But if wasted, thwarted, abused, or misguided, it can respond like "the dream deferred" in the Langston Hughes' poem "Harlem":[41]

> Does it dry up
> like a raisin in the sun?
> Or fester like a sore—
> And then run?
> Does it stink like rotten meat?
> Or crust and sugar over—
> like a syrupy sweet?
>
> Maybe it just sags
> like a heavy load.
>
> *Or does it explode?*

What is the source of all the other instinctual drives in humans that we read about in popular science magazines and books?[42] When these purported instincts are described, most sound suspiciously like emotional attributes. Not being able to perceive emotion and thus properly incorporate it into their ideas, many scientific writers have lumped their conceptions of emotions into a generic pool of innate elements labeled "instincts." These "instinctive emotions" are then errone-ously relegated to explain the actualization of innate patterns of behavior.[43]

Human beings pass through a much longer period than animal beings of vir-tually complete dependency on their elders for survival. We have to learn a great deal more in order not only to survive, but to thrive in an overall sense. Rather than hypothesizing we inherit skills and patterns of behavior genetically, like we do blue eyes, red hair or brown skin, it makes more sense to posit we learn them through influences of those around us and through the images and stories of our culture. Rather than hypothesizing that we inherit grammar or that it is drilled into us by parents, it makes more sense to posit the universality of the basic lan-guage grammar is rooted in our physiological and psychological similarities and in the particular dynamics of how we function to learn. As we will explore in the next two sections, we can discover a solid basis for not only the main components of the sentence—the subject, verb, and object—but also for its dynamics in the cycling through four distinct dimensions of self-consciousness.

B: <u>Language</u>

5

Reflections on Learning a Foreign Language

'What's the water in French, sir?'
'L'eau,' replied Nicholas.
'Ah!' said Mr. Lillywick, shaking his head mournfully. 'I thought as much. Lo, eh? I
don't think anything of that language—nothing at all.'
(***Charles Dickens,*** **Nicholas Nickleby**)

I have collected a montage of personal experiences in learning a foreign language. Learning one, especially one from another language family, is an arduous chore for an adult. For many Westerners it is virtually impossible to learn an Oriental tonal language. Yet if they were to drop any of their children—the younger the better—into that linguistic environ, the child would learn that language as easily as a new game. You would think an educated adult who has already mastered one language and understands basic grammar would have a head start. But many adults have forgotten how to play.

Relearning to Play

Actually the difficulty in language learning starts much earlier than adulthood. Notice among your immigrant friends that those with an accent are those who arrived in your country after puberty. Those who arrived before puberty generally do not have an accent at all.

If you had not learned your first language by puberty, you would not have been able to learn one at all. Over the last few centuries scientists have encountered and studied a handful of children who were separated from all other humans at a very young age and either raised by animals like Victor, "the wild boy of Aveyron,"[44] or kept incommunicado in an attic room until past the age of puberty. None of these children, even with the most intensive and individual tutoring, could ever become fluent in any language. Was it that they were past the primary experimental stage of making sense of the world? Were they too far beyond those childhood experiments for the modus operandi of those experiments in the invention of subject, verb, and object? Rooms no longer change shape as the teen walks through them. The quantity of a volume of water remains the same when poured from tall thin glasses into short stubby ones. The prepuberty child lives primarily playing in the flow of the present moment. The teen already in an advanced state of self-consciousness is separating out between feeling, thinking, conceiving, and his intentions and aspirations, as though they were unrelated to each other, except in theory. Puberty is a natural 'age of no return'[45] for first language learning.

Puberty is the beginning of the age when we can start taking language apart into pieces and thinking purely abstractly. Physics isn't taught at elementary levels, not because children need more time to learn the mathematics required, but because they have only limited ability to focus their efforts on only one mode of self-consciousness. Young children can, for example, learn to appreciate and name gravitational and centrifugal forces through physical interactions but cannot conceptualize them into comprehensive mathematical abstractions.

After puberty,[46] even second-language learning becomes more difficult. When we as adults first hear the verbal stream of our chosen foreign language, our first impulse is to try to make sense of it, and we fight to achieve that through vocabulary studies and grammar books. But language must be heard as recognizable bits. Our ears pick up only a continuum of sound. We have to break it up into discrete pieces—individual words—before we can then understand in the context of collections of them—sentences. As those of us who have learned a foreign language have found out, our ears are completely useless in determining how to break up a continuum of one sentence of unfamiliar sounds into individual words. We cannot divide that stream of exotic sound into the units of words until we can at least recognize most of the words in that sentence. Then we will be able to interpret the unrecognizable pieces in between as other discrete units, which we can then ask about or look up in a dictionary.

If we give up in despair, we rationalize by saying we do not have a gift for languages. Well, we all had this gift when we were children, and there are a number of adults who do learn foreign languages very well. Why did those adults not lose the gift? How do they retain or regain the gift for language learning they had as children?

The typical adult language learner has the same problem as someone who has never learned how to type attempting to write an essay directly on a word processor. This novice typist would be struggling with the meaning of what to write while at the same time struggling with learning the physical manipulations necessary to get it down. It is amazingly frustrating to learn how to type if you are also concerned with the meaning of what you are typing. In fact the effort devolves into a stalemate, a paralysis of both thought and action.

The novice typist starts out properly by focusing on one letter a time, one finger practicing one letter, and within the first lesson gradually expanding to use the full hand for four letters. Instead of focusing on the meaning of what is being written, she focuses strictly on the feel and action of the fingers, forming relationships between those and the meaningless individual letters she is copying. Similarly, the smart novice linguist starts out practicing hearing and repeating the sounds of that foreign language not worrying about their meaning.

During my years in Thailand, I discovered that none of the first-rate Thai-language schools for teaching foreigners supplied textbooks. At first I suspected they wanted to keep their teaching methodology secret from the other schools. We students wanted texts so desperately! But later I realized their methodology was simply to force us to practice listening to and saying words and phrases.

It is so undignified! The adult is ordered to abandon his need to make sense of what he is doing and forced to mumble strange nonsense syllables like some babbling idiot or little child—exactly like a little child. We were forced to first learn to enjoy making those peculiar exotic sounds and how to blend them until we acquired some approximation for the internal rhythm of the language. Only gradually, as they became part of our physical skill, could we be concerned about their meanings and act dignified about it. Like a child we have to learn to lose ourselves in an action game for which we do not understand the rules, and enjoy exploring its strangeness.

Learning language is much more a sport than a mental game. How to enunciate those strange sounds and even learn to hear them is a physical art. Could you learn to play soccer by reading a dozen books about it?

This might seem ridiculous to you. Why do we need to start at the very basics again with learning a second language? We already know one language and are they not all fundamentally the same? They are, but they are also very different. Though all languages have subjects, verbs, and objects, at their roots, they also have thousands of different grammatical rules. Have you tried to learn French verb conjugations? Even more confusing, even though we might know the literal meaning of, for example, several Thai words, what they mean in combination in Thai has often little or no relationship to what we mean by that same combination in English. Furthermore, the exact same form of many words in Thai can be used as an adjective, adverb, noun, or verb, all depending on where it is in the sentence. This complication is further compounded by the particular etiquette of any particular culture that delineates what matters are polite to speak about explicitly and what can only be alluded to and how—the whole emotional ambience associated with all words and expressions. It is impossible to grasp these complications intellectually, until after you have learned to speak that new language in the context of its native speakers.

Emotional Rhythms and Punctuation

Every language has it own rhythm. Have you ever listened carefully to two foreigners speaking a totally strange language? Of course, you cannot have a clue what they are talking about. But just try focusing all your concentration only on the emotional aspect. Listen to it as you would to jazz. In jazz it is as though the different instruments are playing with each other as friends and lovers do. The more animated are your speakers, the more you can pick up parallel patterns. Of course if you are eavesdropping on two lovers, it might sound more like "Il Silencio."[47]

In my fourth or fifth month in Thailand, I discovered myself cuing in strictly on the emotional dimension to be able to "communicate." There were many times in that early period when I had no idea what people were even talking about. But I could fit in and be part of the ongoing emotional rhythms of those around. I had begun to apprehend the emotional rhythms of their language and very crudely emote in symphony. On the one hand, since I often did not even know the subject of conversation, you could say I was faking it. On the other hand, I had found a way to be a dynamic part of a real aspect of what was happening and delight in the company of these friendly peoples.

I was reminded of one of the most important techniques of cross-cultural communications by a headman in a remote village of Sarawak. I was there for a brief tour and had no idea of their language, communicating exclusively through an interpreter. At one point I was asked to summarize my impressions to the group of villagers assembled. Out of habit, I turned to the interpreter and started my summary. Immediately, the village headman spoke up, insisting I turn toward him, addressing him and his friends directly. Later I realized that only in that way could they at least get the direct emotional impact of my feelings, which they could then splice onto the intellectual content from the interpreter.

This lesson was often reinforced for me when working overseas through interpreters. If either one of the single-language speakers focuses exclusively on the interpreter, the depth of communication is poor. Too much of the emotional content of the speaker gets lost in the process. If both speakers address the other

solely through the interpreter, communication easily breaks down into the acrimony of mutual incomprehension and disrespect, especially if the interpreter is
merely summarizing the information instead of embodying the same emotions as
the speakers. Outside of the context of emotional content, neither can put the
other's thoughts into perspective.

Parrot or Genius?

In second-language learning, it is safer to start out cooing and babbling as a child
and gradually, after a great deal of blood, sweat, and tears, end up being a genius
in that language. As long as you insist on tackling it as a genius, you will be lucky
to end up as fluent as a parrot.

Actually that is probably good advice about anything learned. Even if we are
expert at something, the only way to understand that subject from someone else's
point of view is to leave our own understanding behind. Anyone who brings his
own framework along to understanding the other's will only get caught up criti-
cizing the new framework as invalid and unworkable, and never get through to
what the other means by it. Or in the case in which we know what the other has
meant and we do not like it, we react by attacking his conclusions as being totally
unrealistic in terms of our old framework. In the case of language learning, I have
heard learners seriously complain about how irrationally the Thai grammar is
structured!

Advice on language learning is a lot easier to give than to take. In fact it is
excruciatingly difficult to carry out. When I was learning Thai, I was so slow they
had to make a special class of one to keep me from holding up the rest. The only
way I became proficient was by being lifted out of Bangkok and dropped into a
rural setting where I could not possibly perform any work without learning the
local lingo. Once there, I was trapped between my aspirations to accomplish
something and the enormous difficulties—linguistic, cultural, and otherwise—in
being able to do anything. Luckily the emotional excitement in living in such a
strange and wonderful place and wholehearted morale support from local persons
gave me the energy to hang on to my aspirations and struggle through the seemingly insurmountable linguistic and cultural barriers.

"Mathein Pathein"[48]

The dynamics of learning that seemed so natural in childhood become very difficult in adulthood. As adults we have forgotten how to learn from scratch. Luckily
the infant cannot conceive the impossibility of learning something for which he
does not yet have any skill, much less the faintest preconception. Naïvely he

charges ahead step by step sustained throughout his many trials and tribulations by enjoyment in the gradual accumulation of competency in communicating with an ever-widening world of other persons. In contrast the adult has to first rid the self of an accumulated baggage of pride and preconceptions and overcome his self-consciousness of ignorance and lack of skill in forging a new path. Real learning for adults is dirty, undignified, sweaty work—our sacrifice. If we do not have the sense of humor to appreciate and accept the ridiculousness and absurdity of it all, we are totally stymied and fail to discover the phoenix rising from the ashes.

In forging through the awkwardness of learning a foreign language we gain an appreciation of some of the basics of what language is. But for a more intimate appreciation we should start with the one we know best, as we will do in the following chapters.

6

The Syllable: Marriage of Consonant and Vowel

To see the world in a grain of sand.
(William Blake)

In the next chapter, we will work toward appreciating the origin of the structure and dynamics of language. But here we will focus on vowels and consonants at the level just below the meaning of words. The mystery of the relationship between vowels and consonants in the syllable is as intriguing as that between verbs and nouns in the sentence. Whereas verbs describe the relationship of the subject of a sentence with its object, vowels bridge consonants within a syllable. With an understanding of the parallels between these two, we will have the license to permit us to better appreciate the synthesis between the emotional and perceptive faculties at the roots of consciousness and its communication.

The Alphabet and Phonetics

The most obvious phenomenon about vowels and consonants is that vowels are vowels and consonants are consonants right across the spectrum of languages. Generally, what is a vowel sound in one language is not a consonant sound in another language. Vowels in any one language are only variations of the vowels in any other. Consonants in any language punctuate those vowels, or vice versa, the vowels are the particular sound made in connecting any two consonants. Though the particular combination of vowels and consonants used in any one language is different from any other language (or most other languages), what makes the difference between vowel and consonant sounds is common to all languages. This phenomenon has allowed phonetics to create a universal phonology or alphabet of vowels and consonants that can be used to spell the words in all languages.

It is difficult for nonlinguists listening to a foreign language to accept the idea of a universal alphabet. Not only are the vowels not quite the same sound, but also different languages do not use the same selection of vowels and consonants from the linguist's universal alphabet. The number of syllables available to any particular language is limited to whatever fraction of the whole possible range of all vowels and consonants that a cultural group has selected to use and combine.

The difficulty for the layperson in accepting the idea of universal phonetics is further complicated by the fact that the first level of interpretation within which we self-consciously distinguish between sounds is not that of vowel and consonant sounds as separate entities but in combination as syllables. By themselves, vowels and consonants are merely so much meaningless noise. Learning the English, Thai, or Arabic alphabets has little to do with learning the real essential sound of vowels and consonants as used in speech. Just try spelling a word super fast, even a phonetically correct word like "string" or "crap," and then listen to the differences between the overall sound thus produced and how the real word sounds as spoken. They are very different.

Take the letter "b" of the English alphabet. When you say the letter, you are actually saying "bee," which includes both consonant and vowel sounds. When you try to separate out the pure "b" from the "ee" and just sound the "b," all you get is a puff of air. Many linguists argue that consonants do not have any sound in themselves at all. To them only vowels are audible. Linguists also assure us that when we say or "spell" the letter "a" we are actually saying "ay," the "y" being termed a "glide" consonant. If we shorten the vowel sound to avoid this glide we find we have to use a "stop" consonant like "p," "d," "t," or "k."

It would appear that in general we cannot sound a letter without expressing a vowel and consonant together. Professional linguists themselves are as mystified by this relationship between vowels and consonants as are physicists with the relationship between their conceptions of light as a waveform and as a quantum of energy. For instance, Edward Callary, a phonologist, ascribes the difference between the two by how they are made: "While consonants are made with some kind of obstruction in the oral cavity, vowels are 'open' sounds made with a relatively free flow of air." [49] Of course this statement begs the question, "Can sound occur only as the result of interference with airflow?" He could just as well have said something like "consonants are made by fixed shapes that the vowels are forced to connect, or vice versa..."

From Cooing to Babbling

Linguists have named the child's first major step in native language learning as *cooing*. During his second month of life outside the womb, the infant has begun with some serious experimentation in producing vowel sounds similar to those heard from his guardians. A few months later he begins *babbling*, punctuating those vowel sounds with more and more distinct consonants. We can think of this play with consonants as analogous to adding specific prefixes and suffixes to the vowels. Rather than having clear sounds in and of themselves, the consonants are merely variations on how to begin and end vowels, to punctuate and isolate them from other vowels so we can more sharply experience and enjoy their interplay in longer words perhaps.

"One of the grand mysteries of language concerns the nature of vowels and consonants. Are they really different entities processed separately by the brain, or just artificial labels developed for convenience?" reads a recent edition of the *Harvard Gazette*.[50] Apparently these scientists were fortunate enough to discover two head injury patients, one who had trouble speaking vowels and the other consonants, and then study them together. The conclusion of their studies is that vowels and consonants are processed in different areas of the brain. "We're excited about answering a question that has been around for such a long time, excited about reaching a definite conclusion that people possess separate mechanisms to process vowels and consonants."

Let us take a somewhat different path and instead of wondering if they are produced in different places, rather speculate that their origin is of a totally different nature. After all, one of these scientists, Doriana Chialant, goes a step further. She "believes that vowels give speech a pattern the way harmony structures music." Why not go with vowels as the archetypal expression of the emotional wave and consonants as that of discrete bits of sensory information? The vowel is the energy that connects the consonants together through time. In this interpretation of the relationship between vowel and consonant we can see it as a microcosm of that between the verb and its nouns and see the evidence of their origin in the interplay of the emotional and perceptive aspects of our nature.

Language as Tool or Archetype?

Academics often fall into treating language either as a mere mechanism or as an innate artifact to fit into the limitations of their research tools and methodology. But language is not a mechanical tool like a hammer or typewriter activated by manipulating physical materials. The act of conversing in the present moment is the everyday expression of intelligence as rooted in the very dynamics of our psyches, both in physical and emotional dimensions. Its manifestation and development, whether in oral or signed language, is the flowering of our profound duty to, desire for, and fulfillment in communing with both the self and the other.

Thinkers like Michael Polanyi argue for language as the expression of the emerging evolving nature of man. "The operations of a higher level cannot be accounted for by the laws governing its particulars forming the lower level. You cannot derive a vocabulary from phonetics; you cannot derive the grammar of a language from its vocabulary..."[51] Studying the relationship between consonants and vowels gains us some preliminary insight into the larger picture of language on a grammatical level in the following chapter.

7

Capturing Language Alive

I am still studying verbs and the mystery of how they connect nouns.
(Sandburg) [52]

As infants learning to talk, we could not understand linguistics research. And if an infant "mewling and puking in the nurse's arms"[53] can learn how to do it without knowing anything about it, do we need to spend a great deal of our time and energy floundering through tomes of hoary academic jargon in order to come to terms with it?

Mind you, some linguists might not like my approach. They might insist on having us try to pin language down, formulating it in their specialized language until it cannot wriggle any more in the museum of objectivity. They need to dissect it and name all its parts within the confines of abstract theories or hierarchies of factors to explain it away. Like other scientists, they want to avoid the contamination and distortion of their study materials by subjective or emotional elements. The theorist wants a consistent logical theory, while the empiricist wants a cool objective hierarchy of factors.

The theorist's problem comes when he wants to take all his interesting ideas and put them back together into a workable reflection of how language functions in reality. In having focused his apprehension strictly on the universal structural elements of language, he no longer has the dynamo of emotion that made it all work in nature. So, he concludes that language grew out of an innate software program.

The functionalist's problem is in getting his facts to work organically. He interpreted and translated all that emotional energy into statistical data and cannot change them back. Besides, having restricted his observations and thoughts strictly to what stimulated the listener and what he said as a result, he could not have any idea of what went on between the listener's hearing something and subsequently his mouthing a response. The pragmatists, knowing both are only partially right, are left seesawing between them.

But we are zookeepers. We want to capture language alive, emotions and all. We want to see and feel the various parts of language and how their juxtaposition reflects our experiencing of everyday life. We are prepared to see it and feel it in its mystery and paradox. We are searching for meaning that makes sense in the physics and poetics of the present moment.

Poetic vs. Prosaic Language

Before we really get started, let us make sure we are talking about the same thing when we talk about *language*. A few linguists theorize that animals can talk. They are very inventive in interpreting an animal's signaling system of squeaks, squawks, and growls as words within a grammar. There is no doubt that animals, and even to a lesser extent plants, employ deep and complex communication systems. For instance, Monty Roberts describes the sequence of signals through which he can develop a trust relationship with an unbroken horse in less than an hour.[54] He has demonstrated and proven his technique on tours around the world by encountering strange wild horses in his specially designed ring and then riding them without any of the traditional whips, breaking bits, and other conventional techniques used to break a horse's spirit in order to dominate and subjugate it to the trainer's iron will. But there is a qualitative limitation on these signaling systems[55] as compared to what we can do through human language.

Of our pet dogs barking together, we casually say they are "talking" to each other, because there is an obvious exchange of sounds and an ongoing communication between them. At first glance we identify this as the same framework of communication we experience many times a day in our interaction with persons. Whereas there is no doubt there are a great variety of sounds made during animal communication—whether of emotional affection or disaffection, or even while showing the young how to do certain tasks—barking is not considered language by the majority of linguists, because it does not have the same internal structure. Rather the sounds are merely a series of signals structured not through a natural grammar, but through the dynamics of what is happening in the moment of that time and place.

A linguist, R.L. Trask, describes it as follows:

> Can you imagine being able to talk about nothing but the present moment and about nothing but what you can see at the present moment?...And yet this unthinkable state of affairs is exactly the way animal signaling systems appear to work...So far as we can tell, mice do not swap stories about their close encounters with cats, nor do bears soberly discuss the severity of the

coming winter…Virtually all "utterances" by nonhuman animals appear to relate directly, and exclusively, to the time and place of uttering.[56]

We can also operate in a primeval or emotional "utterance" mode like that of animals in present time and space. Most obviously we had to as infants before we learned language. We could choose between contented gurgling sounds, crying, or one of several hundred variations in between to demonstrate our particular feeling about what was happening at that moment. We also experienced it as children or even much later as adults playing a fast-paced sport and entirely focused within the tempo and rhythm of the action, exclaiming, warning, encouraging, fooling, or intimidating other players. When we are playing totally in the zone we are not self-conscious of the time and place. We assume all the players are preoccupied within that same present moment of time and space, so we do not have to use whole sentences to spell out what we mean.

In that situation, or in any other in intense moments of interaction when we are totally in a groove with someone else, our sentence patterns can dissolve into almost pure signals, like the kaleidoscope of images in a poem. What is perfectly and totally intelligible to the two involved in such an interaction is often complete nonsense to any outsider who happens by. The outsider's first question is "Hey what's going on here?" The outsider has to get the two to explain their frame of reference in time and place in order for him to understand what it is all about, to get them to start using "proper" sentences to enable all three to carry on conversation.

In fact that is why when we really want to get to know someone, we choose a private place in which to do it, a place where nobody can disturb us. Then we start out with clear full sentences. But as we begin to find a mutual rhythm and tempo, a groove begins to grow, we lose self-conscious track of where we are in time and space, allowing ourselves to slip more and more into stream-of-consciousness type utterances, signaling within a sharing of feeling and understanding…

Such are the dynamics of poetic language. What most obviously distinguishes the linguist's idea of "real" or "literal" language from these poetic signaling systems is the human's strange power of being able to separate a happening into two parts: time and space. In fact, what we humans do when we talk clearly and explicitly is take the external sense of space and internalize it into the noun, and the sense of time—as seen in the importance of tense—into the verb. Only then is it possible for us to sit around the fire at night and tell stories about our animal friends. Language in its prosaic use is a reconstruction of reality in imaginary time, outside of real time and space.

Nouns as Ghosts of Space

First, let's reexamine our schoolbook definitions of noun and verb. A huge stumbling block in appreciating language is being stuck in hackneyed definitions. Like whales beached on the sands of Peggy's Cove, ideas abstracted from real experiences soon lose their elegant shapes and fluidity of motion. They need to be constantly reimmersed in their natural element to stay alive and meaningful for us. Take for instance the word *noun*. We define it as the name of a person or thing. Well what "thing" are we talking about when we use the word *dog?* Can you make even the foggiest picture of what that thing is? You can conjure up pictures of particular dogs, Snoopy or Lassie, but the more you try to make up a generic picture that includes all the dogs you have known, the more you end up with a very ghostly configuration.

What does one generalized picture of all the dogs we have ever known look like? Try and make one generic picture of the lean mean Doberman pinscher, the friendly short-legged Jack Russell, the hairy Shetland collie, and the affectionate giant St. Bernard. It is totally futile. The closer we get to something we can visualize, the less it looks like the collection of physical characteristics we mean. Yet in everyday speech we speak confidently as if we all have the same meaning for "dog" in mind. After all, is that not why we have only one word for it?

Young children have a lot of fun trying to come to terms with how adults use nouns. I suspect that is where they get the idea of ghosts. We keep telling them there are no such things as ghosts, but every time we speak we use nouns that have no definite body or color or any other sensible property to them, just a sort of vague indeterminate shape floating in midair. And we use them as though these words refer to something that really exists.

To make it even more confusing, we use many nouns with no physical characteristics at all, words referring to ideals like liberty, democracy, and justice. And how are we going to classify those nouns that appear more like verbs, purely emotional words like love, caring, disgust, and hate?

What about the verb? Take any verb and try to perceive it by itself as we define it: the expression of action or being. It is impossible to perceive anything without using a thing or person as a form within which it can be expressed. The verb seems to be pure spirit, a purely abstract conception. In dealing with nouns and verbs we are grappling with ghosts and the spirits that animate them. We know clearly only what they mean when combined together and used unself-consciously.

What reality is there in this thing, a thought, that we can turn over and around in our minds to look at from a thousand different angles, and even pull apart into little pieces like a mechano set and then put back together again as if it were a substantial whole? And what about those emotions the poet professes to be real, which he spins into poems for us as "dwellings" to be experienced in a dazzle of feelings?

Subject-Verb-Object

Linguists agree that every language studied is rooted in sentence structures employing a subject, verb, and object. Though every language has thousands of unique grammar rules, without exception, whether of the most primitive peoples in Papua New Guinea, or those arisen from the grandest of ancient civilizations, or those spoken in the most sophisticated cities today, all languages use this trio as the nucleus of sentence building. It is the heart of Chomsky's "universal grammar."

Most of us remember parsing sentences in English classes. But it might not have occurred to us then that we could easily have divided the sentence into two main types of parts: the modified and the modifiers. Only the subject, main verb, and object of the sentence are not themselves modifiers or part of a multiword modifier like a phrase or clause. They form the central dynamic of the sentence. All the other parts, whether adjectives and adverbs or phrases and clauses, merely modify, that is, more sharply delineate, them. The modifiers merely give us more detailed information on the what, where, when, who, how, or why of the subject, verb and object.

There are differences in how these three key parts are ordered in the format of sentences in the various languages. For example, English speakers use the order subject-verb-object, whereas Japanese speakers use subject-object-verb. Basque and Latin speakers can use either subject-verb-object or object-verb-subject, since they use special suffixes to differentiate between object and subject. Thai speakers can make virtually any word a subject, verb, or object simply by putting that word as it is into the right place in the sentence. But whether a language uses word order or suffixes to differentiate between object and subject is irrelevant to us. The essential aspect is that each is clearly "tagged"—whether by its position in the sentence or the use of suffixes—so the speaker can easily designate what he wants the listener to take as the subject and what as the object of his meaning.[57]

Flexibility within Universal Grammar

The universal grammar of language has to be very flexible to accommodate using either a noun or verb as the subject, object, or the verb of the sentence. It has to accommodate all four members of our quartet to encourage them to talk to each other, no matter how confusing.

The most difficult if not impossible words to pin down are words of emotion. After all, their true nature is that of the energy of a verb, of very specific different kinds of energies—pure delight, sadness, love, hate, indifference, mischievousness, et cetera. Yet the empiricist insists on treating even emotions like objects, so he uses them as nouns and ends up defining them as manifestations of the activity of this hormone or that. But this is only fair. The artist insists on using her actions—the empiricist's conceptions of motions—as metaphors, as mere surrogates for expressing his real feelings.

The empiricist views all the parts of the world as objects in interaction with each other. She wants to use the word "love" as a noun, as the behavior effected by a particular hormone circulating through the blood system. The artist is adamant on his right use of *love* as a verb, as the powerful feelings he experiences within its embrace, whether as the tortured captive of an uncaring other or the supreme blissful participant of ecstatic union with a responsive lover. The idealist's use is not this simple. She wants it both ways. She likes using it as a noun too—as an ideal toward which she is aspiring to embody as the predicate that will consummate her actions. The theorist's use, like the idealist's, is not simple. But unlike the idealist who at least can use it clearly both ways, he makes his rather vague.

The theorist is naturally vague when it comes to putting his thought processes into words. He works on a metaphorical level—one that precedes the literal world of language. Einstein describes his mental activity on this level, "The words of language, as they are written or spoken, do not seem to play any role in my mechanism of thought,"[58] The empiricist is a thinker too, but on a different level. She works at the level of notions she has already named. She names her objects and the manifestations of their interactions and then works within this familiar context trying to see the relationships and sort out the contradictions she can find between them. In debate, she insists on her opponent first defining his terms. She is most perfectly relaxed in thinking through things with words adopted from the language heard around her, insisting on a "literal" meaning of her universe.

The artist, like the theorist, is also a "preliterate." As a poet, the artist's only use for words is in how he can use them to construe the sequence of images he feels will convey the characteristics and impact of the emotions he feels. The artist as painter, musician or sculptor has an easier time of it, circumventing the use of language altogether. The poet must use the words adopted by the idealist from those she has heard to name the parts of her world, or occasionally invent new ones. Like the artist, the idealist is also a feeler, but on a different level, one within which she has named all the parts. Like the empiricist she is comfortable working only within a literal understanding of her universe.

But even the empiricist and idealist are opposites in their literal approaches. Whereas the empiricist wants to treat both subject and object as objects she is observing, the idealist wants to treat them both as subjects she is feeling. In communicating with each other, do these two merely compromise and split the difference? Do the theorist and artist even care? Is the artist-as-poet just making fun of their straight-laced prosaic efforts in exercising his poetic license in variations of rhyme, meter, onomatopoeia, broken grammar, and so forth to get the idealist into a metaphorical flight of emotion? Does the theorist lose himself in spontaneous and ungrammatical streams of consciousness just to tease into awareness that one great metaphor that, if he could only get the empiricist to dwell in it long enough, would enable her to imagine a whole new dimension of physical reality?

In earlier chapters about the art of dune buggy racing and of learning to type, we made some crude attempts to integrate opposite frameworks of perception and emotion into one. Now with language, we can do the same with the structure and dynamics of a sentence. The idea behind the *subject* originated in the relationship between the theorist and empiricist, the subject being the perception in which the latter can dwell. The emotional energy of the *verb* originated with the artist dwelling in his feelings—feelings the empiricist conceives in the motions of her *objects*. The idealist ties them all together, through her intentions for the subject and her aspirations in the object, to guide the action.

Verbs as Spirits of Time

We can watch from our backyard as the train flashes by on the nearby track across the horizon, while all those things around us—our house, our yard with all its trees, and the track—appear motionless. We can easily identify the train part as separate from all those motionless parts. But what can we label as *flashing* in and of itself? Everything we see in the landscape is already labeled as either part of the train or part of the surrounding area. Really there is nothing that is a referent of flashing. All we can do for now is tie the label onto the train, because all motion is coming from it.

But when we ourselves are riding on that same train looking out the window, it appears the surroundings are moving backward, and the train itself is quite still and motionless. In this case we automatically associate the motion with those objects, like trees and houses close to the track, that keep flashing by us. We associate the verb with the frame of reference of the object, and thus get the predicate—the verb and object. The framework from which we are observing is the subject.

If we are in our backyard, it is the train that is moving. If we are on the train, it is everything else that is moving. As such the motion, expressed in this case by the verb *flashing,* is rather fickle identifying with whatever framework is convenient from our vantage of perception. No wonder we have such a hard time labeling what is the motion-the verb Our differentiation between subject and object is an implicit way of stating our physical orientation, of whether we are looking at the moving train from the backyard or looking at our moving backyard from the train. The verb does not seem to have anything to do with what the nouns are in themselves at all.

Newton's Third

But verbs really only make good sense when connecting nouns. Take for example Newton's pure verb, his Third Law of Thermodynamics: "For every force exerted by one object on a second object, there is an equal and opposite force exerted by the second on the first." If we try to understand Newton's Third in its bare literal sense, it does not make any sense. Logically, if there is an equal and directly opposite force for every force exerted, how could any motion take place at all?

Anybody's first response to hearing Newton's Third Law should be to declare it a totally ridiculous statement. But since we would not be able to find even one physicist who questions this paradox, we would be wiser to grapple with it ourselves first. The Third Law is a concept, not a theory. As such it is incomprehensible without imagining it functioning within the empiricist's forms through time. Through exploring what this law means through examples of a rocket's flight, we can see the result of the interaction between the two opposite forces depends on the shape of the forms.

Take for example the physicist's explanation for the flight of a toy water rocket fuelled by compressed air.[59] The force that propels the rocket in flight is exactly equal in magnitude to the force expelling the water from the rocket and propelling it in the opposite direction. The physicist conceptualizes one force in the compressed air as pushing against the nose of the rocket while another force in the compressed air is propelling the water out of the opposite end. For nonphysicists, this duality of forces sounds somewhat suspicious, because both forces are completely dependent on each other for working. In fact they are perfect mirror images of each other, even to the point of losing their force at exactly the same rate over the course of a launch.

The non-physicist could easily argue that the identification of this exact mirror image relationship between the two forces is too much of a coincidence to validate the physicist's conceptualization of them as being separate and distinct. These two forces being so similar, why are not they conceptualized as merely opposite effects of the same quanta of energy—one verb? Energy by itself has no direction, except as explosive or implosive. It is the form or shape of the rocket's body that channels the energy into particular directions and consequently appears as two apparently opposite forces—that of action and reaction.

We can also apply Newton's Third Law to attractive forces, for example, gravitational force. The force of attraction between the earth and any object in space is exactly equal and opposite. The gravitational force the earth exerts on a falling feather is exactly equal in strength, though exactly opposite in direction, to the gravitational force the falling feather is exerting on the earth. Neither force exists without the other, and both increase at exactly the same rate, as the earth and feather approach each other. But where is the form within which these forces are channeled? Since there is not an obvious one, the physicist had to invent one: gravitational waves.

Taken by itself then, Newton's Third Law appears nonsensical. Focusing only on that conception, we are stuck in a motionless world of an equal and opposite reciprocity of forces, in a pure verb isolated from the rest of the sentence. Maybe that is the best definition of a concept: a verb with all time squeezed out. We can realize and understand the validity of the concept only through the device of animating the empiricist's forms through time.

Foxy's Tail: Subject or Object?

Why do we choose one noun as a subject and the other as an object? As we explored above with the verb *flashing*, part of the answer is just to communicate our choice of frameworks, the "from-to" direction of our activity. For the other part, let us continue with Newton's Third Law.

We can study Newton's idea of the reciprocity between forces in our everyday use of action verbs, for example in the sentence, "Foxy is wagging her tail." Let us start with the speaker's actual situation. Imagine a mechanical toy dog wagging its tail. Now pick up the toy by the tail and, voila! the tail is now wagging the dog. Now, if you go back and closely observe the real Foxy wagging her tail, you will see her body is wagging too. There is just as much force there as in the tail, but it is much less evident because the body is so much larger and heavier. A larger mass requires much less movement to achieve the same force. The muscles connecting the body and tail are doing the work. They are pulling just as hard on the body as they are on the tail. The muscles are merely playing off the inertia of one against the other. But all we can see is reciprocity between a small highly energetic tail flashing back and forth and a large slowly oscillating body and we call it *wagging*. In a Newtonian sense, it is just as true to say, "The tail is wagging Foxy" as "Foxy is wagging her tail."

Consider any sentence with an action verb, and you will find a similar inverse relationship by applying Newton's Third Law. But it is more difficult to see it in sentences like "He said, 'Stop!'" The reciprocal would be "'Stop!' said him." At first glance it might seem ridiculous to consider that the word spoken, "stop," takes just as essential a role in the action as the speaker. But in order for the speaker to have said "Stop!" he had to perform the specific physical requirements of correctly vibrating his vocal cords and moving the tongue through several contortions along with varying the position of his jaw relative to the roof of the mouth exactly as required by that word. If he failed in this, he could have come out with "Go!" or "Phooey!" instead. In order to pronounce "Stop!" he had to conform to the necessary vocal constraints imposed on him by that particular word. Whereas the speaker provided the energy for the word "stop," the word complemented that energy by dictating the pattern he had to follow in using that energy. In a way, "'Stop!' said him" makes just as much sense as "He said, 'Stop!'" though it does not sit very comfortably. And neither does "the tail is wagging Foxy."

We can nominate Newton as physicist of the action-reaction verb, but he fails to give us a way of dealing with the difference between the subject and object of the sentence. For him, the action of subject-verb and reaction of object-verb are but mirror images and interchangeable. All the initiative comes from forces outside the verb. Using his approach we are able to objectify our sentence into one framework of two interacting objects and thus freely substitute them to be either subject or object. But the fact remains that in originally speaking or writing that sentence, we make one noun the subject and the other the object.

We do have a subject and an object here, and they do not sit very comfortably when we switch them around. There is a decided from-to motion in going from subject to object. In the moment during which we are saying, "Foxy is wagging her tail," we do not notice that the body is oscillating because we are looking toward the tail from dwelling in the framework of her body. This is why we normally notice only the motion of the wagging tail, not the body. If we had said, "The tail is wagging Foxy," we would imply we are seeing Foxy from the still framework of the tail as we did when we picked up our mechanical toy dog by the tail, or as a writer would in imagining life from the vantage point of a flea living in Foxy's tail.

But what shall we consider the cause of the motion if it is not in the tail or the body? Should we claim the muscles are the cause of the motion? The problem here is that if we could use X-ray vision to watch the muscles, we would see the muscles on one side contracting and relaxing in alternate sync with those on the other side as they relax and contract. Again we find perfect symmetry between equal and opposite forces. What is the cause of their reciprocal actions?

The speaker is attributing action to an unbalanced force—an external agent or cause. In this case we would understand him to be implying the cause of this mischief with the laws of physics is in the dog as a whole, as an expression of the animal's decision to be friendly. Though Foxy initially had been caught between her friendly nature and her general wariness of strangers, she had decided to reciprocate the stranger's apparent friendliness with her own amiable side and hope for some pleasure from his petting. Thus, we have discovered our idealist, the believer in her decision-making.

Instantaneous vs. Momentous Time

Every great poet is remaking the world, for he is trying to see it as if there were no Time, no History.
(Mircea Eliade)[60]

What happened to our artist? How does he fit into the sentence about Foxy? He is the verb itself, "wagging" in its spontaneous expression of friendliness. In our ideal sentence, whereas the idealist is expressed in how she frames her intentions and goals through the subject and object, the verb is the expression of his emotions in how he feels in his relationship between himself and the stranger.

To get a clearer picture of the verb as the true embodiment of the artist, we will examine the difference in meaning of two sentences, between one using a verb referring to an action in one particular instant with that of the most general verb of all, *to be.*

Superficially, we associate time with the verb only through our use of tense. But this is a natural bias, especially of adults. Whether the action is taking place in the past, present or future is only of importance for the empiricist and the idealist. The empiricist is most interested in the facts of the past and how they will impact on the future. The idealist is primarily focused in what shall be, in how the "what should be" can be realized through action in the present as rooted in her beliefs of what she has intended or willed in the past. To complement this pair, we will explore two other dimensions of time in the verb.

In contrast, as artist and theorist, we distinguish between more particular and more general time, for example in the two sentences, "He played hockey yesterday," and, "He plays hockey." In the former, we are referring to the fact that he was playing during a particular period. The latter sentence refers to a much more generalized sense of time. We mean he has played in the past and also will play in the future.

We can take the first two examples, "He played hockey," and "He plays hockey," and take them to their extremes, to the most particular point in time and the most general: the universal. "He scores!" expresses an instant in time, and in the opposite case, "He is hockey" refers to someone who plays only hockey, talks only hockey, thinks only hockey and dreams only hockey. In the first example of referring to one particular time isolated from the rest of time, we have changed the verb from the more general "play" to the more specific description of what he was actually doing, "scoring," in the present moment. In the second, in referring to a period of time from in the past through the present into the future, we have to change the verb from "play" to the least time-specific verb of all, "to be."

As we go from describing what happens at a particular time to more generalized statements, the nature of the verb becomes more general too. It is apparent that we used the verb *play* in a more general sense than *score* but in a more specific sense than *is*. Being intermediate between the two, it is more difficult to pin this use of the verb *play* down as being an action verb like *score* or an immanent one like *is*. In the particular action he was doing something to something, he was backhanding the puck into the net. In the most general statement, action has disappeared completely. He *is* being defined by or equated to his activity or more accurately his obsession, *hockey*. In the intermediate generalization of using the word *play* there is reference to action, but we do not have one clear action in mind, just a general sense of all the various actions that hockey players do. Besides, he is not doing anything *to* hockey.

As we move from pinpointing time in the instant of a concrete situation in "scoring" through intermediate ones in "playing" to the most ubiquitous one in "being," we are finding ways to make the verb reflect the differences in overall time.

On the one hand, in the instant Johnny backhands the puck into the net for the winning goal in the championship game, his mother exclaims, "He scores!" On the other hand, as a wife exasperated with the weekly task of picking up the beer cans and vacuuming the pretzel crumbs after her husband's and his pals' enjoyment of a televised hockey game, she declaims the theory, "Men are slobs!" The instant of action and the universality of an idea are at opposite ends of the time spectrum. In crying out, "He scores!" she is capturing a moment of triumph in a memory she can feel and remember forever. In using the purely immanent verb, "to be," she is capturing infinity in one instant perception.

Mother as Poet and Theorist

Though this mother would not qualify as a leading poet or theorist of our times, her pronouncements have all the earmarks of poetry and theory.

In shouting, "He scores!" she is not telling anybody at the rink anything they do not already know. The words are a vehicle for expressing her realization of the instant of triumph, her reward for all those hours of sorting through used hockey equipment to find the best she and her husband could afford, of pushing herself to get up out of bed in the wee hours and dragging Johnny out of bed for the hundreds of trips to and from the rink, of freezing for hours on end waiting idly in the cold dampness of many arenas, of the innumerable exchanges with him in which she was either scolding, encouraging, disparaging, praising, discouraging, or advising his efforts.

In saying, "All men are slobs!" she does the opposite. She is concentrating all the weekly facts of cleaning up after men in time and space into one metaphor. Another woman could just as easily not have associated cleaning up the house only with the men's carelessness in particular, but as just part of the endless cycle of her husband, herself, the kids, and visitors dirtying up the house: "There's no end to cleaning a house!" This second woman's realization is much broader and thus more valid in a universal sense, summing up her exasperation for this endless and often thankless task. But both theories of cleaning are clearly ideas that attempt to explain a series of physical events happening over an extended period of time and space.

Remember our earlier discussion of language's nature ranging from one extreme—that of a pure signaling device when playing in the groove, or in the kaleidoscope of images in poetry or in the intimate communication between two persons—to the other extreme—that of a descriptive device in cool objective prose frameworks? In the heat and groove of action, the speaker ends up focusing all energies on the action of the present instant in capturing it by making an association between it and the summation of all her associated emotions. In contrast, in pure thought, she ends up focusing to encompass a whole series of perceptions in one metaphor.

Emotional Tension within the Verb

In poetic language, tension is compressed in the buildup of emotion between opposite emotions within the person. Let us look closer at the nature of the formation of the emotional complex expressed in "He scores!" The hockey mother is ecstatic her son has shot the winning goal not only because she has been so hopeful he would luck out by doing just that, but also because she has been worried he might screw up to allow the other team to score and win. The emotion of triumph is victory over the fear of defeat, not only his victory, but her struggles through all the emotional ups and downs of supporting his efforts over the years.

Imagine, too, the emotions of defeat on the losing bench. They have played just as hard. Their hopes were as high. In the loss they realize all the worries and fears they had about losing. But if they had not had any hopes of winning in the first place, their realization of loss would not be devastating. The emotion of defeat is losing in the hope of victory. They, as their opponents have played and all the fans have watched through this game, were poised between the tensions of hope and fear.

The triumphal emotion in Johnny scoring that winning goal gradually fades from daily memory. But the mother can always recall it clearly and vividly as long as she can remember the associated incident well enough to relive it in memory. The emotional impact will always be the centerpiece of the fact of doing it. It is as though that memory of the details of that incident serves as a formula that preserves the exact description of that emotion, and a hook to let her pull it out and reexperience it and maybe compare it with other triumphs later on.

She may modify that emotion later if she changes her interpretation of the event in which it was formed. If during the next season of play Johnny losses his eye in a stick-fight during a game souring the hockey mother's attitude toward hockey, her emotional feeling about that winning goal at the end of the previous season might well change to one that is bittersweet. She knows Johnny would not have played another season of hockey and subsequently lost his eye if he had not got that winning goal that made him so popular and convinced him to play for another year. But as long as she can return to the memory of that winning goal and isolate it from its relationship to the eye-losing incident the following year, she can still experience it as she did originally.

The Middle Way[61]

The sentence implicitly reflects emotional dynamics through the tension between the intentions of the subject, the spontaneous emotion of the verb, and the aspirations for the object as they are related to the physical action explicitly expressed. In everyday life, at one extreme we often allow our emotions to direct our actions; at the other we merely use them to drive ourselves toward goals we have set. But bravely and innocently striding down the middle of these two extremes are the noble hero and gracious heroine of the best folk and classical literature whose words and actions embody emotions arising spontaneously out of an integrity of their best intentions and goals.

That sounds too beautiful to be true. But that is why literature is called "fiction."

The classic ideal is that our words and actions project the spontaneous expression of our highest intentions. Our highest hopes are to experience that mutually in our relationship with another. The everyday reality is that the expression of our actual intentions, which are not very high or ideal on a whole array of matters, is not what is necessarily acceptable to the other or even our own consciences in that situation. We are continually caught in a tension between what we really feel and what we actually express in that situation because we know what others in our company expect us to feel and how to behave, what our own consciences tell us should be the case, and what we really are feeling and doing.

We become most acutely aware of these tensions at major events like weddings and parties when our feelings do not seem to jibe with those of the others. "Why do I feel so depressed at this wedding? Don't I care about this person's happiness?" Or, "Why do I find this party so dull? Everybody else is having a great time, or is everybody else faking it too?" But even though we generally are not self-consciously aware of it, we experience it continually in everyday life especially in interaction with others. The better we know them, the better and deeper we can do it. The more we trust someone, the clearer we allow that person to see the nature of that tension within ourselves. For dear friends we work to be transparent. We need their help to sort it out and get our balance. For strangers or others of whom we are wary, we "muddy the waters" to disguise it, putting up as many barriers as possible to prevent them from penetrating our personas.

We want to be like those heroes and heroines, knights and ladies, one in unison and devoid of contradictions within our deepest intentions and how we project them. But in the experiences of everyday life we are aware of a whole range of conflicting emotions on every topic. There are very few things about which we can absolutely say, "I totally love that, period."

Have you ever gone to a funeral and found you had to "fake it"? You never knew the person who died…the reason you went was the only surviving dependant was your boss with whom you don't really get along all that well…but it wouldn't have looked right if you didn't go…everybody would have talked about it the next day if you didn't…but you still felt you should not have come and pretended to feel sad…in fact you had a sneaking feeling it served her right…you told yourself, "It's not right to feel like this…It's not Christian (or Buddhist, or Muslim, etc.)…What if my best friend died?…How would I want the boss to feel? Would she recognize my sorrow and could she realize it as something real and important to me? Or would she come just faking it because as my boss she knows she has to come? To and fro, from I to her and back from she to me, and around we go."

Whenever we are faced with a dilemma, we have a whole pageant of miscellaneous scraps of feelings creeping in from the various nooks and crannies of our memories. And how we view them depends greatly on our general mood or intention of that time, whether optimistic or pessimistic, merciful or hard-hearted, charitable or miserly, loving or hateful. Sometimes, when we have to make a very important decision, we put it off because we are very confused or depressed in our general mood. We then wait until the confusion has cleared and we are in whatever we sense is the right mood to consider the question properly with the best intentions to make the most balanced decision on the matter and take the right action.

We strive for understanding beyond both an insight into intellectual questions and reciprocity of emotional stimulation and response. Through the action of language we attempt to orchestrate all four of our quartet into one whole expression of who we have been, are, and hope to become.

C: <u>The Quartet</u>

8

The Sensation of Communication

Whose speech Truth knows not from her thought
Nor Love her body from her soul.
(Dante Gabriel Rosetti, from "Love-Lily")

Some psychologists, as pure scientists, have used rats, pigeons, and computers to invent models for human learning. But we are philosophers. Instead of elucidating a model from the behavior and functioning of computers or animals, we will come around to examining how we relate to them only after we get a handle on the art of communicating with each other. Whether we are a primitive bushman living totally within the environment of the Kalahari Desert, a university professor at an elite school, a farmer, or a factory laborer, the art of communication is the central and most intimate pivot in all our relationships to others. As such, it must reflect our inner workings. Once we get a grasp of the interplay between idea and emotion, as rooted in the duality of sensation, we will not have to worry or wonder whether what we have learned about learning is the same for us as for animals and robots. We will know.

The Robot Model

It is most frustrating that as we grow into middle age it seems harder and harder to learn new things. How many people give up after a few language lessons, or are totally frustrated after taking the first twenty? How many despair of ever being able to keyboard at a computer or even just hit that tennis ball right? And when we fail, we tend to blame it on our lack of willpower and self-discipline. We usually fail to question our understanding and method of learning. We have adopted half-baked ideas of how learning works and channeled our learning efforts through them.

In these times, images of the computer—where and how it works and what it is increasingly able to do—pervade our thinking. Every day we read and hear praises of its ever-widening applications and the increasing powers of its chips. It is often compared to the human mind, and we have great debates over whether a computer can think. Many researchers have adopted the computer as the model by which they study learning, just as a previous generation of researchers adopted rats. Scientists like Stephen Jay Gould are enthralled in comprehending the human brain as "the most complex computing device ever evolved in the history of our planet,"[62] just as many scientists have adopted the terminology of computer operation and applied it to ourselves in everyday life. They talk about "inputs" and "outputs." They talk about knowledge as "bits and bytes" of information we store in "memory" and "retrieve" when needed for "interfacing" and "networking."

When it comes time to study something, many of us carelessly adopt this idea of the robot, a computer directing a machine, as a simplified mirror of ourselves, as a brain directing a body. We work toward the idea of ourselves becoming rational logical thinkers who, after having abstracted the key principles from our lessons, can in turn come up with rules we can then apply to direct and control our actions. Emotions, whether of like or dislike, fear or comfort, anxiety or pleasure, happiness or sadness, doubt or confidence, are considered to be incidental phenomena that arise spontaneously and generally must be overcome, like glitches in a computer program, so we can encounter learning in a cool and objective manner. With a logical grasp on our learning materials memorized in one corner of the brains, we attempt to run the gauntlet of learning how to do something, trying to take into account the various sensations that bombard us from the outside while channeling the chaos of emotions arising from the inside.

These mind-as-a-computer researchers picture the mind as a storage container for files of information from the past. The artist and the idealist are the ones who know how to reenergize those memories and incorporate them into the present experience of living in real time. Only when we are totally attentive and absorbed in creative action in the present moment does the felt distinction between our bodies and our minds totally vanish.

Two Sides of "Good Morning!"

Though we can instantly distinguish between the elements of emotion and thought in language spoken to us after the fact of experiencing it, both elements are indispensable in making the expression meaningful in that particular time and place.

The use of language, as any other art, requires action integrating thoughts and emotion. Take for example the greeting, "Good morning." If your boss is having a bad start on the day, she might say it quite flatly, or even crossly. Or if she is downright mean, she might say it in a way that implies, "Good morning, a-hole." If she is good-natured and had a good start, it might come out light and merry. Or, if she is afraid or too shy to express her true emotions of the moment, it comes out with that false heartiness of someone who is either just pretending or earnestly trying to be happy to meet you.

Whatever way she says it, whether she is expressing feelings based on the nature of her relationship to you or feelings reflecting more her own state of mind, whether the emotion is spontaneous or contrived, sincere or insincere, you get a different meaning. The better you know, or think you know her, the more shades of meaning you hear or read into what she says. She can, through the one expression "Good morning," communicate virtually thousands of different meanings by varying the emotional mix that is part of the whole communicative effort. Of course whether these shades of meaning are actually communicated to you depends on your sensitivity and understanding.

Conversely, just as the boss can vary the meaning of any single phrase through emotional variations, she can also keep the emotion constant and vary the framework. For instance, she can express affection by the way she says "Good morning" or "Good work" or "How are the kids?" Or she can use these same words in a sarcastic tone to express her dislike and disdain for you. We can list hundreds of different feelings—love, tenderness, fear, hate, disdain, superiority, inferiority, excitement, boredom, delight, happiness, joy, sadness, hollowness, pettiness, peevishness, piety, shyness, boldness—to start, with which she in turn can create an infinite number of permutations of feeling to color any framework she sets out in words. To make it even more complicated, other than the main emotion of the verb in every sentence, she is also projecting emotions of intention in the subject and aspiration in the verb. Of course, I do not mean to suggest she is a consummate actress. She is merely acting out her feelings and thoughts as learned in the years of the development of her character and her interpretation of the world in her particular relationship with you.

The romantic poet is tempted to view words and expressions as merely a neutral vehicle for the communication of emotion. If we focus on the emotional content of "Good morning," its literal meaning seems totally irrelevant. But this is not so. What if the boss had instead said "Gluckity gluck" with the same emotion, and after you stared back in surprise, she added as an explanation, "Gluck it for ell"? In this scenario, you would despair of making any real communication, beat a quick retreat, and send for the shrink. Even if the boss had said something comprehensible like "I love you," you would still be thrown off track because that framework is entirely inappropriate for that time and place, and you would focus strictly on what was behind the meaning of what she said instead of getting into an emotional groove with her.

Thought and emotional elements only make sense and meaning in combination with each other when we apprehend them as one whole.

The Gauntlet of Emotion and Thought

In communicating what we *really* mean, we strive not only for the right balance between emotions and thought but the right synthesis. In the worst extremes, we are just using one to sell the other. In the best of moods, we spontaneously create the ideal synthesis.

At one extreme, we do not spontaneously feel the emotion we are projecting, but merely simulate it. We pretend to feel it because we are trying to manipulate somebody into doing something for us, as a seducer wanting sexual stimulation, as a waitress working on a customer's feelings to get a big tip, as a child being friendly to get more candy, or as one spouse softening up the other to get a new carpet. On the other extreme, we spontaneously feel the emotion we project, but are merely finding excuses or pretexts—contrived contexts—for expressing it, as an angry child irritating its parents about their choice of clothes, as angry spouses fighting it out in heated arguments over the telephone bill, or as a lovesick man giving flowers to complete strangers in the park.

In both extremes, the action and emotional elements are related only through an ulterior motive. One is being used for the sake of the other. In one, we are calculatingly simulating some emotion to get something. In the other, spontaneous emotion directs the thrust of our words. In the former, the emotion of kindness or tenderness is merely a simulated vehicle for our real objective—what we think or feel we have to do in order to get something from someone, whether a thing or a change in that person's behavior. In the latter, the situation of the style of clothes or the expensive telephone bill is merely a convenient vehicle to vent or express whatever emotions we feel about that person.

We do not necessarily experience such extremes every day. For example, though the motivation of getting a tip stimulates them to try a little harder to please their customers, most waitresses already enjoy their jobs and feel good about serving and earning a living for themselves. But there are days we feel completely flat, as though we had no feeling for anyone around us. And there are other days we feel strongly emotional about everything and fly off the handle. Some persons are more one way than the other, depending on the situation. The more discrepancy or lack of balance we detect between a person's words and emotional impact, the more we tend to question that person's character and intentions and label him accordingly as calculating or naïve, devious or gullible, manipulative or foolish, objective or subjective, cold-fish or hot-tempered, cold- or warm-blooded, nerdy or whimsical, in the particular context in which we are talking or thinking about him, as to whether he responds to those situations with his head or his heart.

In contrast to those extremes, sometimes we wholly feel the emotion that most perfectly reflects the thought, as in that moment and situation when we feel totally in love with someone and discover ourselves affirming it with the spontaneous statement, "I love you." In this case our intentions and aspirations in making the statement are identical with the verb of its expression. There is no covert agenda to attain an end. In fact all aspects are so intertwined we find it impossible to distinguish between them. We do not even *want* to analyze it.

Of course years later during the divorce proceedings, if we are so unfortunate, we may start to analyze it and see this memory merely as the record of the naïve impulse of hormone-charged youth trapped in the wrong time and place. And maybe it was so. But those of us who are lucky, foolish, or determined enough in our first marriage cherish that memory as a whole, and occasionally return to it to help us maintain our morale in the many battles of marital life.

There are many variations intermediary to the two extremes. For instance, as with my "Good morning" example, we might feel an emotion opposite to that implied by the words. We could say, "I love you," in a very sarcastic tone of voice. Or, in an ironic mood we could say, "I do not love you," in a loving way. Or maybe we are earnestly trying to feel a particular emotion because we think we should be feeling it toward someone even though we do not, like when somebody hands us a baby and it pees on our shirt or blouse. Or we might feel a particular emotion and are earnestly trying to fit it into the present context, as when we feel attracted to the idea of kissing the person whom we should know is not yet ready to accept such an intimate sign of affection in a public place. We can only make our way through these complications in communicating, because as listeners we can compare our felt emotions to the emotions we can read through our perceptions.

But we strive to achieve the same spontaneous expression between emotion and thought as in the ideal example of "I love you" in our communication, at whatever level of intimacy, when we do what we think and feel what we should, not in order to get something but just what is right at that moment. For instance, when wet upon by a baby, the Thai people employ an interesting expression: "When a baby pees on you, it is showing its love for you." Of course, Thais do not believe this as an objective truth. But it is an apt metaphor to steer the adult into feeling the "right" way about it. If successful, the adult feels the warmth of the baby's water in his clothes as the warmth of its feelings toward him. And the baby in turn feeling the warmth of his response, answers with a smile. But conversely, when we feel the right emotion at the wrong time, like the lovesick lover, we are urged to remember another saying: "There is a time and place for everything," and strive to create the right situation or at least keep our attention open to the right way in which we can properly and sincerely express it, and hope for as truthful a response.

The Astute vs. the Sensitive

We can characterize many everyday conversations into two categories. On the one hand, we have those wherein we are trying to persuade someone about something. On the other hand, we are just sharing a moment of enjoyment whether purely physical or intellectual. On the surface they have a similar pattern. Dialogue at its most shallow is moving back and forth between these two modes during a conversation. At the most fruitful level it's as though we are doing both simultaneously.

When we analyze our everyday conversations, we can characterize the thought and emotional elements into two distinct patterns. Thought proceeds in skips and jumps to develop a picture of a situation. Emotions ebb and flow as waves. One speaker introduces a particular framework. If the other accepts it as a topic he elaborates on it, and the two keep up a back and forth within it until they become satisfied or bored and frustrated. Then one of them either quits or introduces a new topic and so forth. But the emotional element for each topic is like a complex wave of different emotions that gradually builds to a climax and then gradually fades. Some topics do not generate much enthusiasm and can be characterized as short-lived shallow waves. Some topics are very exciting to both participants and can go on for much longer periods.

We can characterize the stage or depth of the dynamics of any conversation in terms of the extent of the congruency between the participants' understanding of what the other's framework is, and the similarities or disparities between their feelings about it. The more congruency felt by the participants as the conversation develops, the more they feel they are on the same wavelength and communicating. The less of both realized, the more they feel there is confusion and a lack of communication. At this level we can pinpoint the key difference between argument and empathy.

In argument, whether we are a mother determined to get the kids to brush their teeth twice a day or a salesperson selling the idea of how exciting and useful a brand new car would be, or a political debater arguing for a particular action, we have a fixed point of view we want the other to adopt. We want the other to appreciate and accept, intellectually and emotionally, our point of view as hers. Neither as mother or salesperson or debater are we ready to accept the skepticism of the other. Whatever objections or reservations they raise, we study the other looking for cracks in reasoning or softening in emotional objections but mainly for the incongruities between these two, to find a way to burrow through for the persuasive punch line that will show her she is wrong. Astute mothers, salespersons, and politicians have such sensitive antennae that they can spot "weaknesses" from fifty yards out and effortlessly attack with brazen importunity. When we are the initiator of such an argument, we do everything we can to have the other move to our way of looking at and feeling about something.

On the other hand, in a mode of pure empathy we are trying to appreciate the congruency of the other's emotions with his thoughts and actions about something. We can apprehend and empathize with a child's aversion to brushing teeth, a voter's acceptance of the opposite political stance, or a buyer's affection for his old jalopy.

In dialogue, no matter how strongly we think and feel about something, we try to do both. We are open to what the other has to express both emotionally and thoughtfully, as fully as we can be. Instead of zeroing in only on their weaknesses as we see them, we also seek out their strengths. Through alternating back and forth between expressing our own ideas as clearly and emotionally truly as we can and then assuming the other's ideas and feelings about it to see our own idea from his perspective, we gradually work toward a new understanding. In this form of communication, when both participants are in a dialogue mode, both move toward becoming one in mental framework and emotion, through a much more complicated dynamic than that of either argument or empathy alone.

In argument, we distinguish between the other's thought and emotional content and focus on incongruence between them. In conversation with someone with whom we have no real sympathy, for example a persistently disobedient child, we might treat him as though the feelings he is expressing are inconsistent with his behavior. In contrast, in empathy, we accept them together. We accept that the child must have a valid rationale for behaving the way he is, for relating those emotions with those thoughts, as irrational as it may seem to us. In dialogue we shoot at the least for a practical compromise, and at the most for new mutual insight into the matter at hand.

We can sense immediately when someone is treating us as a known and fixed quantity they can then work on to change to their point of view. They just have to figure out how to manipulate, dominate, and teach us in argument and debate.

In contrast, we also know those who treat us as fellow travelers in life and can readily share their puzzlement, disappointments, and hopes about the trip. In the argumentative mode we treat our opposites as known entities whom we have to teach. In the second, in sharing, we "forget" we know them already since we realize that which we know about them is only a partial view, and holding that view of them in mind only hinders our ability to interact with them as the whole they are. So we forget or ignore those distracting bits we already know in order to search for the stranger we realize we do not yet know.

Relating to Mass Media

What is the difference in relating to some form of media, whether print, sculpture, television, or even interactive computer software, with relating to a living being—whether student, teacher, friend, or pet? No matter what the nature of the medium, it cannot argue or empathize with us as we really are in present time. Rather it exists only in imaginary time and only to the extent we can relate emotionally to it.

The artifacts of media are merely the inanimate residue of human efforts. This book itself is merely a hypothesis for a way of thinking about learning in its broadest sense, just as an ad might try to sell the ownership of a car as an exciting love affair with a particularly beautiful model. Though this book is more complex in intellectual aspects, it does not allow you any more interactions with the writer—me—than the television commercial does with its producers. The words of this book will not change the least bit, no matter how strong your opinions or feelings, any more than the advertisement will change its absurd claim to the elixir of new life. You as the living being have only two choices in responding: to argue by asserting your skepticism and viewing the whole thing quizzically, or empathetically accepting it and seeing your own world through its mental and emotional assumptions. But in neither mode do you have a real live partner with whom you can struggle through the ideas in present time, only a paper tiger—an imaginary construct. In effect, in the act of relating to media, we are essentially only arguing or empathizing with ourselves, between who we are and our image of the media piece's author to the extent we are capable of imagining this other, this author.

Whether in watching a television show or a live theatrical performance, we can take either of these two approaches. If we dislike the show, we view it critically in an argumentative or comprehensive mode, focusing our energies in dissecting its banalities, excesses, contradictions. But if we really like the show, we lose ourselves in it in a spontaneous absorption or apprehension of what is happening and its emotions. Of course, even in the comprehensive mode we first have to apprehend it, but instead of working to tune into the ebb and flow of the particular emotions aroused within that particular set of events and allowing ourselves to absorb it as one whole, we perceive only particular pieces of it from the viewpoint of what we already know or believe. The most insightful critic, as opposed to the wittiest, is the one disciplined enough to maintain an apprehensive mode during the performance, attempting to comprehend it only afterwards. He moves to a dialogue within only after putting down the book or shutting off the television, when he can study his own reactions. Only in reflection can we step outside our reactions and see ourselves in the new light, moving back and forth between the two, effectively dialoguing with ourselves.

Computerized Bells and Whistles

What about the nature of learning in the case of a student working with an interactive computer program with all the latest bells and whistles of simulated emotional inserts? Really, by all the evidence for how difficult it is for children to learn anything of any complexity through them, by themselves computer programs are much less effective than interaction even with a teacher who is merely going through the motions. Just as that teacher is acting out a role in a mechanical way, the computer program is following the dictates of its own programming instructions. Both are merely transmitting and receiving messages. Neither is communicating with their subjects, except in a mechanical sense.

The advantage of even the most bored skilled teacher, though, is that he, even as a mere transmitter, still has an infinitely more sophisticated program than any computer can yet simulate. But more importantly, that teacher might wake up to take a real interest in his students and inspire them to higher achievements. There is not the faintest chance a computer will ever wake up to the shy excitement of a student in love with a subject and intellectually and emotionally dialogue with her through the inevitable yet unpredictable series of trials and tribulations in its hot pursuit. Nor is there any way it can empathize with and console the tearful frustration of the child totally stymied by an inability to deal with the intellectual task at hand and lead her gradually out of that misery through the complicated emotional path to an ease and confidence in doing it.

Even when computers are used merely to communicate, as in messaging, there are gross limitations and constraints on what can be transmitted between the two communicants in comparison to face-to-face interaction. In *High-Tech Heretic*, a book of droll humor on the limitations of computers for learning as told through a series of anecdotes and observations, Clifford Stoll—Internet pioneer and astronomy professor—writes, "If we wish to create a world of isolates—a society where people cannot get along with each other—I can hardly think of a better way than to shove children into cyberspace and tell 'em to communicate electronically."[63] We have been massaged by commercials to think in glowing terms of the value of fax machines, camera-phones, and streaming audio-visual communication through the Internet. The commercials emphasize how much communication they allow us with our loved ones or our business associates who are located elsewhere. What we forget is how their limitations restrict us in terms of the full range of communication possible in face-to-face situations. Telephones allow us more flexibility than fax machines, and audio-visual meetings allow us more than telephones. But the man stuck overseas calling home once a week yearns for personal one-to-one real life contact. He wants the real thing in blood and flesh—the whole ball of wax.

Communication implies a union or sharing not only of intellectual comprehension but also of intention and aspiration. When the cruel prison guard in the movie *Cool Hand Luke* exclaims, "What we have here is a failure to communicate!" what he means is not that the prisoner, Luke, has failed to get the drift of what he wants, but that Luke is refusing to accept his intentions and aspirations in saying whatever he did and behave accordingly.

Sometimes in working with computers we become so enthralled and mesmerized by their incredible wizardry, we forget they are merely sophisticated calculators with bells and whistles. Intelligence is in the harmony of and balance between thought and emotion. Though computers can be aids in learning, their not having any ability to spontaneously emote or express any intentions or aspirations leaves them at a real intelligence of zero. Computers can no more replace the role of teachers than even the greatest books can, because the potential for emotional conflicts and caring to generate the excitement of spontaneous communication is absolutely nil. Students cannot begin to relate to computers meaningfully through all four dimensions of our quartet. Our favorite schoolteacher is more real and precious to us than Shakespeare's plays, or Euclid's theorems, or any computer program.

Pets, Infants, and Teachers

Many of us experience a strong communicative bond with our pets. In contrast to various learning media to which we relate in imaginary time and space, we relate to animals only in real time and real space as we do infants. In fact both animals and infants appear to be conscious only of the present moment and the immediate situation. We cannot address them by asking about their sickness of the day before or their concerns about the snowstorm forecast for tomorrow or even what happened ten minutes ago. Yet as totally wrapped up as they are in present time, they have an incredibly uncanny sense of our ongoing emotions and intentions toward them, and even appear to sympathize with us. Dogs try to draw us into sharing their delight and excitement in the chase of almost anything that moves. Do pet pigeons hope for us to share their delight in flight?

Many of us have read the famous case of Hans the Horse that took place during early last century in Europe. For years the horse amazed audiences with his ability to do arithmetic. He could apparently add, subtract, multiply, and even divide. His handler would ask him the question and the horse would start pawing the ground and keep pawing until he reached the correct answer. Even when the owner was replaced at the horse's side by an impartial scientist so the owner could in no way affect the outcome, the horse still answered correctly. However it was discovered that when the questioner himself did not know the answer, the horse became confused and did not know when to stop pawing. The scientists studying this phenomenon decided the horse's apparent brilliance arose entirely out of his ability to read the body language of the questioner. But it would be more accurate to say Hans had become adept at feeling out his handler's emotions and wanted to please him.

Infants have a similar uncanny sensitivity. Many years ago I noticed a pattern: the day preceding the departure of my wife on another field trip, our first born would become very upset. He could not have had any clear idea of her pending departure the next day, but I surmise he could sense her emotional withdrawal from the everyday domestic scene as she began preparing herself mentally and emotionally to address the issues she was going to meet somewhere else. He could feel that even though she was still behaving toward him in the same way as any other day, her actions had become mechanical. He was no longer the center of her thoughts and feelings and expressed a visceral disapproval of her lukewarm interest in sympathizing with his delight in his toys and his fear of being abandoned.

The successful teacher, whether a professional in a school or a father teaching his daughter to ride a bicycle, initiates an emotional and physical dynamic that excites student effort and aspiration. In moments of true inspiration they move into a mental and emotional synchrony like dancers to music they are creating together in that moment.

Running the Gauntlet

The root problem with the robot modeling of human activity is its total inability to incorporate the emotional half of communication. It cannot begin to duplicate the gauntlet of thought and emotion through which Cornelia has to run when talking with her husband, Jim. She knows herself and how many times she can shift from one perception to another and also how variously her moods can shift through the event of even one conversation. For each mood she might have a different intention and aspiration. She knows Jim's are also in constant flux. The mystery and excitement in relating to others is the constant exploring to discover whether the other is feeling and thinking the same as I about the same thing. What does Jim feel? Why does the other feel differently? Can she really appreciate how Jim feels? Should she feel the same as he does? What would make Cornelia feel the same about it as Jim? How can she make him feel the same about it as her? Is he even talking about the same thing? And if it is the same thing, is he looking at it through the same conceptions? They go back and forth and in and out around the four quadrants. Their ability to keep track of how to remain in enough synchrony with each other for a mutually intelligible and satisfying conversation is based in the simultaneous receptivity of both perceptive and emotional elements of sensation.

Pinning Down the Spirit of Emotion

Why is it so difficult for scientists to deal with the communication of emotions? Being so elusive, it is challenge enough just trying to get a handle on them, much less figuring out how they could be communicated.

Emotional aspects of communication are often only vaguely acknowledged, since they are too elusive for conventional scientific analysis. The problem is that we cannot observe emotions as we can, for example, the physical form of a child. In fact if we try to visualize emotions for what they are in themselves, we cannot get any image at all. Take the verb *delight*. We can conceive of it as embodied in the actions of children happily playing together. But once we take the observable forms, that is, the subject, "children," out of our mental picture, we have nothing left. We cannot perceive the *delightful* nature of this energy in and of itself. We can conceive of its existence underlying the motion we observe. But in the end we can only really "feel" it, either in the moment of first discovering it or through recalling it from memory.

How can scientists deal with what cannot be perceived in and of itself but only directly felt and named? Since they cannot solve this mystery of how to pin down and formulate the feeling of emotions, they cannot treat them experimentally in a scientific manner within a laboratory setting. This limitation has steered some psychologists, the behaviorists, to study emotions by focusing strictly on the physical evidence of that energy in the stimulus and response of behaviors, evidence that can be measured and thus quantified. Thus, for example, rats can be timed to see how quickly they learn to work their way through any particular maze, or students can be tested and timed at intervals to see how quickly they learn to perform certain tasks to assess the effectiveness or efficiency of different stimuli. Physiologists take this empirical approach a step further by identifying hormones in the blood and relating them to the particular actions during which they are most likely to be present. But what is the initial source of stimulation for the release and dispersion of those hormones? Is it completely internal or do external factors have a direct effect as B.F. Skinner so insistently implied through his "stimulus-response" construct or as Merleau-Ponty contends in his expression of the "blind apprehension" of emotions?[64]

The Double Whammy of Sensation

To explain and rationalize the direct emotional communication we feel with others, some writers have developed concepts such as a "sixth sense" or "extrasensory perception." But we do not need such esoteric concepts to explain it. The reality is much simpler. Neurophysiologists are proving that all our sense organs are wired directly into both perceptive and emotional centers of the brain, feeding both simultaneously.

Our sensors—ears, eyes, nose, skin, and mouth—are our main communication portals to the outside world, both for our perceptions of it and the emotions that stimulate us. All the sense organs—even the nose and mouth—have lines of transmission to both cognitive and emotional centers of the brain. Both centers are activated simultaneously by sensation. Dr. Stanley Greenspan, a child psychologist, maintains that as infants, our first lessons were in making associations between what we perceived and what emotions we felt being communicated to us in the same moment. We label each experience "both by its physical properties (bright, big, loud, smooth, and the like) and by the emotional qualities we connect with it (we might experience it as soothing or jarring, or it might make us feel happy or tense). This double coding allows the child to 'cross-reference' each memory or experience."[65]

For an intriguing scientific metaphor on the dual communication of perception and emotion, go to physics. A hundred years ago our physicists already accepted the dual nature of light as both wave and energy. In *The Dancing Wu Li Masters,* Gary Zukav asks, "How can mutually exclusive wavelike and particlelike behaviors both be one and the same light?…They are not properties of light. They are properties of our interaction with light." Based on that metaphor, as we will explore in a later chapter, through our experimentation we apprehend the sensation of light simultaneously through firstly what we perceive as a wave and secondly, what we feel and then conceive as energy. As applied to human audio sensation, we could say, for example, a listener isolates and perceives the spoken data, "I like you," from the flow of sound reaching her ears regardless of whether the words are spoken in a high-pitched shrill, a soft whisper, or a heavy accent. But simultaneously she feels the energy, the emotion, with which it is said, whether heartily, facetiously, ironically, sarcastically, tenderly, flippantly, carelessly, or shyly.

With the advent of brain-imaging and various electromagnetic scanning studies of the body, neuroscientists are continuing to discover more of the physiological bases for the dual perception and emotional receptivity of sensation. Not that perceptions and emotions are transmitted as discrete entities from the other to us. Rather we receive sensations of sight, sound, taste, smell, and touch through our sense organs, and then perceive ideas while simultaneously feeling the nature of their energy through our emotions.

Take for instance the research work with the sense of touch in the organ of our skin. We sometimes use the verb *feel* as what we do through touch. But we can divide how we deal with tactile sensations into both what we perceive and the emotions we feel. For example, one Swedish-Canadian team discovered a woman whose fast sensory nerves for the sense of touch had been destroyed or at least inactivated, leaving intact only the slow nerves feeding into the area of emotional receptivity.[66] The woman could not perceive the stroking of a feather, nor the texture of its bristles on her skin. She could not perceive where on her skin it was happening. But she distinctly experienced the emotion of pleasure as it was happening.[67] Of course, the healthy adult gets both messages, though the emotional is usually much more subtle and subdued, as are the various emotions stimulated through the eyes by different colors.

The interior decorator specializes in knowing the direct emotional effect of color. She is sensitive to the shades of feeling evoked by different colors and their various hues in painting the walls as backdrops to the furniture. She designs to get the optimum balance between the dual perceptive and emotional effects of her creation as a whole. For her, as with any artist, dealing with sensation through both its cognitively-perceived and emotionally-received effects is only a matter of common sense.

Many psychologists contend that we apprehend emotions exclusively through an ability to read them first, that is, to perceive them. Once perceived, we can then secondarily feel them. Of course this cannot be so. By their natures, they are totally different qualities. Besides, if we could not get a more immediate access to another's emotions, we would have had to spend time every day of our lives studying video clips to first learn which facial expression and which tone of voice should be associated with which emotion. And would those associations be the same for the many persons we meet? How does the newborn relate so immediately and intimately to his mother and father? How can children play so spontaneously and creatively together? Reading someone's emotion perceptually is merely a secondary check of the emotion's manifestation in the other person in order to confirm what we already are feeling when we are surprised by the response. We can read emotions perceptively to a limited extent, but only through the interpretative background of initial experiences collected through the dual coding of perceptions and emotions in primary sensing. Without that background, we would be totally autistic—a robot incapable of even beginning to communicate, much less have the desire to do so.[68]

The idea of this dual purpose sensory system, as substantiated by physiological studies, makes so much common sense, that the "burden of proof" is on those scientists who claim that only half of it—the perceptive half—is real. We have to ask these academics, are they so caught in words and ideas they have overlooked or dismissed the simultaneous communication of the very emotional context within which they can directly grasp the intended meaning of the words they hear? Why do they find it so easy to accept the mystery of how we can transmute the raw perceptual data from all the senses together to originate those ghostly abstractions we call "ideas," but hesitate to even acknowledge the mystery of how we transmute all the various emotional elements from those same senses to experience the spirits we call "emotions"?

'The Girl Is Mother of the Woman'[69]

Even though the neurological evidence for the functioning of the senses as dual-purpose portals has been accumulating for quite some time, psychological research has focused almost exclusively on elucidating their perceptive aspects.[70] The cognitive bias of assuming all emotional communication takes place through faculties of perception has misled many scientists into accepting an electronic conception of mental functioning. For them the brain is a chaos of inner emotional energy stimulated into animation and actualization by incoming perceptual data. To explain and bring order to the interaction between these most dissimilar aspects, these scientists have then to postulate an extremely complicated and comprehensive system of instincts or "genetically-inherited software." Thus we end up with a brain modeled on the computer: the energy of emotion is akin to the electricity of the computer that energizes neural software which in turn processes the incoming digital perceptual data. This cranial neural software serves as the interface between the perception and the emotion we have about it. On a superficial level, this model seems to work well to describe the apparently effortless functioning in activities at which adults are already skilled and merely performing mechanically, but it has no power to explain creativity. It begs the question: if we inherited the software for a universal language, did we also inherit the software to type, ride bicycles, sculpt, peel apples, and use computers?

Is the software for our skills inherited through our genes, or is it developed by us? Is learning merely a series of trials and errors in applying inherited software, or do we create our own programs? Of course, I am arguing that the child is the programmer, albeit not self-consciously, but consciously in the natural cycling through a quartet of functioning.

Introvert and Extrovert

Through the nervous system we perceive the world. Simultaneously, through the limbic (emotional) system, we feel it. To distinguish between them, we get into the false habit of thinking of perceptions as originating from "out there" and emotions from "in here." But the original stimulation for both perception and emotion comes from "out there." Our sense organs, as active receptors, split raw sensation into two very different streams of inputs. At the response end of our activity, our motor system recombines the two streams into action, as is so evident in our expression of language.

This reception of dual elements of sensation and their reintegration in action is at the roots of the split in psychology into two main streams of study by theoretical cognitivists and the empirical behaviorists. We can discover this psychological pair in understanding how our mental faculties mediate the interaction between our sensory and motor abilities, between the moment of spontaneous sensing and that of purposeful action. This is the task of the next chapter.

9

The Roots of Idea, Motion, Ideal, and Emotion

I had to abandon the idea of the superordinate position of the ego.[71]...I saw that everything, all paths I had been following, all steps I had taken, were leading back to a single point—namely, to the midpoint. It became increasingly plain to me that the mandala is the centre. It is the exponent of all paths. It is the path to the centre, to individuation...I knew that in finding the mandala as an expression of the self I had attained what was for me the ultimate.
—C. G. Jung. [72]

If we have a clear idea of the origins of our quarrelsome quartet and see the quartet operating within the context of biology, it will be easier to appreciate their character. We will try to flush them out from their dwelling place from within our personal camouflage of flesh and blood, nerves and hormones, bones and brain waves. We are seeking to catch a glimpse of them emerging from the natural functioning and interaction of body and mind.

The Biological Gauntlet of Nerves and Hormones

Admittedly, biology is a dangerous place to start. We could get so mired in dwelling in the idea of the physical body and the interactions of the nervous system and hormones, we might forget to appreciate the very self-consciousness that allows us to be aware of its existence and functioning in the first place.

We are an enormous complex of cells organized into organs connected through a cobweb of nerves transmitting electrical data while simultaneously being bathed in waves of constantly changing combinations of hormonal impulses. It is as though we function through a "digital" nervous system interfaced with an "analogical" hormonal one. The nervous system functions through networks of very fast nerves insulated from the rest of the body to carry specific

97

quanta of energy from one specific part of the body to another. In contrast, the hormonal system works through hormones in the bloodstream and literally bathes the whole body in its messages. Thus body cells, or organs as a whole, get two completely different types of messages in different ways. A select part of them get the electrical pulses on the inside, while all of them are being massaged by various mixtures of hormones from the outside.

Sensory perception works on the basis of collating series of discrete bits of information from our sense organs at the high speed of neural impulses. This is the whole basis for information theory. But it is only half the basis for our communication theory. All the sense organs, whether of smell, taste, sight, sound, or touch, are wired directly not only into cognitive or thinking centers of the brain, but also into our limbic or emotional centers.

Whereas the artist is the antenna for the dual purpose portals of sensation, the idealist is the transmitter at the other end—driving action in the motoring department. The idealist not only sends out discrete packets of nervous instructions to the muscles, it gives these instructions a stability and rhythm through hormones pumped through the blood around the system. Remember the concept of an integration or skill we developed earlier as a fusion of idea and emotion? We could say on a biological level that this integration directs the hormonal bathing of the muscles responsible for the motions it has simultaneously stimulated from inside the cell through the nerves. Thus slow subtle waves of "feeling" are generated in the infinitely varied combinations and proportions of various hormones. They might be slow, but this emotional energy contributes all the continuity and style to the bare bones instructions from those discrete packets of instantaneous nervous information.

On a physical level we can study the evidence of this underlying dual activity. For example, though all of us walk erectly in balancing the forces of gravity on all sides of a center of balance through perception, each of us have a different style in doing it, such that we can identify close friends in the distance just by the way they are walking. As they approach, we can even sense the particular mood they happen to be in.

The nervous system has a tempo very different from that of the hormonal system. For example, the nerves that carry signals from the sensory organ of the skin to the cognitively perceptive centers of the brain operate at 60 m/sec. The fibers that carry a very different kind of signal from the same senses to the emotional centers of the brain operate at much slower speeds. This "dual tempo" characteristic is also reflected in the "action" half of our activity in using our integrations of skill. The nervous system is the conduit for Morse-code-type messages comprising on/off signals through nervous fibers at instantaneous speeds to the muscles. Simultaneously, hormones are transported by the blood in waves of infinitely variable proportions (there are dozens of hormonal types) to the muscles at momentous speed. The nervous system stimulates the muscles into patterns of activity. The emotional system through hormonal flows gives them a personal style and continuum over time.

The Theoretical and Empirical Duo

Crudely, we could say that the theorist and empiricist are the idea originator and the image processor squeezed into the brain between the antenna and transmitter of the body.

We find the empiricist ensconced inside a 3-D viewer, observing and measuring the motions of the objects she is conceiving. We know she cannot really see what is out there in reality. For example, outside her self-consciousness of it, there is no such thing as color. Color is something she only imagines. In fact, absolutely everything she observes is what she is conceiving in her head to be out there. Whoever put the idea into her head there was something really out there anyway? The theorist did, of course. All her observations originate in his ideas, within which she is dwelling to be able to conceive what is out there. The theorist's ideas in turn originate in the artist's dual coding of the emotional and perceptive aspects of sensation from all the sense organs. The artist himself is stimulated into activity by raw sensations. The idealist from her well of purposes will assign the proper intentions and aspirations to the forms the empiricist is observing—or rather conceiving—giving direction to the cycle through action to bring it back to the artist in order to rediscover the immediacy of his feelings—the energies underlying the motions conceived by the empiricist.

This cycle, from artist to theorist to empiricist to idealist and back to artist, is the natural innate cycling of consciousness in us as children. As teenagers we begin to become self-conscious of particular dimensions and begin to control them to some extent. As adults we can become so self-conscious of one or more of the different components of the cycle that we virtually focus all our energies there.

Train-Car: From Balloon to Box

Take a deeper look into the relationship between the theorist and the empiricist—the processors of idea and image. How do we "see" things in everyday life? Do you remember as a child looking down a stretch of train tracks and being surprised that the further away you looked the thinner and closer together the tracks appeared to get? It puzzled us because we knew they were not really like that. We had a very different idea in our mind. We were convinced the tracks remained the same thickness and distance apart at all points on the line. We had an idea of the tracks as they really were as emerged from the gradual accumulation of the perceptions from all the senses together and the ideas they engendered. It is only by dwelling in this idea or perception (the subject) that we can conceive of those tracks as one and the same object from any of the infinite number of vantage points we can use to look at them (as the object) in perspective.

What does a passenger train-car look like? It looks like a sturdy, oversized, elongated shoebox with rectangular windows and a door of equal size at either end, does it not? But now imagine sitting in the middle of an empty car. All the other passengers and seats have been removed for our thought experiment. From where we sit, the ends of the car appear much narrower than the middle where we are. The sides and roof of the car get smaller as they recede from us. Even the windows get smaller. Really, if we did not know we were sitting in a box-shaped car, it would be easy for me to convince you otherwise at this point, and make you question that you could ever get through the small doors at either end without getting down onto all fours and crawling through.

It only becomes stranger; when we start walking up the car to one end, if we focus solely on our actual perceptions, it is as though that part of the car is expanding around us as we approach, and the part we are leaving behind is shrinking. And when we turn around and start back the other way, that end starts to expand around us while the one behind us begins to shrink. It is as though the car is a balloon of curved space that expands and contracts relative to our position in it. Remember your delight as a child in running up and down a train or plane aisle, making it expand and contract around you?

What happened to our oversized shoebox? No matter to what viewing point we move inside the boxcar, it never looks exactly like a rectangular box. We can only conclude that before we started to focus our attention solely on how we actually perceive it, we must have imagined it!

Of course, as experimenters, we can now get out our measuring tapes, chalk lines and squares, and check out all the dimensions of the boxcar to confirm that our imagination was correct. And we can go further, and discover the infinite number of distortions in our perceptions was caused by the simple fact that the closer an object is to us the more space it takes up on the retinas of our eyes and thus it appears bigger than the same object further away. So the windows closer to us appear much bigger than those further away, and alternately increase and decrease in size as we first approach and then retreat from them.

The only way we could theoretically get to the idea of the perfect shoebox boxcar is to visualize the boxcar from a particular point in space, from an infinite distance away from it when all lines of sight are theoretically perfectly parallel and present us with a perfect object.

Or, from an infinitely close presence. By dwelling in the idea, we can combine every single possible different point of view into one, as if we were totally absorbed within the idea of the car's shape as a whole. It is impossible for us to visualize any forms as they truly are. Visualization requires a point from which we are viewing. But in our idea of it, we are not limited in that way. While we were perceiving the boxcar as an expanding and contracting balloon, we were imagining it as temporarily freed of the shoebox idea we had assumed for so long.

Remember now how you experienced the boxcar before you tried this experiment, or any room you have entered and walked through? You will realize you do not usually see them as being wider in the part where you are sitting (or standing), and getting narrower at the ends. You usually only notice perspective if we sit down and concentrate on actually seeing it as if for the first time when we are confused in identifying something in our view. It is only then we realize that all along the omnipresent view is the one of which we were conscious in our minds in orientating ourselves within it.

This is how we share the same orientation of things with others on the train, all of whom have a different angle of perspective on it. We are all using the same artificial construct—our conception of the train-car as an oversized shoebox—as if we were bypassing our personal perspective, as being able to see it from every perspective that exists at once. Only, from our actual pinpoint perspective of where we are on the train do we see it differently from the others.

No matter in what place in that car or room you are, you normally conceive it as a rectangular box. From your perspective of being in a particular place within it, you can visualize the characteristics like the color of the walls and the location of the furnishings and windows. This visualization fills in the details of your omnipresent experience of the idea, just as it did for the railroad track. You can spin around slowly on your heels within the room and have no problem relating to all its contents as part of one whole. That one abstract whole is our pure idea of what a room is.

Just consider the efficiencies! While we were perceiving the train-car as an expanding and contracting rubber balloon, we had a different perception of shape and size of the whole car and all the windows and doors in it from every different vantage point. But by dwelling in the idea of a shoebox car, we can now imagine all the different parts of it as one stable whole and implicitly deal with any distortions as that due to perspective. Instead of having to store a million images in memory, we can now relate all our sensations of color, texture, sound, and smell in that car around one idea as we spin on our heels, just as we will learn to do with the "three-baller" in a later chapter. That is the theorist's job—to reduce and distill millions of perceptions into the most concise idea. In this case he took a sequence of all those flat-screen perceptions absorbed in walking up and down the car and found the key to understanding them as part of one whole.

Perceiving and Conceiving

Idea takes its characteristics from the perceptions that gave birth to it. Perception consists of a sequence of stills—each instant snapshot marking a point or break in time. Each comes to the brain and fades in turn to be replaced by another milliseconds later. How much time, distance, volume, and direction can we find in these instant snapshots? Even though they took a discrete duration of time to develop, there is none at all left in any still. If by "instant" we mean a small fraction of time, whether a second, millisecond, or even nanosecond, an arrow in flight would still have been able to travel some fraction of distance in that time, whether a meter, millimeter, or nanometer. In a perfect still, as Zeno cannily pointed out about our mental image of an arrow caught motionless in full flight, the arrow, not having had any time to move, could not have traveled any distance or in any actual direction! Continuous time has all been completely squeezed out of the idea, leaving it punctuated only by breaks in time with only the logic of direction derived from the sequence or order of the perceptions.

In effect, it is not the theorist, but the empiricist who learns to conceive of continuous time, distance, volume, and physical direction in her imagination of the motion and interaction of objects. But only by dwelling in or knowing the idea of a boxcar can the empiricist, our experimenter, invent and whip out her measuring tools to check it, just to make sure. Without the theorist's ideas, she would have been able neither to observe a box to measure nor to study the motions and interactions of any objects within it.

It is difficult to appreciate the activity of perceiving ideas as a self-conscious activity separate from the activity of conceiving it. We prefer to live in an apparently seamless whole of consciousness. We get a sense of the activity required to perceive only when we discover something brand new outside our experience. Then we need to look at it very carefully from many different angles, play with it, listen to it, and even smell and taste it to get a good idea of what it is, to perceive it for what it is. We need to get all the senses involved.

We see but we do not see. The skilled botanist can see the differences between a thousand different species of grasses, but we others are able to distinguish only between crab- and bluegrass. The skilled doctor can see the differences between the ailment as of fungal, bacterial or viral origin, but we others see only a general sickness. Depending on how we make our livings and even our cultures, each of us has learned how to observe different aspects of the world based on what aspects we were pushed into perceiving, into questioning what it was, and forcing hypotheses out of those questions which in turn our "observer" could try out by dwelling in them. As adults we are highly selective in what aspects of our external reality we choose to try to perceive and thus dwell in to make our observations.

Our Emotional Pair

What is driving and directing these two characters of our quartet? Without our emotional pair—the antenna and transmitter—neither would have gotten off the ground. The artist in bonding strings of raw perceptions to raw emotions makes them stay around long enough to be accessible in memory[73] to allow the thinker to work out an idea about the perceptions. And the idealist, the embodiment of all purpose in conscience, guides and directs the action.

The relationship between the idealist and artist is analogous to that of the theorist and the empiricist. Whereas the theorist works toward discovering an idea through which everything can be observed and studied, the empiricist is observing everything from only one particular vantage point in her reality. Whereas the idealist works toward one omniscient conscience that can guide all her actions to realize her most profoundly felt ideals of intention and aspirations toward fulfillment, the artist is focused on expressing the emotion of the present moment.

We can say we feel, but we do not feel. The various connoisseurs of classical music, alternative rock, jazz, and country and western have developed a sensitivity to appreciate the varied emotional nuances of their favorite music. But only a small selection from all these different styles can be appreciated by all. We begin life with a very limited capacity to appreciate the broad range of emotional stimulation. It is only through the turmoil of struggling with the everyday exigencies of living that we grow to appreciate and express the subtleties of an amazing range of emotional communication. But to which aspects of the whole stream of sensation we become emotionally sensitive and which emotions we attach to particular ideas and observations, is limited to the comprehensiveness of our relationship to the range of character in our guardians and of whatever friends, mentors, and interests color our experiences within our particular culture.

As adults, most of us are much less self-conscious of the activity of the artist and the theorist than of the empiricist and the idealist. Whereas the first pair—essential for the primary discovery of the world—is much more active in childhood, the second pair—working with what we have discovered and wondering what to do with it—tends to preoccupy us much more in the later more practical-orientated adult life.

The quartet is only made possible at the one extreme through the initial splitting of raw sensation into two streams, one to cognitive and the other to limbic or emotional centers of the brain, and at the other extreme in action in we how we recombine them in the motor centers. The artist and theorist represent our introversive half in contrast to the extroversive empiricist and idealist. The extroverts are preoccupied with recombining the products of the first pair through conceiving forms and deciding how we should feel about them in order to best project ourselves outwards into the world through action.

From Dualism into Four Dimensions

Scientists acknowledge the dualism and interaction of nerves and hormones, of cognitive and emotional centers of the brain. The neuroscientist Antonio Damasio[74] even argues that without an active interrelationship between them we could no longer function creatively. He has studied a few patients in whom the intersection between the emotional and cognitive centers of the brain is damaged. At first glance, these persons appear to be physically and cognitively normal. They are able to pass a whole battery of skill tests with flying colors. But they are rather dysfunctional in everyday living. They cannot work productively enough to hold a job nor can they carry on normal personal relationships. Apparently the key to the creativity required in these situations is a healthy dynamic of emotional and cognitive interaction.

At this "dual" level of interpretation we can appreciate the validity of the syllable of consonant and vowel as the synthesis of emotional and cognitive elements. How do we jump to a higher level of organization to derive the four components for the structure and dynamics of the sentence?

It is not as if there are two systems—one of nerves and one of hormones—operating in separate corners of the brain that then meet at one point, and poof we get creative! Not only does the brain have different structures stimulated by nerves while bathing in hormones, but also a whole range of brain wave activity—typically divided into four frequencies: beta, alpha, theta, and delta. Scientists haven't yet figured out what role these waves play in the communication or coordination between different parts of the brain. What about the rest of the body? During sensing and physical activity, we are as present in our skin and the muscles of our hands and feet as anywhere else. Rather than in one poof, we could think of the four types of self-consciousness of our quartet integrating different parts of body and brain together, both through nervous and hormonal pathways discovered through anatomical dissections and brain waves as detected in living organisms.

Why not use the functioning of our "bodily" pair—the sensory and motor systems—and our "brainy" pair—the idea originator and image processor—as the basis for finding our psychological quartet? After all, what is self-consciousness? We will explore it as manifestations of ourselves "dwelling-in"[75] each of these four natural functions.

To see how this could be, it would be useless to start by digging further into the brain with scalpel and probe. We will not find any feelings, thoughts, conceptions, or purposes in that grey and bloody mass with its multibuzz of brain waves. The only rational way to start exploring this conundrum is through studying how each member of our quartet is self-conscious of its particular take on reality. Inevitably, no matter what we want to know, we always have to work backwards from our self-consciousness of what we sense, think, conceive as real, and do about it.

10

Four Characters in Search of One Author

By dark gropings, by feelings not wholly understood, by catching at hints and fumbling for explanations.
(Alfred Adler, on the search for meaning)

All four of our quartet can function semi-autonomously: the artist intoxicated with an infinite variety of emotion in the spontaneous combustion of sensation, the theorist mesmerized in piercing the veil of sensation for ideas, the empiricist coolly observing and quantifying the motions of her objective conceptions, and the idealist striving to bind all her ideals together into one overall purpose. How can we get this quarrelsome quartet literally to work together?[76] First we will pin down their individual characteristics. At least then, can we understand why they have so much difficulty working together within the basic structure and dynamics of the same sentence.

A typical epistemological approach is to consider idea and emotion as opposite sides of man's nature. But let us assume, like Immanuel Kant, they are inseparably linked in consciousness, as the two sides of one coin. In fact, let us assume consciousness is the two in synthesis and focus on how we combine them in different ways. After all we have both four very different ideas of what time—the continuum of emotion—is, and also four different approaches in relating to our sensory perceptions. We will explore these four pairs as modes of self-consciousness, and how one person relates them together through a pyramid of four "double-sided coins," or like a working windmill with four vanes reaching out to catch all the wind that blows, into full consciousness.

Time as the Veil of Emotion

Time and emotion are intimately related. Emotion gives instantaneous perceptive data momentous punctuation and continuity.

At the least we can begin by agreeing Mary does learn at a particular time—the present. It is obvious Mary can only learn in the present. That she has learned in the past is obvious too, but she learned only at intervals in the past when she was present in the moments when it happened, when she wanted to know "what is real?" The questions, "what *was* real?" and "what should be real?" are another matter altogether. Besides, those questions will only be finally answered or revised by reference to the present, to what she believes *is* real.

Learning is through "what is" in present time. We can experience the reality in which we exist only in the present. Any speculation outside the present into the past is based in memories. Any speculation about the future springs from our hopes and fears. All we really have to explore to discover "what is real" is that in present time. We cannot assume time outside the present even exists. In fact, it is obvious neither the past nor the future exist in present time. The past and future have no more real life than do memories and dreams. They only exist to the extent we can dwell in them to more broadly and deeply relate to our world in the present moment.

The historian puts great store in past realities of "what was." Jim picks over bones found in graves, tar pits, and landslides, and explores the ruins of old structures and the tools humans used to build, decorate, maintain, and destroy them. He studies old manuscripts, themselves but shadows of a reality a known or unknown person aspired toward through mere words of a perhaps now-dead language. Through this debris the historian sorts, painstakingly reconstructing a memory of their "reality." But for us laymen and laywomen living in the present, those past realities are meaningful only for how they help us deal with "what is." If somebody were to invent a time machine that would allow us to go back and live there, then we could take a real interest in history for itself. But nobody will ever be able to invent such a machine, because of course the past does not exist in the present so there is no way we could get there from here. Our present or "presence" is in the space between our memories of the past and our dreams of the future, between the facts of our experiences and the dreams we want to explore through the questions and emotions that puzzle and energize us.

Can we define *present time?* How long is it—a second, an hour, a month, or an eternity? In modern life we are so used to dividing time into artificially uniform bits we sometimes forget emotional time—how it can drag on or race by, become an insurmountable barrier or suddenly vanish into thin air. We describe time through its moods and swings, in a myriad of emotional terms as slow or quick, jittery or smooth, rough or calm, troubled or peaceful, happy or sad, despairing or hopeful. Curiously, we can describe time with any adjective describing any emotion. We can feel time's ever-changing frequencies, speed, and periodicity with our ever-changing and unpredictable humors. But when we try to perceive it, it vanishes. As St. Augustine wrote, "I know what time is, if no one asks me. But if I try to explain it to one who asks, I no longer know."

The empirical scientist, using clocks and calendars to invent time as artificially equal bits, explores the mathematical dimension of time in concepts of speed, acceleration, energy, efficiency, et cetera. She reduces time to a dimension with which she can deal through the device of clock and calendar. In contrast, the theoretical scientist sucks out all the duration of time leaving us with a grey theory incorporating only its direction, the "arrow" of time. Whereas the theorist and empiricist think in shades of black and white schematic and mathematical shadows of time, the idealist and artist enjoy a much more colorful dimension.

On the one extreme, time can be characterized as flat endless boredom. On the other, time vanishes with the sudden onset of a delightful insight or deep sorrow. It disappears in those moments when we lose ourselves in strong feelings, when we realize only afterward from a clock that a whole hour had passed or even a whole evening, or even twenty years when we rediscovered a wonderful childhood friend. Where did "time" vanish? It did not. We only experienced her true colors in those emotions. Through what device did we drop our guard in time to discover she had dropped her veil?

The artist, a mischievous fool at times, insists on looking directly at naked time to capture it exactly as it is in that moment or eternity of emotion, in a sculpture, painting, or poem. The idealist, the woman of purpose, jumps on its bare back and rides it through adventures in once-upon-a-time to bring her ideals into reality with that energy. She focuses her intentions and goals during the action to find her way back to the artist, who is intent on the nature of the actual emotion energizing the self in the moment of the action.

That Was Then or What Should Be; This Is Now, Forever

The empiricist is the historian of facts and the idealist is the visionary of the future. But our metaphorical pair pioneers the present. The theorist concentrates all time into one idea that can be grasped in the instant and the artist searches for the perfect emotion that can be treasured for all of time.

The empiricist puts no stock in the present at all. There is no room for it in the infinite continuity of clocked time. All duration of time is either in what is past or in what is in the future. For her, the present is no more than a dividing line between what has happened and what will happen. Having reduced the duration of the present to nothing, she can overlook her own presence in time and relate to it at arm's length through the contrivance of cesium-atom clocks within the larger frameworks of the daily, monthly, and yearly cycles of the sun, moon, and stars, the mechanical clocks of the universe. Having reduced time to an objective ruler, she can now conceive its motion instead of feeling it. She can now proceed to subsume her interpretation of all time to these contrivances, delighting in the statistical measurements of speed in accomplishing discrete amounts of work and the frequency, juxtaposition, and periodicity of particular events.

The pure idealist has an extreme discomfort with the present. She concerns herself primarily with what is wrong with it. She is obsessed with replacing it with her vision of what should be according to her ideals. Having rooted her idea of time in the cyclical clock of living beings—of conception, emergence, growth, fruiting, dying, and death—she argues the value of ideals in stories of the birth, growth, flowering, and consummation of an ideal in an emotion-packed train of action, with a once-upon-a-time beginning in the paradise of the greatest intentions in the good old days, through great difficulties in the middle—the present—to a happily-ever-after end in an oasis of joy and peace in the future. This woman of purpose, our woman of action, is intent on laying the groundwork to prepare the living world for the embodiment of her ideals in the future. She imperatively asserts which emotions of intention should be associated with which subjects of perception and which emotions of fulfillment should be associated with which objectives.

Whereas the empiricist organizes the facts that stimulated her in the *was* of the past to the *therefore will be* in the future, the idealist is rooted in a belief of what *shall*[77] *be* in the future despite what *is* in the present because of what was intended in the beginning. The empiricist believes in a future of consequences based on the established facts of motional cause and effect or of the emotional stimuli and responses she discovered in the past. The idealist assigns intentions to the past in order to give meaning to the ideals she is dedicated to realizing in the future.

In contrast, our metaphorists—the theorist and artist—focus on the present, reducing the past to the status of mere memory and the future to that of dream. The theorist Albert Einstein writes, "The distinction between past, present, and future is only an illusion, however persistent."[78] The theorist illuminates the logic of the path, whether that of living beings toward increasing order and sophistication or that of the inanimate world toward entropy. He wants to capture the whole logic of its developing patterns in one overwhelming hypothesis that can be understood in an instant. In a reverse parallel, the artist wants to capture his most profound emotions within the still framework of a painting, poem, or sculpture. He strives to discover the purest, most momentous emotions and then declares them eternal for all time "as it was in the beginning, is now, and ever shall be."[79]

With this understanding, we should not have any trouble getting our quarrelsome four working together in time. The theorist fits exactly into the slot of the empiricist's dividing line between past and future. Since this dividing line—the present instant—has no duration of time, it is the perfect place for him. He provides the empiricist a present in which to live, and the empiricist provides him a past and future in which to make use of his arrow of time. Similarly, the artist complements the idealist by linking the latter's past intentions and future aspirations with the present moment. He completes the idealist's half-empty glass with one half full. The idealist completes the artist with a beginning and an end to give him a comprehensible framework from which he can apprehend the moment.

The Four Dimensions of Cognition: Objectivity vs. Subjectivity

The roles of scientist and artist are reversed in the domain of the sensory perception. Whereas the idealist and artist preoccupied with the emotional aspects of sensation declare that time is but the veil of emotion, the scientist preoccupied by perceiving and conceiving declares that raw sensations are merely the veil of perception.

The theoretician, peering through the confusion of primary sensory data, perceives underlying patterns and comes up with ideas. The empiricist dwelling in those ideas conceives the interaction of forms and divides the action into causes and effects, stimuli and responses, which she can then measure and quantify over time. The root difference between these two scientists in cognition—knowing—is in the very different ways they are being objective, just as the artist and idealist know through different ways of being subjective.

Take the example of the different ways in which our quartet members relate to an infant playing with a ball. Consider that at an early stage, when the ball roles away to end up hidden behind a box, the infant seems to completely lose interest in it and starts to play with something else. Only at a later stage does the infant actively try to find that ball. The scientists want to understand what happened to change the child's behavior in the interval.

The cognitivist, the theorist, argues the infant only starts looking for the ball after its thought processes have developed to a point wherein it can conceive of the ball as having an existence outside the instant of its perceiving it. Before that point, the infant had perceived of the ball as existing only during its interaction with it. Thus, when the ball disappeared earlier, it no longer existed for the infant, so it could not even have occurred to the infant to look for it.

The pure behaviorist, our empiricist, argues that during the interval between before and after, the child was finally conditioned positively enough toward that ball and thus is interested enough to try to find it. At this point the behaviorist can set up an experiment to measure the degree of "ball conditioning" various stimuli have on the infant. She identifies the differences between stimuli given to infants who learn it quicker with that given to those who take longer to learn it. She uses the length of time it took the child to change its behavior from not-looking to looking-for as the measuring stick for testing the effectiveness or efficiency of various stimuli in effecting this change.

Notice the empiricist tries neither to quantify nor describe the stimulation the subject itself senses nor how it works to prepare a response. Like the physicist who according to Newton's Third Law considers all action-reaction energy instantaneous, the pure empiricist's approach takes into account only the stimulus itself and the effected result. She does not try to differentiate between perceptual and emotional stimulation, nor between conceptual understanding and belief in the response of her subjects. In effect, as defined by her scientific method, she takes a purely objective point of view through her experimental method, observing her subjects as objects conditioned by external operant stimuli to result in concrete elicited responses.

The cognitivist like Piaget has a different orientation to objectivity from the behaviorist. He treats his subjects as dualistic life forms—the engine and its fuel. His objectivity depends on his ability to separate out between cognition—the engine of his "objective" half—and its emotional fuel—the "subjective" half, and focus solely on the first. In contrast to the behaviorist treating the subject as a whole, Piaget splits his subjects into two halves, and focuses solely on elucidating the changing perceptions of the infant experimenter to the apparent exclusion of the emotional pair of functions. The theorist discovers the child's cumulative discovery of ideas, whereas the behaviorist ensconced in her 3-D viewer—dwelling in the theorist's idea that the child already knows that objects exist outside of the moment of its perceiving them—is intent on testing the idealist—our child of action—measuring only the results of its efforts to learn in the past and collect her facts.

In contrast to our objective researchers who study the other in interaction with objects and others, the idealist and especially the artist explore the human being through direct emotional interaction with the other and within themselves. But this subjective pair also demonstrates a similar divergence in how they explore their fascination through this opposite orientation.

As parents of the child playing with the ball, on the one hand, as artists we try to empathize with its spirit as much as possible. We strive to apprehend the same actual energy, the infant's emotions, in the present or presence of its playfulness. On the other hand, as idealists, we struggle to fathom the intentions behind the infant's desire to play with that ball and the fulfillment resulting from its actions.

The artist in focusing on the emotional content, is the complement of the theorist. He also turns inward, but to the experience of the other half—pure emotion—and how to embody it fully in the moment of action. In playing with the child, he is striving to empathize fully with the child's train of emotions by feeling them himself. As such, the artist is content with the superficial aspects of perception. Since emotions cannot be perceived, the parent—as artist—only wants as detailed a physical impression of his perceptions as possible as the "hook" to recall the emotions of similar memories to help in intensifying and clarifying the ones he is experiencing in the present situation. Joseph Conrad writes, "All art...appeals primarily to the senses, and the artistic aim when expressing itself in the written words must also make its appeal through the senses, if its highest desire is to reach the secret spring of responsive emotions."[80] Instead of penetrating the superficialities of the perception like the theorist, the artist uses them merely as mnemonic hooks to relate his emotional experiences in the present with those in memory.

The idealist as the complement of the empirical behaviorist does not distinguish between pure emotions and ideas. She turns outward in combining them into ideals of the most righteous and just intentions to achieve her goal. In playing with the child, she is searching for the right actions through which she can best interact with the child to help the child achieve its goal—finding the ball. Her ultimate act is to give her own life to the cause that will bring the world closer to her ideal consummation. She uses the empiricist's observations of forms in motion merely as symbols or vehicles to embody the ideals she is pursuing. Whereas the dictum of the empiricist is "seeing is believing," that of the idealist—for example Miguel de Cervantes' Don Quixote—is "believing is seeing": "The whole point is that, without seeing her, you must believe, confess, affirm, swear and uphold it [that in the world there is no maiden more beauteous than Dulcinea del Toboso]...If I were to let you see her, what merit would there be in confessing so manifest a truth?"[81]

Our incredible quartet! They each have different types of questions arising from their different ways of approaching the subject, and of course different answers. Each one has become stuck in exploring his or her particular central "duality," whether of relating idea to action, making connections between cause and effect, filling the gap between intention and aspiration with the "right" action, or getting the true fit between feeling and perception. Throw a metaphorical thinker and a literal behaviorist into the same learning ring with a zealous believer and a romantic poet, and observe the confusion—a fascinating but troublesome lot.

The Quartet and Language

Above, in a literal way, we broke down the functions of each member of our quartet to fit into a cycle of activity. But we need a metaphor within which they can be shown to work together simultaneously. In an earlier chapter, we worked through the idea of how language develops through the interaction of the quartet. The sentence provides us with the ideal framework for a suitable metaphor. The artist's spontaneous emotion fits the verb. The theorist, our deep thinker, provides the ideas for the subject in which the empiricist can dwell. Of course, the empiricist, our experimenter, by dwelling in ideas discovers objects and conceives of their motions. To complete it, the idealist provides the intentions for the subject—the agent of action—and the aspirations for fulfillment in the object.

Our difficult four communicate with each other through the language formed through the integration of all four into the components and dynamics of the sentence. It is a common language, but what a difference, between the poetry of Shakespeare and the text of Newton's treatise on gravity! The different styles reflect the difference in how they embody time, emotion, space, and perception. But as we have already explored in trying to capture language alive, the ingenious flexibility of language's universal grammar allows them to try to relate to each other through it.

The most congenial relationships are between the theorist and the empiricist and between the idealist and the artist. As pairs they complement each other naturally and pair up to form the basis for the activities in the Science and Arts faculties of our universities, respectively. The theorist provides the perception as subject and the empiricist fills in with the predicate. The empiricist needs only an imaginary verb of energy conceived of as distances over time periods in various directions to completely describe the motions of her object relative to the subject in which she is dwelling. For our Arts pair, the artist provides the felt verb, the present moment of feeling as composed of whatever infinitely possible combination of emotions. The idealist directs the subject with the right action to fulfill her aspirations in the objective.

The most difficult communication is that diagonally across our learning ring in the Social Sciences, for example that between the theorist and the idealist. The first has tied the meaning of his ideas to the perceptions from which they were derived while the other has extracted abstract dictionary meanings and insists on wholly subsuming these in the emotions she has assigned them from her experiences with them. The artist and the empiricist have an even greater difficulty. For the artist the experience of the feeling of his emotions is the meaning of the verb. The empiricist studying only emotion's manifestation in how her objects behave effectively reduces emotion to what is observed. As you can see, the matchups between these diagonal relationships we typically find in the most acrimonious debates in the Social Sciences—the intermediary between Arts and Sciences—results in the most confusion and thus an extremely wide diversity of opinions on each and every issue.

It is obvious none of our four caricatures could exist alone as real persons. We only become caricatures in self-consciously limiting ourselves to less than all four modes of knowing, and by our reluctance or inability to integrate and synthesize them into our thoughts and actions. In unself-conscious action we survive into oneness by blurring them together: new perceptions modifying older ones remembered, new variations of emotional receptions revitalizing our stores of emotional memories recalled, new conceptions of understanding the changes happening around us, and more comprehensive beliefs to reorient our activities to a deeper and more-encompassing purpose.

D: <u>Dancing</u>

11

The "To-Fro and Around": Who Cares and a Catch-22

"What then is Love?"…
"…He is a great spirit, and like all spirits he is intermediate between the divine and the mortal."
"And what," I said, "is his power?"
"He interprets," she replied, "between gods and men, conveying and taking across to the gods the prayers and sacrifices of men, and to men the commands of the gods and the benefits they return; he is the mediator who spans the chasm which divides them, and therefore by him the universe is bound together…"
(Plato: Symposium)

The learning dance step is "to-fro and around," whether for poetry or physics. The only real difference is the scientist starts out with an idea and then works toward conceiving of the energies animating it, whereas the poet starts out with the energies he feels and works toward an appropriate action. The problem of students is to figure out how relate to their metaphors, facts, and ideals to make sense of what they are trying to understand and communicate within the experiences of their lives.

Mating, Nostalgia, Shy Love, and Caring

We should be very cautious of talking about scientists and poets in the same breath. Traditionally there has been a great deal of misunderstanding between the two. Take for instance poet William Yeats's tirade:

> Those learned men who are a terror to children and an ignominious sight in lovers' eyes, all those butts of a traditional humor where there is something of the wisdom of peasants, are mathematicians, theologians, lawyers, men of science of various kinds. They have followed some abstract reverie, which

stirs the brain only and needs that only, and have therefore stood before the looking-glass without pleasure and never known those thoughts that shape the lines of the body for beauty or animation, and wake a desire for praise or for display.[82]

Perhaps he was thinking of Isaac Newton, that dour man caught laughing only once in public life when someone suggested he did not know his geometry, who insisted on calling great works of sculpture "stone dolls," and summed up poetry as "an ingenious kind of nonsense."

Few poets dare write anything about the relationship between scientists and poets. As a group, they are not nearly as understanding as Samuel Coleridge who contended the best poets were those who were also good mathematicians, and especially Walter de la Mare, who wrote the following poem, "The Happy Encounter":

I saw sweet Poetry turn troubled eyes
On shaggy Science nosing in the grass,
For by that way poor Poetry must pass
On her long pilgrimage to Paradise.
He snuffled, grunted, squealed: perplexed by flies,
Parched, weatherworn, and near of sight, alas,
From peering close where little was
In dens secluded from the open skies.

But Poetry in bravery went down,
And called his name, soft, clear, and fearlessly;
Stooped low, and stroked his muzzle overgrown;
Refreshed his drought with dew; wiped pure and free
His eyes: and lo! laughed loud for joy to see
In those grey deeps the azure of her own.[83]

Did you enjoy the poem? I had fun trying to figure out what images through which to see the two characters. Now it is clear Poetry is female and Science is male. At first I thought of Science as a near-sighted pig "squealing" in the rooting pursuit of some rubbish in a barnyard infested with flies (or poorly-lit laboratory), with Poetry a sad sparrow perched on the eaves of the barn (or shelf of the laboratory) watching him, knowing she will soon have to get down to the same task to do her thing. But in the second stanza, they are more like dog and master on an early morning walk because now he has Poetry "stooping," and Science has a "muzzle," and that "dew" definitely pins it to morning. But the dog's muzzle is "overgrown," like a beard he has forgotten to shave—are they now people? In the two last lines it is not clear whether his eyes are laughing or it is she who is laughing, and then they get lost in each other's eyes—Poetry and Science are lovers? So does that mean when she "went down and called his name" maybe it was he that stooped low and stroked the fuzz on her gro…, er, I mean, "muzzle overgrown." Is Science now the female and Poetry the male? The imagery shifts around, and we can do different things with it at different times.

A good poem is like a well-cut diamond. It is only beautiful when in motion, as facets sparkling on a loved one's hand—a jigsaw puzzle of a kaleidoscope of images. A poet wants you to have fun, too, especially if he is very serious about keeping you interested long enough to find out how he feels about life to buy his latest collection.

There are many different kinds of poems—mischievous ones like "The Happy Encounter" and cheeky ones like Ogden Nash's "Candy is dandy, but liquor is quicker." There are Gerard Hopkins' poems with smashing images of piety, or those by others of Bacchanalian debauchery, John Donne's cerebral metaphysical sermons and John Keats's sensual lyrics. You can find long rambling sentimental poems like Robert Frost's in the stoic language of straight backwoodsmen or callous ones by city-dwellers like T.S. Eliot's "The Love Song of J. Alfred Prufrock" that snake around and through the despair of lost men rummaging the rubbish heaps of their memories for shreds of hope.

The various moods aroused by different great poems can always be traced back to an emotional tension. Take for instance D. H. Lawrence's "The Piano":

Softly, in the dusk, a woman is singing to me;
Taking me back down the vista of years, till I see
A child sitting under the piano, in the boom of the tingling strings
And pressing the small, poised feet of a mother who smiles as she sings.

In spite of myself, the insidious mastery of song
Betrays me back, till the heart of me weeps to belong
To the old Sunday evenings at home, with winter outside
And hymns in the cozy parlor, the tinkling piano our guide.

So now it is vain for the singer to burst into clamor
With the great black piano appassionato. The glamour
Of childish days is upon me, my manhood is cast
Down in the flood of remembrance, I weep like a child for the past.

Start with the view from the rafters of a darkened concert hall. You see a man in the audience apparently mesmerized by a woman singing softly to a tune on a piano. The emotions evoked recall to his memory those wintry Sunday evenings when as a child he played at his mother's feet while she played the piano and sang hymns. Suddenly, the opera singer breaking out into a passionate love song breaks into his happy reverie. Her interruption makes him aware of himself again as an old man. He realizes he can never return to those days and breaks out in tears.

The man is entranced with his memories. They evoke a deep yearning for a return to those youthful years. But age has put an insurmountable barrier between him and the hope of recovering them. On the one hand he cannot forget and lose them. On the other he cannot get any closer to them than his memories. He can only circle around his childhood memories like a lost lamb. He cries. The common point around which the emotional force revolves is nostalgia. Appropriately, the word "nostalgia" is rooted in the Greek words for "return home" and "pain."

Another well-loved poem is Carl Sandburg's "Maybe":

Maybe he believes me, maybe not.
Maybe I can marry him, maybe not.
Maybe the wind in the prairie,
The wind on the sea, maybe,
Somebody somewhere, maybe, can tell.
I will lay my head on his shoulder
And when he asks me I will say yes,
Maybe.

From the vantage point of dwelling in her emotions of loving him, she wonders if he really loves her. While dwelling in her imagination of his emotions of loving her, she wonders if she really loves him. Imagine two planets circling each other deep in outer space and name them "His" and "Hers," or even better "You" and "I." We feel a strong pulling toward each other, but our uncertainty of our own and the other's motivation keep us shying away. The mystery of the emotion is that the power of young love not only attracts, but also repels by making the lovers unsure of themselves and each other. The paradox is that love evolves through this tension between curiosity and fear.

The best poetry, by crystallizing a dilemma in which we can become the main character, guides us to a keener awareness of the underlying dynamics of a balanced emotional life. What could be a better balance to the attraction of love than a fear or shyness that bids us to be patient while getting a deeper and more circumspect sense of it all before committing ourselves irrevocably?

Another great poem is Walter de la Mare's "Listeners." We meet the "Traveller" at midnight, as he is knocking on a door of an unlit house deep within a forest. We have no idea from whence he came or where he is going, nor any idea of why he stopped here except that he had promised to do so. Who are the "Listeners?" We never hear a peep out of anybody in the house. They do not get up to greet him or to quibble about the racket he is making, or even to yell at him to go away. Do they hate him, despise him, pity him, or think he is ridiculous? The only thing we can surmise is they do not have the faintest interest or curiosity about the Traveller. They appear frigidly indifferent. They have no care in the world for him. But the Traveller cares, daring to knock three times at this house isolated in the wilderness. At first he is perplexed by the lack of response; after the second time he is aroused, whether in anger or frustration or desperation we do not know. In the end we hear him riding away on his horse in haste. All we know is that he still cares. Otherwise he would not have insisted upon shouting out that he has kept his promise.

Without a context, it is impossible to attribute a particular meaning to the poem. It is as though the poet stripped a story of all its plot and theme and characters and left us just one isolated incident, ample scenery, spare but intense emotions, and a few lines of monologue. No reader can have a clue what it is all about because it does not seem to be about anything.

The poem is a naked metaphor of the mystery of the caring of one for another and the absolutely indifferent response of the other. The carer is perplexed, then makes one last appeal and finally leaves. We wonder why he knocked so many as three times. Or, if he *really* cared, why did he quit trying to reach them? Going back and forth between his feelings for them and their indifference to him, he ends up like a sun caught in an orbit around a dead planet. He is drawn to it by his caring. But he holds a wary distance, because his warmth and desire are not eliciting a likewise response from that frigid planet. Being a bare metaphor, the poem virtually forces us to clothe it with whatever experiences we ourselves have experienced to be able to understand it in a context.

"A Private Universe"

Exploring the application of the "to-fro and around" idea to science is more problematic than that to poetry. It is naturally easier to appreciate poetry than make intelligible conversation on scientific issues. First of all we need to identify a subject with which we all have some familiarity and interest.

Why not start with understanding the basics of the solar system? There is much anecdotal evidence about how few people regardless of educational achievement understand it. An award-winning video entitled *A Private Universe*[84] laments how few correct answers the interviewer got in asking twenty-three seniors, alumni, and faculty at the 1987 Harvard University convocation to answer the following questions:

"Why is it warmer in summer than in winter?"
"Why does the moon have a different shape each night?"

To the amazement of the interviewers, only two of twenty-three of Harvard's finest were able to give correct answers. The interviewers found little difference between the wrong answers and those of the grade nine students in a neighboring high school. How do we explain this? Despite the fact that all had been exposed several times during their education to scientific descriptions of the major movements within our solar system, and the implications for earth thereof, it only really stuck with two. Most forgot their education right after the exams!

Who cares?

Of course, a major part of the problem is that few of us have any real interest in the matter to begin with. Consideration of the movements of the sun and moon has virtually no importance in our daily lives. We work and live according to the calendar and the clock. They have replaced our former need to monitor the heavens for time. Weather-tight houses, warm clothes, cheap energy, and light bulbs have released us from overdue consideration of natural light and dark, warmth and cold. And since most of us live in cities, sunrises and sunsets (and the moon) are mostly obscured by buildings. Consequently, in modern times, even though we are obsessed with weather forecasts, most of us do not bother to monitor the actual movements of sun and moon in our lives. In fact we do not even capitalize their names despite our total dependency on them for sustaining natural life on earth. Our modern attitude is very different from that of the traditional Inuit[85]:

And I think over again
My small adventures
When with a shore wind I drifted out
In my kayak
And thought I was in danger.
My fears,
Those small ones
That I thought so big

For all the vital things
I had to get and to reach.

And yet, there is only
One great thing,
The only thing:
To live to see in huts and on journeys
The great day that dawns,
And the light that fills the world.

Talk about being intoxicated with sunrises! How many people questioned on the street in Vancouver or Bangkok could even see a sunrise, much less describe the back and forth wandering of sunrises and sunsets across the horizon over the year? The peculiarities of how the celestial bodies move and their effects are mere curiosities that rate below the level of "Ripley's Believe It or Not." Not having any need to monitor them and make sense of it, we have not, and thus modern man, as opposed to our ancestors, brings relatively few relevant personal experiences to interact with what is being taught.

Not only that, the abbreviated solar system model of three balls representing the sun, earth, and moon is something strange to behold. It has no resemblance to anything we have ever experienced from here on earth. What we have noticed is a sun apparently circling us once a day and some of us have noticed that the moon seems to be roughly following it in the same direction. In contrast, in the scientific model, the moon takes about twenty-eight days to orbit us and in the opposite direction, and the sun apparently does not even orbit us at all. According to the scientists we on the earth go around the sun and take a full year doing it! The scientist explains that our illusion is due to the rotation of the earth, which is really very confusing to us so it is better just to accept this objectively true Copernican ball-bearing solar system for now to serve as the scientific model. It will surely all become clear later on, but as exemplified by interviewing Harvard's finest, it rarely does…

The Three-Baller as Object and Subject

Consider the moon and its different shapes. We are all familiar with the three-balls model of sun, earth, and moon. The stationary big one at the center represents the sun. The one revolving around the sun represents the earth, which of course makes a revolution once a year and rotates to mark off the days; a third ball represents the moon, which takes about twenty-eight days to revolve around the earth, in approximately the same plane as the sun's orbit. Once we can make this model work with the right orbit periodicity in our mind, and simulate the light of the sun reflecting off the moon to earth, we can see why the moon changes shape each night. Knowledge of this model is sufficient for us to answer the question: "Why does the moon change its shape each night?"

But this memorized model tucked away in one corner of our memory does not have any affect on our past perceptions of the real solar system as we have perceived it from being on the earth every single day, of the sun and moon following each other in circling around the earth. At this stage, what do we really know? We know on seeing the moon how to figure out why it is in the phase it is in by reaching into memory for the relevant memorized simulation and puzzle through it backwards to explain what we are seeing at that moment. In other words, we still do not really know it. We just know how to choose the correct simulation—and run it through our mind—in order to get to the "right" answer.

At this level of learning we are mere technicians of knowledge. We are like the typing student who in her first week of practicing thinks she knows how to type because she can quickly go through all five steps to type each letter to eventually copy a whole sentence onto her paper. But all she knows are the five steps of typing. Like her, we have not yet internalized the simulation of the three-baller into one step—one skill with all the various memories of our experiences. The problem is that neither she nor we have yet put the self inside the simulation.

How can we resolve this conundrum? Actually, we have two problems now: the motivation to learn this thing and the problem of how to integrate our sensory experience with scientific simulations. Let us deal briefly with motivation first.

The Father and Mother of Learning

How many thousands of times have we either overheard or taken part as students or workers in the following conversation?

"Did you understand that?"
"Who cares? Why does it matter?"

That question is the beginning of learning, when we are considering whether or not to make somebody or something "matter" to us. Choosing to care is at the beginning of making or remaking the connections between our emotions and thoughts. Choosing not to care is the end of it, except when life keeps throwing it back into our faces. Then we respond by entering into an interest in it, finding another way of temporarily wriggling out of it, or building a negative attitude of anger, disgust, fear, distress, disdain, and hate to keep it out.

How can we be inspired by a subject enough to study it if we have little or no idea of what it is? It is impossible of course. What we do not feel any relation to or interest in cannot turn us on. External necessities like future examinations, or any form of duty toward a particular job, or urging and inspiration from friends, or strong reaction to our enemies provide external motivation to push us into the direction of learning something.

These external forces are sufficient to get us into absorbing a collection of data mapped over a framework, like the names of the capitals of our nation's provinces or the model of our solar system. Knowledge learned in this way often stays around only as long as the external forces driving them. So we might learn to clean our room from being pushed into it by parents. But as soon as we leave the home this practice falls apart if it has not already been transmuted into one we have learned to realize, accept, and enjoy on our own terms. We will also forget our scientific solar system after the examination, unless we have reached the point of "real-izing" and believing what it is in terms of our own sensory experiences. This second stage of motivation toward realization is guided mainly from within.

Overall, external forces are needed to get us off the ground. External necessity is the father of learning. But internal initiatives are needed to make it all stick to our ribs, to convert all this objective knowledge from the filing cabinets of our minds into subjective knowing as part of the very operating systems through which we perceive reality everyday. This is why we call our courses of study *subjects*. We have to work hard to convert them from strange cold objects into familiar constructs in our imaginations and then into comfortable subjects through which we can spontaneously string our experiences. Enjoyment, sweat, love, play, challenge, and curiosity are the mothers of knowing.

In my recent foray into higher education as an older learner, I was often completely bored by work assigned. Despite the pressure for high grades and the associated pride, I would initially be unable to force myself into doing anything with it. But at some point I would take the idea of an assignment and some experience to which it related and turn them over and over in my mind until I discovered an angle, or more accurately a question that intrigued me. Often this question would have little relationship to that on which the course was focused, but at least I was now motivated, churning on the inside, and ready to follow that idea. It does not matter at which point or how we enter into our explorations—through memories of our experiences with it, or from an interest in the basis for the logic, content, or even the implications of the theory used to integrate the experiential components in our imaginations.

Whether we start at the beginning, the middle, or the end with memories of our experiences or the theory, is relatively immaterial to the outcome. What is important is that we have experiences to which we can relate, that we are able to distinguish between facts and patterns, and that we get excited wondering how everything fits together. Of course, I cannot find the question of interest to determine the best point of entry for you. How you work to inter yourself in the subject at hand is up to you.

But the art of caring in itself has two sides. On the one hand, as the poet, we can see our subject entirely through the energies of our emotional commitment to it. On the other hand, as the scientist, we can strip our subject of all emotional connection to us and see it totally indifferently or dispassionately as a purely physical entity. It is in rocking back and forth between too much and too little, between total obsession and total disinterest, we discover the proper balance between caring and not caring for that subject in any particular time and place—whether real or imaginary.

A Catch-22: Common Sense vs. Science

Our everyday experiences lead us to a very different picture of the relationship between the sun and the earth than the science version we are taught in school. Whereas we have the distinct and direct impression that the sun revolves around the earth, the teacher tells us we are wrong. Apparently science has proved the earth goes around the sun. Such experiences in school inadvertently teach students to mistrust the evidence of their own senses and experiences and begin treating science as dogma handed down by teachers. From an early age we are asked to give up our own common sense in exchange for the knowledge of "higher learning."

This idea that the truth is something to which we cannot relate with our common sense can be devastating to learning. It puts the student into a catch-22: if he follows his sensual perceptions he will be wrong; if he follows the canons of science he will never be able to verify them because he cannot trust his sensual perceptions. In effect, the more problems he meets like the one of the relationship between the sun and the earth, the more he is forced to put science into a compartment separate from his everyday reality. Thus he retains the category of common sense for what he can relate to spontaneously, and creates a new one called "theory" for "highfalutin stuff" that is probably true but is nonsense to his everyday experiences. Since he cannot really understand the second, he works toward memorizing it just long enough to be able to answer the teacher's questions and pass the exam.

The challenge for the student is to be able to experience the earth as rotating and also revolving around the sun from where he is on the earth and be able to merge it seamlessly with his everyday experiences of the apparent daily revolution of the sun around the earth. This is what we will do, and more, in the following chapter.

12

The Rock 'n' Roll of Physics

We shall not cease from exploration
And the end of all our exploring
Will be to arrive where we started
And know the place for the first time.
(T.S. Eliot)

We will explore the "to-fro-and-around" dance in the basics of perceiving and conceiving. In studying physics, you as a student who experiences the earth as flat are asked to suppose the scientific image of a three-body solar system of earth, moon, and sun. You will be guided through a series of steps to go back and forth from seeing one body from the other, and integrate that with your memories of previous experiences. Then you will be guided to comprehend the basic facts of gravity to discover the nature of the forces controlling its motion. The integration of the "to-fro" with the "around" is spontaneous.

Images from the Past

The ancient Greeks thought the sun was a ball of fire dragged across the sky by a team of horses driven by Hermes. Every year they sacrificed a team of their best horses in his name to ensure he had enough horsepower to keep doing it in the New Year. Now whether or not they thought their gift of horses drowned in the depths of the Aegean Sea would be up for the job, at the least they felt it right to express their thankfulness to the bearer of the sun for light, and plead for his continued support.

My favorite belief is that of the Ancient Egyptians. They thought of the stars as lights decorating the sky, which was really the belly of the Goddess Nut. She stood bent over the earth, supported by her legs in the east and her arms in the west. Every morning she gave birth to the infant-god Ra, who would sail in a boat across the sky giving daylight to the earth. By evening Ra would have grown into an old man and she would swallow him back. Through the night he would travel in the chaos and turbulence of the underworld through her intestines to be reborn in the morning as a baby.

Not only did this image give the Ancient Egyptians an explanation for what was happening in nature, it also gave them a metaphor for their daily lives. In the morning we wake up refreshed, as though born anew. We feel we can tackle anything. But as the day wears on it gets more complicated and wearisome, until the evening comes and we find ourselves resting, whether as our ancestors around a communal fire, or today in an easy chair puzzling on the confusion of the day's events. It is a relief to finally get to sleep and forget it all. Forget? All night we move from dream to dream in the chaos of a world apparently gone mad in the intestines of our subconscious.

The scientist objects to bringing such superstitions into discussions in the realm of physics. He is right. He does not have the tools to deal with myths. What we cannot tackle without measuring tapes and protractors we have to abandon right now as useless in our pursuit of elegant simulations and equations. In pure science we do our best to strip reality of any and all its emotional value, except maybe that of pure aesthetics. We want to see the thing raw, naked, no matter how embarrassing, inane, or futile it might seem to our emotions.

Where shall we start? Before we can go to the sun, we have to be aware of where we are coming from. I mean do you really believe this stuff about the earth being like a big ball? It looks pretty flat to me. Our ancestors believed it to be flat. They talked about traveling to the far "ends" of the earth and believed long-distance voyagers to be crazy to risk going so far they might fall off. Of course, if those travelers did come back, instead of being treated as crazy they were welcomed as the bravest of the brave. So our sailor ancestors went farther and farther into unknown waters until one ship, the Spanish *Victoria,* by continually following the sun in its westerly course around the detours of South America, the Philippines, India, and Africa, eventually arrived back at the place it had started, which is what we want to do…

We know that kids like the flat-earth theory. The sun looks like a huge light bulb rising up at the edge of the earth every morning in the east and floating over them in an arc, until it disappears in the west. Really, that is how most of us still experience it every day. Even on highway or air trips, when we are traveling in curves we look at flat maps and think of ourselves as moving in straight lines. Of course, we know the earth is not flat; but most of us not being astronomers, rocket scientists, or pilots have not been forced into dealing with it as a huge ball we work to circumnavigate. That way of thinking then does not come naturally.

The only way we can move from a flat earth to a round one is to jump in and go for a spin.

Actually, the ideal way to approach this task would be to take an infinite number of individual observations from particular points in space and time and integrate all these into one. In a way that is what we ended up doing in our omnipresent viewer. But we cannot start there.

The physicist P.W. Bridgman wrote about the creative endeavor in science: "There is no scientific method as such, but that the most vital feature of the scientist's procedure has been merely to do his utmost with his mind, no holds barred." Theoretical scientists create an idea through unifying a series of perceptions into one. Through this perception, the empiricist can then imagine the pattern of the motions of particular objects. The latter can now come up with conceptions about the energies that guide them. Empiricists have a whole methodology called the "scientific method" for quantifying those energies to compare and contrast them with all the other energies they know. But there is no method to come up with either the theoretician's perceptions or the empiricist's conceptions. All they can tell us is it takes a mountain of focus and concentration through blood, sweat, and tears. We, as students, can only accept the three-baller as a gift, test it for its validity in our backyards, and then try to grasp the conception of what drives and holds the whole thing together.

To the Stars and Back Using the Pole-Hug

At night time, most of us have observed that the stars appear to move around. They appear to be circling an axis extending from the North Pole to the North Star, Polaris,[86] taking about one day to make a complete circuit. Now the physicist claims this star movement is only apparent motion. Really it is the earth that is rotating. So our first task is to apprehend the rotational effect of the earth relative to the stars.

First, we need to find Polaris. If we were lying flat on our backs on the ice at the North Pole looking straight up, it would be in the center of our vision. But all of us are somewhere else and cannot afford a trip up there. Find the Big Dipper in the northern sky. It has seven main stars—three in the handle and four in the cup. Take the line of the two stars in the cup part that are on the opposite side of the handle, and extend it five times in length above the Dipper to reach a very bright star. That is Polaris. It is so far away that all lines drawn from anywhere on earth to it are virtually parallel. This line will become our axis of rotation.

Get yourself a nice comfortable lawn chair and sit down to watch Polaris. It will be very boring, and you can nod off every once in awhile because no matter when you wake up it will always appear to be in the same place. In fact, many thousands of years ago, our ancestors had already named it "Nail in the Sky."[87] So we will use it for a benchmark. To mark the spot get yourself a pole at least four or five meters long and thick enough so that when you hug it, you can shimmy around it like a monkey. Sharpen the end into a point and then plant it in the ground with the sharp end pointing right at Polaris. Now no matter night or day for the next hundred years at least, you can rest assured it will be pointing at that star. Done? Okay, now we can observe the rest of the stars.

For the next step, I advise wearing a heavy shirt or blouse and jeans. Hug the pole and hold your left cheek flush against it and get a bead on a star straight ahead. As you hold completely still to watch it, you will notice it moving very slowly to your right. In fact no matter which star you get a bead on, they are all moving together in circles at an angle perpendicular to the axis of your pole. Now follow one as it moves around that axis. Over six hours, you will find that, along with all the other stars, it has moved about one-quarter of the way around the pole. And as you watch it for another six hours (in winter of course when the nights are long) you will end up clinging to the underside of the pole.

Over those twelve hours of painfully slowly following the star around the pole, by holding yourself still in respect to the stars, you are able to cancel out the effects of the rotation of the earth. Glancing down from your crawling round the pole every once in a while, you can apprehend the earth slowly turning around you in a counterclockwise motion. This gives us another piece of the jigsaw puzzle on the motions of the earth and sun. A rotating earth is making some sense now. But, more importantly, you have now found another way to observe the sun from a nonrotating framework. Next let us use the moon to get some more practice at pole-hugging to strengthen our new skill.

To the Moon and Back

In the usual way of seeing the moon from the earth's surface, it rises in the east, travels through an arc in the same pattern as the sun during the day, and finally sets in the west. But when you watch it from your pole-hug while following the movements of a star, you will see something very different. It is seven o'clock on a December evening, and the moon is rising. You are at the pole. Align yourself toward a star you have chosen directly above the moon. Hugging the pole, rotate around it keeping your eyes aligned with the chosen star. After an hour or two you will begin to notice something is strange. The moon is not moving to the west as normal. Relative to your line of sight, it has apparently reversed direction to the east, and at an extremely reduced speed. Over a period of six hours, it has barely moved 2 degrees relative to your original line of sight.

The next night, align yourself with the same star as the previous night, and you will find moonrise occurs an hour later than it did on the previous night, and it is now about 13 or 14 degrees to the left of the star. The next night the moon will rise still another hour later, and is now 27 or 28 degrees to the left of the star. At that speed, it will take the moon about four weeks to make one whole "backward" revolution—360 degrees—around you hugging the pole on a "still" earth.

By compensating for the earth's rotation, you are actually watching the moon revolving around the earth at its true speed of about twenty-nine and a half days per revolution. Not only that, you see it revolving in the opposite direction to what you normally perceive, in its true direction.

About four weeks for one revolution of the moon around the earth? But is not that how long it takes for the moon to wax and wane from new moon to full and back to new? On reflection, you have discovered a consistency with something else you already know.

Before we go on to the next step, we should make note of something rather interesting that might otherwise go unnoticed.

Apprehension vs. Comprehension

We think the way we hunt moose. Never in a straight line because then the moose knows where you are. You go around and around the moose, coming closer all the time until you finally close in on him.
(An Amerindian guide)

Above I insisted that you, the reader, act out the part of the astronomer hugging the pole. Why not just ask you to watch me or some imaginary character do it? Am I just being cute? Or maybe I did it because the latest fad is reader participation, to get the reader involved in the material so she will retain the information a little better? Actually my primary motivation is neither of these.

Acting out the part, experiencing it, is absolutely essential to realizing an observation. Imagine yourself merely watching someone do this astronomical pole-hugging thing. In this way could you have the experience of seeing the moon move backward at that lunar month rate? You could comprehend intellectually why that someone is experiencing it. But it is impossible for you to have the same immediate realization without doing it yourself in your imagination. Of course it would be even better actually doing it outside in your backyard. But that is not essential, only helpful.

In fact, doing the pole-hug in your backyard is no guarantee you would perceive the true revolution. You might just assume the moon's true revolution because that is what scientists predict would happen, and be so wrapped up in figuring out the mechanics of the degrees of difference in speed and relating it to this and that as consistent with particular isolated observations, you would devote no time to actually watching what is actually happening. Besides, we cannot really trust our senses, can we?

Experiment with the difference in feel between the results of the two ways of doing it: one working to comprehend it by thinking it through, and the other of apprehending it through the senses, even if only imaginary. In the first instance, we end up with the idea of the lunar month as something we figure or think is right, based on calculation and deduction; but in the second instance, the observation of the lunar month is a direct experience of it, and thus has the feel of real life. In the first instance we learn to rationalize the facts of the relationship between earth and moon explicitly, whereas in the second we learn to know this relationship implicitly in such a way it is now intuitively related to our actions. By reading about it, we can learn to accept the physicist's image of the moon's orbit around the earth; but we can come to "real-ize" it only by reconstructing it in our imaginations through a double act of going to the other through direct experiences and coming back to seeing ourselves in our imagination.

To the Sun and Back Again

Now what about following the sun? Unfortunately, we can see the stars only at night and the sun after the stars have set, so we have a problem in coordinating our observations, and that is why we have been practicing on observing the stars and moon. By now you are able to rotate at the exact speed of the stars, even after they fade away at sunrise, to eliminate the effect of the earth's rotation. Hugging the pole, start an hour before sunrise to get into the right speed of rotation. Choose a star that will have you eyeing the horizon exactly at sunrise through welding glasses to protect your eyes.

Over the first six hours it appears your antirotation crawl speed is barely different from that of the sun. The sun is almost keeping up. In fact after the first twenty-four hours you find the sun is lagging only one degree behind your line of vision to the star. Like the moon, it too is now revolving backward. At the rate the sun is revolving, you will be shimmying round the pole for over 360 days before your eyes line up with it again. You find yourself taking one year to make one rotation around the pole relative to the sun, whereas the earth rotated underneath you over 360 times.

In effect, by using the stars as a fixed frame of reference to eliminate the effect of the rotation of the earth, you can now perceive the earth as taking one year to revolve around the sun. But are the stars 'fixed' or are they attached to the surface of a sphere rotating around the earth? That was the debate in ancient times. The empiricists seeing the stars, sun, and moon rise and set daily preferred a stationary earth around which the latter were revolving. The theorists preferred a stationary sphere of stars because then they could simplify and regularize the orbits of not only the sun, earth, and moon, but also that of all the other planets in the solar system into one grand scheme.

The Facts and Mystery of Gravity

So far we have been jumping back and forth between the earth, moon, and sun exploring their visual relationship. We have not even begun to consider the felt relationship between them. What holds these bodies locked together in their stately dance round each other?

We have all heard of gravity, and we feel its effects every day. When we are dead tired after a long day at work or an especially vigorous sports activity, we feel it even more and want to collapse on a couch. But do we know what gravity is? We cannot actually feel it directly. We can feel only the resistance of the couch pressing against our bodies at certain points. Try feeling the force of gravity in jumping up and down. As you are rising, you are aware of a resistance to rising, but you cannot feel the force. As you fall, you can feel faint sensations associated with the resistance the air causes on your falling body. The biggest sensation you get is the shock when you hit the floor. Though we are aware of it, we can sense the effects of gravity only in the particular resistances we feel to its force.

We are not alone. Even the physicist cannot explain its existence. Isaac Newton, who developed the classic equation of the force of gravity,[88] writes, "That one body may act upon another at a distance through a vacuum without the mediation of anything else, by and through which their action and force may be conveyed from one to another, is to me so great an absurdity that, I believe, no man who has in philosophic matters a competent faculty of thinking could ever fall into it."[89] Was he so totally embarrassed by the apparent parallels between his conceptions of the forces of gravity and emotion?

We can feel the attracting force of emotion between ourselves and someone else, but we cannot feel the attracting force of gravity on our bodies. The problem is that on the one hand strong emotions bathe the whole body in hormones, while on the other sensations are experienced only in how they differentially affect specific points in the body. Since gravity acts completely equally on all the parts of our bodies, we cannot sense that it is (acting). We can only hypothesize it is. All we can directly sense are the resistances imposed upon us to the force of gravity by the air as we fall, by the ground as we land, and by the tensing of certain muscles within our bodies as we counteract its effect in riding up in a fast elevator. The only real-life experience we have that actually embodies the same idea of the force of gravity is that of emotional attraction to certain others. The closer we get to them, the stronger is the force we feel, until we have them in our arms. (Of course, for certain persons, we would halt our approach at a discrete distance, despite whatever force we feel, either out of politeness or our fear of what they might exclaim if we got any closer.)

Though the modern physicist still has no idea either what gravity is, he can measure exactly how strong it is. You, too, can do an experiment—in your car. Sitting in it, you can feel the resistance of the foam and springs to your body's weight. This is gravity acting on your body. But as you accelerate, you are also thrown backward, compressing the foam and springs in the backrest. This is the result of acceleration. The faster you accelerate, the harder you are thrown backward. But as you let up on the throttle to travel at a constant speed, the backward thrust disappears. Now you only sense the foam and springs pushing up into your butt, the same as when you were sitting still.

The same phenomenon works when slowing down. If you brake hard, you become aware of being thrown forward. Deceleration has the same effect as acceleration. What counts is how fast it happens. The faster you slow down or speed up, the stronger is the force of which you become aware through the evidence of your sensations of resistance to it. A dragster experiences up to three G's of force in acceleration, three times the force of gravity. Even here, he cannot apprehend the force itself. He can only experience the sensations of resistance to it in the feel of the backrest pushing extremely hard into his back.

Mysteriously, there is absolutely no way for scientists to find any quantitative difference between the force of gravity and that of being thrown around this way and that by acceleration and deceleration. In fact scientists have calculated that when a car is accelerating at a rate of 9.8 meters per second anywhere on the earth's surface, the pull backward on the body due to acceleration is exactly the same as the pull down due to gravity.

It does not matter whether the body driving it is a big one or a little one. Gravity does not pull little skinny ones any slower than big fat ones. It is perfectly democratic. In a vacuum, it will cause a feather to have the same acceleration as a ball bearing. This has led physicists into defining the force of gravity in any particular situation strictly as to how fast it causes all things, regardless of size, density, or shape, to accelerate in a vacuum. It is just that a feather, being much lighter than a ball bearing, has much less force when it falls through a vacuum to bump into your nose than the falling ball bearing, even though the two objects accelerate at the same speed.

You become aware of this same pulling force of acceleration at a steady speed, too, when you are traveling around a curve. Even though you are holding the throttle steady, you are aware of being thrown to the outside of the curve. The change in direction is the cause of the effect. The momentum of your car and body wants to move along in a constant direction. Any attempt to change the direction of you and the car requires the input of an extra force for the whole duration of the changing in direction. Thus, we can understand the earth's steady speed motion in circles around the sun is really a state of continual acceleration.

The "Around" of Pulling Together and Pulling Away

If gravity is not affected by an object's shape or volume, how can we formulate a mental framework within which we can see how it works? We know gravity is "interested" in any object's center of gravity, the exact center of all the mass it contains. The force works as though strictly between the centers of gravity of any two objects like the earth and moon.

Though he could not explain gravity, Newton argued it is a mutual force equal and opposite between any two objects. In effect when we throw a ball in the air, we are pushing down on the earth as much as we are pushing up on the ball. In physics, it is as valid to say we are pushing the earth from the ball as throwing the ball from the earth. When the ball begins to descend, it is as valid to say the earth is rising to the ball as the ball is falling to earth. In fact both events are happening simultaneously. Of course, since the earth is so enormous in comparison to the ball, it moves only an infinitesimal amount.

An early scientist, Archimedes, is supposed to have said, "Give me a lever and I will move the earth!" Newton would not have said it. He knew that every boy and girl throwing apples into the sky was actually doing it already.

We can better test the way in which this phenomenon of equal and opposite forces works with bodies of different sizes, and integrate it with the configuration of a sun and earth. Take a small child—one you can lift easily—and swing him around you.[90] You find yourself leaning backward to balance the centrifugal force pulling him away from you. The bigger the child, you have to swing him and the further back you are forced to lean to create a balance between the force you are exerting on him and the force he is exerting to pull you over. The smaller the child, the more upright you can stand while doing it. In effect not only is the child revolving, you are revolving around the same point somewhere straight above where your feet are planted. It is just that your orbit of revolution is a lot smaller than his. But the bigger he is, the larger the orbit you make as you lean further back, until when you are swinging a child the same size as you, the size of your orbit, measured from your center of gravity to the pivotal point, will match his.

It is the same for the earth and moon. From our visual observations, we think of the moon as orbiting the earth. But it is just as true to say the earth orbits the moon. They are actually swinging each other, like you and the child, around a common center somewhere between them, taking about a month for each mutual revolution. Of course, since the earth is bigger than the moon, the pivoting point is closer to the earth so it makes a smaller orbit. In turn, the earth-moon combo is swinging around a common point with the sun. And since the sun is so much more massive than is this combo, the pivotal point between them is much closer to the sun. In effect, it is as true to say the sun is going around the earth-moon combo as to say the earth-moon combo goes around the sun. They are essentially circling each other. Jumping back and forth in our visual duel between them prepares us for the possibility of this resolution, which we can now understand from the awareness of the forces from the common point around which they are revolving.

Common Sense and Science

Whoa! This is kind of embarrassing for me. We started this whole exercise trying to figure out whether the earth goes around the sun or vice versa, and we end up perceiving both have scientific validity. We now know the view from earth can be as true and false as from the sun. They both go around each other once a year, around a common center. It just appears that only the earth is going around the sun because its orbit is so much bigger.[91]

If you were around 2,300 years ago for the debate on this matter between Aristarchus and Archimedes, or even 500 years ago for the debate between Copernicus and "the authorities," you could have intervened and explained, "Cool off, fellows. You are both right." But you could not have made them understand why, because Newton had not been born yet to propose his conception of gravity.

At this point we have completed the task I set out for us in the last chapter—to resolve our common sense with scientific theory. We now know how to dwell in the theorist's three-baller to integrate our visual perceptions of the relative motions of the sun and earth-moon combo into one whole, and then understand the nature of how they circle each other as substantiated through our tangible perceptions of the resistance to gravity and motion.

We can now imagine these massive balls of gases, rock, and fire circling each other in the vastness of outer space tethered together only by the mysterious mutual force of gravity but kept apart by their motions in different directions. The attractive force of gravity is too weak to pull them together, too strong to release them to their own momentum, but just strong enough to hold them some distance apart in a mutually revolutionary balance as though tied together by a hair.[92]

The Fit between Perception and Conception

We often use the words *perception* and *conception* interchangeably, as though they have the same meaning. But perception is rooted in the idea of perceiving or "piercing" the confusing data of discrete packets of direct sensation, capturing that one whole idea that explains the lot. In contrast, conception originates from the act of conceiving what we cannot really see in the interaction of the very forms we have projected as a result of dwelling in the ideas originating in our raw perceptions.

The model of the three-baller, the metaphor of our solar system, is an integration of all the theorist's daily perceptions over all the years of his life of the millions of different positions of the sun, moon, and stars into one three-dimensional form in motion. As students we can realize the true integrative function of that metaphor through doing the pole-hug crawl. That action, whether real or imaginary, enables us to integrate our personal everyday experiences of sunrises and sunsets, full moons and moving stars from the particular point in which we dwell within the solar system into one comprehensible whole. In effect, the pole-hug crawl enables us to dwell within the metaphor to see the solar system as it is.

It is only because of our ability to now comprehend the regularity of the orbital patterns that we can move to conceiving of the energies involved. But since we cannot perceive energy, we can only quantify it through measurements of distance over time in particular directions of the objects observed relative to each other. Consequently, we end up with a purely mathematical conception of the attractive "fact" of gravity, a force we can feel only in how our bodies resist its attraction.

De Chardin's Emotional Resolution

Perhaps it is this last realization that led the scientist-priest Pierre Teilhard de Chardin to propose:

> Driven by the forces of love, the fragments of the world reach each other so that the world may come to being...Whether as a force or curvature, the universal gravity of bodies, so striking to us, is merely the reverse or shadow of that which really moves nature.[93]

Of course his proposal is totally unscientific, but it neither denies the value of the scientific insight nor contradicts it. In fact, it complements both the form of the three-baller and fills in the conception of gravity—that mysterious shell of a mathematical fact—with some emotional content from the felt emotions of the artist, and gives the whole thing meaning with initiatives arising from the ideals and beliefs of the idealist. Teilhard de Chardin, as a lover of both science and his religion, was working to find the best way to put his scientific perceptions and conceptions and his felt emotions and religious ideals together into one. He wanted to experience running on all four cylinders in unison. That was his idea of ecstasy—of experiencing the whole "Truth."

E: <u>Science</u>

13

The Pigeonholing of Knowledge

A woman can be proud and stiff
When on love intent;
But Love has pitched his mansion in
The place of excrement;
For nothing can be sole or whole
That has not been rent.
(William Yeats, from "Crazy Jane Talks with the Bishop")

Academic battlefields—whether in the Arts, Sciences, or Social Sciences—are littered with arguments between theorists and empiricists, formalists and functionalists over the nature of form vs. style, subjectivity vs. objectivity, matter vs. energy, nature vs. nurture, et cetera. With our four-cycle model of feeling, perceiving, conceiving, and doing, we can integrate these dualities into appreciating the functioning of one comprehensible whole person. After all, persons thought up all these ingenious ways of relating to reality.

Where do we start? The sciences provide us an interesting beginning point: the duality between geneticist and environmentalist on the process of the development of living beings. The first focuses on the development of the physical form of man as directed by the actualization of an internal genetic set of blueprints. The second argues that this form is resultant of the incidental impact of the environment.

The Quartet in Thailand

The geneticist perceives that peoples of Canadian origin are larger in stature than those of Thai origin and wonders if it's all in the genetics. The nutritionist argues that these differences are due to external factors—diet—not genetics. She points to other Easterners, for example the latest generation of Japanese who have grown up larger than their parents since the introduction of more meat into the national diet. Whether the debate is about body size, color of hair or eyes, or longevity, the two scientists can set up studies and actual experiments to determine which factor, genetics or nutrition, is the main factor, or if the answer is somehow a combination of the two.

So far in this argument the artist and idealist have been very quiet. The debates between the two scientists on the physical characteristics of peoples from different geographical origins are interesting but irrelevant to their concerns. In fact they really could care less. The artist has become intrigued by native Thai art and music and is trying to perceive and appreciate them through comparing and contrasting them with his own emotional expressions. The idealist, knowing his morality—of identifying what is good and what is evil—as rooted in Christian beliefs, is concerned that Thais have a different source of religious belief: Buddhism. What morality then guides their actions? The artist concerns himself with identifying the particular mix of emotions most valued by that culture and the idealist is concerned with what those peoples believe in to direct their actions. These two, taking opposite approaches to relating to the Thais, have trouble communicating with each other, and they certainly could not ask the scientists to set up scientific experiments to prove or disprove anything with which they are dealing.

In turn the scientists are not really interested in these emotional questions. They are limited to pursuing questions for which they have the tools to explore and verify. But in the end, like our emotional pair, they push their explorations as far as they can go and each end up including the whole world. Each being boxed within their own framework does not realize he has trespassed onto anybody else's domain until the shouting starts, for instance in the cases of religion, eugenics, language, psychology, and evolution.

With the artist and idealist exploring primarily the emotional realm and the scientists exploring the physical world, it should be simple to keep the four apart in their own corners in their own faculties of study, each doing their own thing so they do not distract and bother each other too much except for the occasional stimulating collegial discussion over a hurried lunch or quick beer. But for the student, being pushed and manipulated by all four into accepting their respective dimensions of reality, this proposition becomes more problematical.

Four Pigeonholes of Knowledge

How did these four views become compartmentalized in the first place? Each of our four, being very focused in their self-consciousness in one dimension of consciousness, has staked out his or her particular dimension and drawn up the rules for making sense of it. The theorist needed metaphors to begin perceiving the patterns in the development of particular phenomena like learning language and gradually developed his organization of metaphors into a full-blown theory to encompass all his perceptions. He had to develop theory to check the coherency between his perceptions—to make sure they were perceptions not observations—and that they were about the same thing and in the right logical order. The empiricist, ignoring the theory, is ensconced only in the theorist's perceptions. By dwelling in them she can conceive of the whole world; and moreover, having refined the correct and exact scientific methodology for testing any and all assumptions made about any form she discovers in it, she can develop her hierarchies of factors around her conception of the energy effecting its functioning. The idealist taking merely the shell of the particular conception of energy then purposely sets out to discover the feeling of its energy guided by her intentions and aspirations. She becomes preoccupied in how she can construe her beliefs into the right actions to discover her grail. The artist, ignoring her beliefs but being stimulated both by the direction of the idealist's search and by direct sensation, delights in the kaleidoscope of feelings. He becomes intent on pinning it all down with any means available—whether paint, sculpture, or poetry—so he can relate it to his other feelings. The theorist in turn, ignoring the artist's feelings, takes only the stream of perceived sensation and tries to pierce it for ideas within the process of developing his theory.

The theorist becomes so engrossed in developing his theory he forgets the real importance of his initial perceptions. The empiricist is so intent on the methodology and statistical quantification of experimentation in constructing her hierarchies of facts she forgets the nature of the energy she is conceiving. The idealist gets so involved in interpreting her beliefs into actions to achieve her purpose she forgets the real-life context within which she is living. The artist, in having created artifacts to evoke his feelings, gets so much pleasure from them himself he is content to make copies of them and forgets to be spontaneous. All members of our quartet can get so involved in their own self-circumscribed dimensions that to keep them functioning creatively the philosopher has to work hard to keep unraveling the resultant confusions and misunderstandings to bring them back into communication with each other.

Spice and Salt: Mystics vs. Bean Counters

Let's focus on the relationship between the theorist and the empiricist.

The theoretician in us believes in metaphorical interpretations grasped in an instant of time. The empiricist in us believes in direct factual experience or a literal interpretation of reality over durations of time. Of course, in real life we are pragmatists. We struggle between the two, continually going back and forth between comparisons and contrasts in both dimensions to find the best overall fit. It is just that some of us tend to lean more one way than the other. Not all of us even acknowledge or promote this seesawing and synergism between metaphorical and literal interpretations of reality to find that middle way toward the whole answer. This is like the concept of light as photon—an anomaly of wave and particle—or evolution as rooted in the balancing act between genetics and the environment.

The pure theoretician, avoiding the limitations of fact, explores his reality primarily in transports of metaphor. The pure empiricist refuses to accept anything other than those hierarchies of factors derived directly from the nitty-gritty of cold hard facts from properly controlled experimentation. These two are the extremes—the abstract mystics and the grindstones of learning. We can usefully learn from both, but how can we get beyond the mere pragmatism of using the theoretician's spice to enliven the grindstone's factors, or using the empiricist's facts to salt our mystic's tail?

The first step is to explicitly acknowledge the paradoxical relationship between the results of the two approaches. Scientific knowledge can be perceived as totally rational, but only while we are looking at different pieces of it separately. When we fail to find a rational way to combine particular pieces, like that of the wave theory with the facts of the particle aspects of light, we have to either assume that one approach is wrong or that scientists just have not got to the bottom of it. Whatever the case, the writers of school texts and teachers of scientific knowledge, especially at lower levels of education, tend to minimize and even overlook apparently intractable paradoxes at the most basic level. Scientific knowledge is presented as wholly logical and rational, and then when students rightly fail to grasp it as such, they feel stupid and question the ability of their own intellect. Many students then decide that science is too complicated or abstract and proceed to merely memorize enough of it to write the exam and forget their miserable experience. On the other hand, if they had been presented with the paradoxes of science for what they are, more would become intrigued enough to explore them.

First, we will try to find the right fit between the theorist's perceptions and the empiricist's conceptions by revisiting our thought experiment with the three-baller and gravity to expose a paradox at its center, and then do the same thing for the wave and particle interpretations of light.

14

The theorist and empiricist of gravity and light

"How wonderful that we have met with paradox. Now we have some hope of making progress."
(Neils Bohr)

How do physicists deal with the duality between their perceptions and conceptions? They tend to see them as complementary entities and thus try to put them into the same framework. But doing so results in great confusion. Not only do we then have to imagine light as particle and wave at the same time, we also have to deal with the impossibility of resolving the motions of our three-baller with the law of gravitation. Only by putting them into their proper places in the cycle can we see that conceptions are what arise out of dwelling in perceptions.

Observing the Solar System from the Stars

We have already explored the relationship between the sun and earth. For the ancient Greek theorist Aristarchus, the earth revolved around the sun. For the empiricist, Archimedes, the sun revolved around the earth. The theorist could make greater sense of the relationships between all the celestial bodies in our solar system if he put the sun at the center of their orbits. But the empiricist was stuck in the fact he directly experienced the sun as rising from the horizon and then falling down to it on the opposite side of the earth every single day of his life. Whereas the theorist starts out with, "Wouldn't it be much simpler to grasp this if…?" the empiricist's motto is, "Seeing is believing!"

Initially the empirical point of view won out and became Ptolemy's earth-centered configuration. Then Copernicus turned the tide for the theorists in a revival of Aristarchus's idea of a sun-centered solar system. The solar system as a whole just made more sense that way. But a true balance between the two debating parties was struck by an empiricist, Isaac Newton, who, dwelling in the theorist's idea of the three-baller, could elucidate the concept of gravity to enable us to comprehend the sun and earth-moon combo as trapped within an elliptical balance of gravitational and centrifugal forces swinging each other around a common focus in a grand celestial waltz.

But what happens when we move into a larger frame of reference, that of the other stars in the galaxy? I'm sure the physicist would be disappointed if we did not go the whole way and try again to see the three-baller as it looks from the stars. We went there in a previous chapter, but at the time we did not stay around long enough to notice something more: that the sun itself is in motion. It is revolving (as well as rotating) but within a much larger orbit through our galaxy. It is moving at a speed several times our speed around it. Of course that would mean the earth is really traveling much faster than that apparent speed of revolution. Not only are we keeping up with the sun, but we are also skating rings around it. What would that look like from the vantage point of the stars?

We have the earth-moon combo weaving in and out of the slightly wavy path of the sun.[94] Of course, we do not want to see this as merely two-dimensional. Try to imagine what it would look like from the direction in which the sun is moving, then from a point at right angles to this motion, and then from a whole series of other angles. We get a different view from whichever of the billions upon billions of stars we choose as reference point. From the "objective" points of view there are an infinite number of scenarios from which to choose. The only way we can get one realistic view of the whole is by combining all of them through dwelling in our creation as though within an omnipresent viewer.

Let us dream that the sun is a ball of fire a million kilometers in diameter careening on a slightly wavy trajectory at 100 km/sec through the cold dark emptiness of outer space, chased in circles by the earth-moon combo, each less than 1/1000th in size, locked in revolving around each other 150 million kilometers away, weaving in and out of the sun's sinuous path. This is really different from what we started out with. We are now getting much closer to the reality of the real three-baller.

To get closer yet, we have to attend to details. Get the earth into the right position, so it is both revolving and rotating counterclockwise, and tilted at an angle so its axis of rotation is pointing toward Polaris throughout its whole revolution. Then, make further adjustments to get the seasons right and gradually get the whole simulation in sync.

Steady State or Pulsating Orbits?

But we are left with a glitch. From the vantage point of the sun, the earth's motion around it is a steady speed orbit, in accordance with Kepler's Law.[95] (We'll ignore the slight seasonal change in relative velocity due the slightly elliptical orbit of the earth.) But when we look from the objective vantage point in the stars, we see the earth is actually accelerating and decelerating as it chases the sun and then circles it. How is that possible? Where is the earth getting or losing extra energy to accelerate and decelerate in its annual circumnavigation of the sun? After all, is not the earth just one huge particle of matter? Why would it behave like a wave of pulsating energy?

It is as though the gravitational force is not in the least interested in the real motion or momentum of the earth as measured from the objective view from the stars. It takes its cue only from the relative motion as experienced within the framework of the earth and sun in themselves, completely oblivious to and unaffected by the fact that the sun is moving too and in a particular direction. It is bewildering to find such a grand conception of what we consider the Universal Law of Gravitation is blind to the big picture.

Perhaps our big overview is wrong. How can we check? It would be nice to have an absolutely still framework within our universe to really pin this down. Remember how we used the stars as such a framework to detect the rotation of the earth? Well, those stars are really moving in different directions and very quickly. We just used their apparent stillness to help us out. There does not seem to be anything out there that is not moving relative to something else in the universe, unless it is that imaginary central point of the Big Bang from which the universe is expanding in all directions. And what is it about the "inside picture" from the common pivot of the forces of gravity and centrifuge? We know this point is not any more still in our wild universe than the 3-D framework from the stars. The only constant here is that all-powerful mysterious force of gravity that holds everything together within a universe expanding around the nothingness of one imaginary point at the center of the Big Bang.

Let's try taking a perfectly objective star view of the earth's orbit around the sun. We can average our estimations of the actual acceleration of the earth from all opposite points of view of the simulation. From one side it will appear acceleration is happening to the right, and from the other side, to the left. In effect they cancel each other out. From any one objective point of view around the simulation we can find its opposite objective on the mirror side, canceling out the first. In effect, as we should have realized in the first place—from considering how the theorist came up with the whole idea in the first place—there is no acceleration or any motion in perception, nor any distance, volume, or direction. When we implement the omnipresent viewer by averaging the infinity of possible objective viewpoints, we can restrict all motion and its parameters to where they belong in conceiving the energy of the verb.

From Equal and Opposite Forces to Gravitational Waves

In a way this is what we do when we consider the issue through the inside-out lens of modern physics wherein everything is conceived as but different forms of energy. It allows us to forget about momentum as a balancing force to gravitational attraction and think of gravity as a single force that holds the sun and earth together but at a distance from each other. Instead of imagining Newton's opposite forces balanced in pulling away with pulling toward, modern physicists substitute an image of the sun and earth revolving around each other within a framework of distortions in space caused by the interference of gravitational waves guiding the motions of the planetary masses through planes of least resistance relative to each other. This interpretation does not contradict Newton's interpretation, but it does nicely cover up the inherent intellectual problem.

Seeing and Feeling Light

There is a similar conundrum in discussion of light. We can apprehend the idea of light by using the metaphor of the interaction of water waves in a ripple tank. In contrast, we can comprehend the facts of its energy through how it effects and affects other things.

Remember the battle over the nature of light as wave or particle of a hundred years ago? Thomas Young's experiment proves it is a wave by showing how two streams of light interfere with each other to produce a diffraction pattern. In contrast, Philip Lenard's experiment proves it is a particle. While dwelling in the idea of light as different wavelengths of energy, he carried out an experiment to show each different color has a different effect on how they knock electrons out of metal strips, as though the whole spectrum of light is composed of billiard balls of different densities. The empirical experiment emerges naturally from dwelling in the theoretician's idea. But when we step back and distinguish between the idea and its energy we end with an idea of light as though it is two different entities.

The theoretician argues that the red, blue, and yellow we experience in our heads are correlated with specific frequencies of electromagnetic wave radiation from "out there." He thinks of light as a wave through the diffraction patterns. The empiricist takes a different tact. He has us understand how light as particles with a particular level of energy impacts the retina of the eye resulting in electrical signals to the brain. Whereas the theoretician argues that the red we see is really something we can only perceive as a wave, the empiricist argues that something we can only conceive as a quantum of energy can impact us as redness, blueness, or yellowness.

Young's double-slit experiment proves light is an invisible wave because of something we can perceive, and Lenard's photoelectric experiment proves it is a particle because of something we can feel. Young's approach is theoretical, revolving around only the pattern of light. Lenard's approach is factual. He gets at the nature of light through its apparent effect on something else—metal electrons.

In Young's double-slit experiment, a beam of light is shone onto a plate prepared with two closely-spaced narrow slits. The light getting through illuminates a screen beyond the plate. The light does not do anything; it is just that some of the light is blocked, while the rest of it is allowed through the slits. All the action takes place in the perceiver's imagination. He only really observes the row of alternating light and dark bands produced on the screen behind the slits, and he interprets this as the same kind of interference pattern he has seen resulting from the interaction of water waves spreading out from two gaps in a barrier placed in their path in a ripple tank. By interpreting the alternating bands on the screen as a similar diffraction pattern, he determines that light must be a wave because that is the only explanation he can think of to solve the riddle.

On the other hand, Lenard's photoelectric experiment, which demonstrates the particle theory of light, fits neatly into empirical mode. In this experiment, a light beam is directed at a piece of metal, and an electronic sensor counts the number of electrons knocked out of the metal by the light ray and measures their velocities. The experimenter then doubles and later triples the intensity of the light beam and finds now twice and three times as many electrons are knocked out of the metal respectively, but their velocities remain the same as before. What is interesting is he always finds the same set of particular velocities. Further, by doing the same experiment but this time using only pure colors of light at a time, he finds each blast of his light gun results in only one particular velocity for the electrons ejected in each trial, but a different one for each different color. Thus he demonstrates light as apparently transferring discrete quantities of energy to electrons depending on their wavelength, the concept originating in Young's wave theory.

Lenard got the results of the experiment through the apparent effect of the action of light on the metal by feeling how many electrons were ejected at what velocities. His results are shaped by the evidence collected, not by an idea he picked up from watching something else like water waves, as Young did. Of course, Lenard did not use his own skin to detect the quanta of energy bounced out. We can stand in the sun on a hot day and feel the sun beating on our foreheads. But to get an exact quantification of the energy detected in the photoelectric experiment, he used a high-tech electronic sensor, a mechanical extension of his skin. He read the answer on its dial visually, but the basic measurement is of energy—a felt, not a perceptual quality.

Unlike the wave experiment, the photoelectric experiment happens and changes with each moment. The longer Lenard ran each experiment, the more results to put on graph paper to analyze. The more variations he performed, the more data of results in particular instances of time and space to home in on light's property of being discrete quantities of energy and its ability to act like a billiard ball on electronic billiard balls. In the wave experiment, whether it runs for only one second or for ten hours the results are exactly the same, no more or less: light is a wave. Nothing is "happening" in it; there is no beginning, middle, and end. It just "is" and sits there like any other idea in our mode of thought. But the photoelectric experiment corresponds with a series of action-reactions, of cause and effect.

From Wave and Particle to Photon

The "father of nuclear physics," Neils Bohr, who agreed on the dual nature of light, "maintained that to design an experiment showing light to behave as both wave and particle simultaneously not only *has not* been done but *cannot* be done in principle."[96] This paradox of physics as enshrined in the Copenhagen Protocol is politely known as the "principle of complementarity." Its paradoxical nature was only confirmed by more experiments like Arthur Compton's. By firing X-rays (another form of electromagnetic radiation), he not only got energy readings of particular electrons emitted, but also a diffraction pattern of how they scattered. Again, the scientist beginning with a perception of waves ends up conceiving it as a particle with speed and direction.

We can understand the physicist torn between describing light as a wave or particle wanting to find a new word for light itself. Remember what happens when a basketball is thrown very hard at your solar plexus? Of course, you react to it, and very quickly with a great deal of energy. The harder it is thrown, the more acute is your reaction. If the ball is merely been handed to you, your reaction is much less energetic. The weight of the ball and the speed with which it is thrown at you are much more important to your reaction than its size or shape. Consequently its energy—a multiple of weight and velocity—becomes the most useful way to characterize it in motion. This becomes even more relevant in physics as it moves away from Newton's mechanical world where energy equals mass times weight to become absorbed in exploring at the atomic level, where physicists cannot actually see anything anyway and energy equals mass times the speed of light squared. It becomes much more useful here to label particles at that micro level by the energies they display in knocking electrons around. Thus the particle of light, stripped of its size and specific location in space, was renamed "photon."

The Metaphysics of Duality

In *The Dancing Wu Li Masters,* Zukav asks, "How can mutually exclusive wave-like and particle-like behaviors both be one and the same light?" He argues, "They are not properties of light. They are properties of our interaction with light."[97] Well, we took his advice and note there are two different ways to interact with light, first using Young's metaphor and then Lenard's experiment as our guides.

But scientists like anybody else hate living with paradoxes. Maybe you want to speculate with Zukav—as a metaphysicist now—that light is not what we experience in interacting with it. Is it something else entirely? What might that be? How can that be at all meaningful in our reality if we have no way of ever interacting with it as it really is? What possible interest could we have in something to which we have no possible way of relating?

As Werner Heisenberg argues, our presence affects the reality of what we are seeing. We cannot abstract ourselves from our involvement in our theorizing or experiments. We are at the center of a paradox. There is no external logical rationale that connects a wave and an energized particle any more than there is one to connect the three-baller and gravity, nor any idea with any emotion. But we find them both together and we need to make meaning of it. We are the mediator between perceiving light's form and conceiving of its energy, while wondering about its place, its purpose, in the scheme of all things while we feel the warmth of the sun's rays on our skin and are in awe of the colors in a rainbow. Only in us as persons are all four dimensions unified in consciousness.

Why does Zukav not just ride the wave and cycle through with Teilhard de Chardin? Would it not be prudent to first get comfortable in the four dimensions we already know before attempting the eighteen dimensions of the "super-string" theorists?

15

Nature and Nurture Meet the Emotional Duo

Life is not a problem to be solved but a reality to be experienced.
Søren Kierkegaard

The tensions implicit in the dichotomy between ideas and facts are played out in ongoing battles between the pure theorist and the pure empiricist not only in physics but also in psychology. In the social sciences the battle is often named "nature vs. nurture." Subtle and abstract theories of emerging self-actualizing patterns developed by the theorists are pitted in debate against statistical hierarchies of factors generalized into laws of behavior by the empiricists. Whatever happened to the spontaneous artist and the conscientious idealist in their modeling of the dynamics of knowing? These debates are so abstruse it makes us wonder, for example, how their knowledge can help us more creatively play and share with our children. Was that not their overall objective? Or was their objective merely to understand in order to better manipulate them?

Self-Actualization or External Discipline?

Dewey conceptualized the central debate in education as between those who argue that "education is based upon natural endowments and that education is a process of overcoming natural inclination and substituting in its place habits acquired under external pressure."[98]

On the one hand, Chomsky's discovery of a universal development of language learning led him to postulate a genetically innate basis for it. On the other hand, the pure empiricists, or "functionalists", deny even the existence of "real grammar," and focus solely on actual minute-by-minute empirical evidence of the external energies at work in conditioning a baby's cooing and babbling into intelligible language. This dichotomy leaves the pragmatic linguist who has no vested interest in either approach seesawing between them. He likes the formalist's theory because it gives him an explanation for the basic grammatical structures he finds in all languages and the pattern through which every child progresses in learning his native one. But he also likes the functionalist's hierarchy of stimulus-response factors because those can explain why one child learns Dutch while another learns Thai, and why a Welsh child speaks with a lilt while British royalty speak as though their mouths are filled with marbles. As a pragmatist, the average linguist knows there is truth in both the theorizing of the first and the empirical observations of the second. The overall study of psychology shows a similar divide between the ideas of the theoretical cognitivists and the facts of the empirical behaviorists.

The Theorist's Thoughtful Robot

The theorists of linguistics put forth that all children develop the same underlying grammar—universal to all languages, they say—in the same order, no matter what language on earth they are learning. Similarly, Piagetian theorists can demonstrate children appear to be guided through the same steps of gradually expanding and extending their physical and mental grasp out into the real world. Linguistic and psychological cognitivists in reflecting on the universality of this logic argue these stages of development drawn from a genetic blueprint.

Some cognitivists are so enthralled with the "universal" sequence of such developments, they feel justified in comparing man to the operating systems of computers. "Since the 1960s human memory has been studied primarily from the 'information processing' approach...The mind is visualized as a computer, with information being entered, stored, and then retrieved as needed."[99] Can you imagine being so in awe and jealous of the filing and calculating powers of a machine you would reduce your conception of how we learn to it?

These latter cognitivists are so convinced intelligent thought is merely a mechanical process, they have dedicated themselves to trying to make computers do it—and have failed repeatedly. All the hoopla around artificial intelligence has spun out only faster and more complicated filing and calculating machines, like "Big Blue" that beat the world champion in a chess game—a game with only one page of rules, played within the confines of sixty-four squares on a piece of cardboard with thirty-two figurines. That has not got much to do with the open-ended rough and tumble of real life, where there are no squares but an infinite number of points, where there are no figurines with only one move each in their bag of tricks, but rather six billion living ones, each with an infinite variety of moves—and rules.

The Behaviorists' Wildcards

A white rat possesses more intelligence than the fastest computer. Imagine doing an experiment to compare their overall life skills by dropping one pair of Cray computers and one pair of rats into a selection of environmental zones—the Laurentian Mountains, a New York City sewer, the Deccan Plateau, Ayr's Rock, and the Patagonian Wilds—and making observations of their survival strategies. You do not need to be a rocket scientist to predict the winner. The computer might be able to calculate the square root of two to one million decimal places in less than one second, but that does not make it intelligent. Even bacteria have more common sense.

Let's face it. Either the computer is not playing with a full deck or the rat is stacked with wildcards. The rat knows emotions and lives through them. Can you imagine a computer being tired, eager, tender, rough, sensitive, aggressive, cowardly, courageous, hungry, glutted, loving, hateful, sympathetic, spiteful, kindly, or demanding?

What do emotions have to do with learning? In Robert D. Nye's book, *What Is B. F. Skinner Really Saying?*, Isaac Asimov is quoted as musing, "Could the behaviorists be saying that it's love that makes the world go round?"[100] Well, you can be assured that neither of the two fathers of behaviorism—John Watson and B. F. Skinner—ever said that. Purposefully, they did not distinguish between the powers of perceptual and emotional factors in stimulating learning. They merely lumped everything together and wrote of the concept of positive and negative reinforcement as the centerpiece of the behaviorist—the purely empirical—approach.

The behaviorists did do many of their early experiments on rats. But instead of trying to read what emotion the rats were feeling at any one time or figure out what they were thinking about the experiment, the scientists focused on measuring their speed in solving the mystery of the maze and getting to the piece of cheese at the other end. By measuring a rat's exact speed in solving any particular maze and correlating it with the size and complexity of that maze, they could come up with exact mathematical quantification of the net energy of the creature's positive and negative emotions. It was a neat way of getting around the communication problem and thus avoiding any possibility of misunderstanding between researcher and subject. They decided to use this totally objective methodology with all their subjects—including us.

The behaviorists delight in the measurement of intelligence in numbers, in those very grades that instill fear and despair into every failing schoolboy who ever hid his report card at the bottom of his book bag right beneath the unwrapped peanut butter and jelly sandwich. He knows all his parents have to go on in appreciating the ups and downs of his fierce and futile battles with fractions and division, understanding nouns and verbs, and memorizing the names of all the capitals of the world, is a short column of grades on his report card.

Did the failing schoolboy not get enough "net love" to make his academic world turn around? What parent can understand his child's emotional and perceptual handicaps after the whole range of positive and negative emotions moving him through that roller coaster of learning has been reduced to several net numbers? Do those numbers quantify the net power of the responsive ability of the pupil or that of the stimuli used by parents and teachers?

Puppet of Nature vs. Nurture or Freedom Fighter?

Are you getting a sense of the dilemma for the student of learning? In his research and writings, the cognitive theorist goes off in a completely different direction than that of the behavioral empiricist. Neither has a common sense understanding of learning. The first analyzes the development of intellectual formation into universal step-by-step processes, and the second reduces the whole range of perceptual acuity and the kaleidoscope of emotional energy that make it work to generic mathematical data. Each has a peculiar validity. But since the resulting models end up contradicting and excluding rather than synergizing each other, we know neither purist has captured the essence of the whole, or even the half.

On the one hand, we have Piaget's theory of learning. Through starting with his own children, he discovered children implicitly grasp concepts of basic physics—of time, volume, distance, direction, mass, et cetera—in the same order and at about the same ages. "He conceived of development as a sequence of stages through which all children pass in order to achieve an adult level of intellectual functioning. Later stages evolve from and are built on earlier ones. No stage can be skipped, and all children pass through the stages in the same order."[101] On the other hand, we have the behaviorist who studies the blow-by-blow series of events of children's responses to all the elements in their environments and generalize them into more and less important conditioning factors in their lives. Piagetians perceive the child through the lens or form of one overall theory to discover their commonalties, while behaviorists view a group of children through all their individual "factual" experiences to discover why they are different. Whereas the developmental theorist is focused on abrupt though universal changes, whether in grammar or idea at particular points in time, the empiricist is concerned with the time between those breaks, with ferreting out why they happen sooner or later for different people over time.

What did we do in the learning event? Trapped in the middle between the evolving shapes of genetic actualization at one end while being positively stimulated into responses by the environment from the other, we would not really have to do anything, except just sit back and lap it all up. Is that the way you feel about yourself as a learner—an organic doll programmed through the grand scheme and plan laid out in the genes and being massaged by external stimuli into the right responses? Just think of all that agonizing energy you wasted in the trials and tribulations of busting your brains out in trying to understand algebra, how to program your VCR, fix the vacuum cleaner, teach your kids to behave, or why your spouse does what she or he does. If you had only read what those scientists had to say, you could have let learning happen to you, effortlessly.

That we cannot be self-conscious of learning in the moment of it happening is at the heart of the problem. Since we can only become aware of it after it has happened, scientists are forced into looking for clues in postmortems, through focusing on either the form of its development or studying the conditions under which it had happened. This is the origin of the "nature vs. nurture" debate in the intellectual wars between the theorists and the empiricists. But in examining only the objective corpse of learning—their corpus of knowledge—scientists can capture only dry ideas and cold facts, losing all the lively and exciting subjective parts experienced in the moment of learning. Their approaches fail to deal successfully with the "wild-cards."

To be fair to the scientists, we have to admit that the artists and idealists of the faculty of the arts also work themselves into a similar conundrum. We have to confess that these academics have both suffocated and dissected to death many works of art, burying the bodies in the arts half of the university library. Ultimately the corpus of the arts is only true to its original creative purpose in how effectively it arouses you and me to go back to apprehending the original works of art and enable us to more fully experience and express our meaning in the here and now.

The Theorist vs. the Artist

Piaget, the theorist, distinguishes between thought and emotion as the engine and fuel of the intellect[102] as though they were separate entities. Though he claims emotion is essential for thought, being separate and discrete quantities he implicitly argues they could not have mutually transformative power in synthesis. For the theorist, emotion is merely a generic fuel that drives thought to develop.

In consequence, Piaget has to postulate a sort of genetically directed development over time of the mental structures necessary for intellectual development.[103] He ends up with a theory of development he calls "genetic epistemology" based on the gradual activation of innate determinants, much as Chomsky did for language development.[104]

In total contrast, the artist considers emotion as the very fount of his creativity. For him, it is not emotion as a generic energy that makes thoughts develop. For him thoughts are only very poor ways to describe the transformations of the emotions themselves. Whereas the theorist perceives the changes in thought, the artist feels the changes in his emotions. Neither purist can see the metamorphosis in the fusion of the two.

The Empiricist vs. the Idealist

When the empiricist, as physicist, studies how physical forces act on inanimate matter and its subsequent reactions, she discovers a direct cause and effect—instantaneous action and reaction. The empiricist, as behaviorist, applies this same idea to her study of people but has to invent a new terminology, "stimulus-response," because she cannot use the physicist's laws to explain her subjects' behaviors. She can only postulate probabilities of how each will respond in any particular situation. Whereas the physical reactions of inanimate objects to forces acting on them can be directly predicted by Newton's Laws, they do not have any power to predict the interactions of living beings, for whether they will respond with an eye for an eye, flee in terror, faint in shock, or totally confound an aggressor's stimulus by turning the other cheek.

To deal with this conundrum the behavioral empiricist came up with the idea of operant vs. elicitive conditioning. According to Newton's Third Law, there is no duration of time in the cause-effect interaction between inanimate objects. But in all her subjects, whether animal or human, she discovers a time lag between the stimulation of a living being and it making a response. To account for it, she complements her facts of operant conditioning stimulating the subject in the past with facts of elicitive conditioning, those drawing the human into responding later on. Thus she conceives of the child as having been operantly stimulated and thus conditioned by playing with a ball in the past, but during the experiment the child is elicited into action by the sight of the same ball. In effect, with these two types of conditioning, she invented an inside-out view: operant conditioning as the stimulus that effected the artist to form his intentions through dual coding, and elicitive conditioning as the response of idealist through her aspirations to give direction to her actions.

Of course, our idealist knows it all from the totally opposite vantage point of the empiricist—from her self-consciousness of purpose. She has chosen which of the artist's feelings and how strongly to associate them with which ideas and objects so that she can act quickly and forthrightly when the time comes[105]. Her environment is stimulating her to act in many different ways, but she prepares herself through establishing a hierarchy of purposes in conscience to help her determine what she feels should be most right in different situations.

Two Styles of Science and the Pragmatist

Thought may begin with its object, and at last, in consistency, try to bring its own mystic reality within the circle of material phenomena and mechanical law; or it may begin with itself, and be driven, by the apparent necessities of logic, to conceive all things as form and creatures of the minds [genetics].[106]
(Durant)

Obviously, the theorist performs his experiments in a different way than the empiricist. Seeking out the forms common to all his subjects, the theorist needs only a handful of subjects to construct a full-blown theory. He can see the universe in a grain of sand. The empiricist focusing on the accidental occurrence of external factors impacting on her subject needs many more to justify their statistical probabilities of chance. She needs a truckload of sand samples from all the beaches in the world to have the confidence to make one statement on the "law" of sand.

The theorist's insights arise from his obsession with metaphors to integrate his stream of perceptions, whereas the empiricist rises from the facts he uses to nail down the action he is imagining. The theorist fits his latest idea into his ongoing grand jigsaw puzzle encompassing and unifying all his previous ideas. His logic is driven by Occam's Razor, organizing his many ideas into the simplest single idea to explicate everything.[107] The empiricist focuses on collecting as many facts as possible to bolster her established hierarchy of factors. Both the pure theorist and the pure empiricist attempt to develop an overall concept of human development from the viewpoint of only one member of our quartet in their particular style of postmortem on learning experiences. The theorists have contributed massive volumes of insight describing the universal series of steps we all take in intellectual development, and the behaviorists have contributed massive volumes of facts on what stimulates us to behave in particular ways. But neither, trapped within the confines of their particular mode of knowing, can be ultimately successful in embodying the overall dynamics of personal growth and development.

From Pragmatist to Philosopher

In the study of humans, we have beings who not only study themselves only as objects but also as from the inside through exploring emotions and acting through ideals. It is little wonder the scientific pragmatist has such difficulty getting the objective pair into synchrony, because he has only two quarters of the whole to begin with. He is missing the dynamic duo. The artist, being as sensitive to his feelings as possible, allows them to transport him spontaneously through the creation of new art forms to express what he is feeling now. The idealist works to get the right orientation between her intentions for action and the aspirations she wants to achieve to change the world into what it should be.

What is the pragmatist going to do with this troublesome quartet? Just two was impossible already! He can only escape his dual bind by becoming philosophical and accepting valid roles for all four in playing with his children. By tossing out the theory of the theorist while dwelling only in his perceptions, then instead of focusing on the hierarchy of the behaviorist's factors, he can conceive of the energy giving life to the whole motion, and in turn tap the idealist for the right purposeful action to rediscover the content of that conception in the feeling of a particular energy captured by the artist. Then he will be playing with real children, not mere figments of theory and hierarchies of factors!

The "genetic" and "conditioning" arguments of the theorist and empiricist by themselves, or even the pragmatic attempts to resolve them in a balance of nature vs. nature lead us to a very distorted and limited understanding of how we interact with the world. This is evident since without the artist and idealist, the theorist and empiricist do not even have any connection to objective reality. It is the artist as the antenna who is stimulated by sensations of reality into activity and the idealist as the transmitter who chooses the action to respond to it. The theorist and empiricist merely process ideas and images in between. In this light, the latter pair are the mediators of the questions apprehended through sensation and answered through action.

Which bias of study do you prefer? The rough and tumble travails of the colorful and emotional dynamo wending a tortuous route of chance encounters with a multitude of thoughts and solid objects? Or the abstract coolness of the pragmatist—the theorist-cum-empiricist of the intellect—juggling ideas and facts while balancing on the high wire strung between the spontaneous combustion of sensation and the hard unyielding drive of her ideals? Or some other combination of our quartet? Or perhaps like Piaget you prefer to perceive humans as thoughtful robots, or like Skinner conceive of our behavior like that of a billiard ball in a game of snooker—viewing all of life from the safety of a single-minded purely logical approach—from only one corner of the learning ring? In the end, the true philosopher strives to make one common sense of all his and her four corners—his deepest emotions and most en-compassing perceptions with her clearest conceptions and highest ideals—toward the consciousness of one reality.

16

War over the Bones of Creation

If God does not play dice, is there a miracle in the works?[108]

Evolution is a very emotional topic so let's start out with a very clear idea of it to make sure we are talking about the same thing. We could try tracing the origin of the idea as implicit in the earliest known writings, for example in Genesis that presents us with a simple order for the creation of life from plants through to animals and finally humans. But we will restrict ourselves to the debate in more recent time.

The idea of evolution is the gradual emergence of more and more sophisticated and complex forms of life starting with the constituents of inanimate minerals, liquids, and gases to single-celled organisms to multicelled plants through to mobile animals and finally humans, the ultimate in mobility in both real and imaginary time and space, encompassing the whole universe with their thoughts and feelings. It is this idea within which we have to dwell to conceive of what energies could possibly make it happen, like Newton dwelling in the idea of the three-baller and then conceiving of the tug-of-war between gravity and momentum.

An Awkward Discrepancy

As epistemologists, we could draw analogies between the evolutionary idea of the emergence of life forms and their multiplication into increasingly sophisticated ones with that of the development of language acquisition by the linguists and thought processing by psychologists. There is also a curious parallel between the ways in which they explain it. Theorists argue for its roots in genetics whereas empiricists make the argument for external conditioning or nurturing factors, except for one rather awkward discrepancy.

The theorist for the genetically-based argument for evolution (the neo-Darwinist) proposes that evolution happened because of the failure in the passing on of a genetic inheritance true to the ancestor. He argues that life-forms evolved totally accidentally. It would have been a much neater solution if he, like the the-oretical linguist or psychologist, could have made the argument that forms evolve because of what was inherited instead of what went wrong in the process of inher-itance, then it would not seem as though they were on opposite sides of the same argument, of course about different things.

This discrepancy is only of academic concern to those of us who have already decided the deterministic nature vs. nurture arguments of these linguists and psy-chologists stem from their failure to include the roles of the emotional pair in their idea of the development of human consciousness. However, that opposite arguments are considered valid for evolution and human development by some scientists does raise a serious question about their overall "theory of everything," with which we will deal in the next chapter.

Anger and Confusion over the Bones of Creation

Should discussion of evolution be considered a purely scientific affair as many biologists contend, or is there also room for theologians to get involved in the dis-cussion? The question is not for the philosopher to initiate. When he hears the noise of battle and smells blood, he realizes there is a real fight happening. First he has to figure out why these two sides are even crossing swords.

The debate on evolution between scientists is centered on arguments between the Darwinians, who believed genes dictate the development of the body, and the Lamarckians, who argued the conditions of the organism's environment are the root determinate of change. The Darwinian theorist argued that the tree-leaf-eat-ing giraffe initially got his long neck by accidental genetic mutation and that the subsequent greater survival and propagation rates of the longer-necked mutants ensured its success. For the Lamarckian empiricist, the giraffe's neck gradually got longer and longer because of continual stretching to reach tree leaves. For her, this neck-stretching was translated back into the genetic code of the giraffe's reproductive cells and thus transmitted to its offspring. Whereas the theorist is content to explain the actual creation of the first mutant as naturally arbitrary and accidental, the empiricist feels the need to postulate an external nurturing cause.

On a superficial level, theologians became involved because evolution contra-dicted one of the literal details of the book of Genesis, in which the whole earth evolved from chaos to a comprehensible order in seven days. But on a deeper and more important level, they were more concerned that both approaches seemed to contradict the very spirit of Genesis: that life has meaning and purpose. In the Darwinian model, all evolutionary developments originate in totally accidental genetic mutations. In the Lamarckian model, they originate purely in how living beings are pushed into adapting to their physical environments.

For the first time in history, contrary to all previous accounts of creation handed down from ancient times in any and all of the many cultures that have arisen, there was suddenly no place for purpose and emotion in the explanation of the origin of life. The scientific proponents of evolution took no inspiration from the poets or idealists in their midst, basing everything on the hard evidence of bones and fossils buried over eons in layer upon layer of soil and rock, as if dry dusty bones and fossilized plant life could tell truer tales than the hearts and minds of men. In his book *The Expression of the Emotions*, Darwin seems to imply that emotions are expressed by organs like the appendix or tonsils—vestigal organs of no use to the man of science.

Not only were religious leaders aghast and incensed, but ordinary people—men and women struggling to maintain strong values and discipline in themselves and also instill them into their children—were troubled by these disturbing ideas. How would their children react to this new knowledge? Would it discourage them from making the sacrifices and pursuing the efforts necessary for fulfillment in their lives? Would their children be induced to just give up their goals and ideals in knowing now that life was just a crap shoot and a dog-eat-dog fight for survival by the fittest and smartest bully, or merely an environmentally-conditioned process of adaptation?

These modern scientific versions of creation—devoid of all mystery and majesty—inspire no one to greater and higher human endeavor. In fact they only really persist in halls of dry academia, storerooms of museums, and a corner of the educated man's mind. By themselves, they fail to touch and induce the emotional impact we not only crave but feel is absolutely justified and right to account for what we have experienced in the ups and downs of births, marriages, wars, diseases, loves, fights, victories, and deaths. These modern exclusively scientific versions are missing the context and the *élan vital* central to the creation myths of our past that make all our experiences significant and meaningful.

What to do? As philosophers, we are not going to dispute the validity of the scientist's facts. For instance, did he really find those bones and fossils where he said he did? When those bones were reconstructed, was there really evidence of a progression from simpler to more complex forms of life from those found in the most ancient sites to more recent internments? We could only question those findings fairly by becoming scientists ourselves. As philosophers, we accept those findings and see how we can best fit the idea of evolution into the constellation of ideals we already hold and with the emotions we most value.

Darwinian Genes vs. Lamarckian Retrogenes

Curiously, despite all the scientists finding and studying the same "bones," their individual ideas about the dynamics of evolution are very different. In fact the debates of the present time are so complicated with so many different strands of thought being hypothesized by so many different scientists we do not have time for anything like even the broadest of overviews. We will explore only the very basics of the scientific debates in evolution between proponents of Charles Darwin and of Jean Lamarck.

Their theories were at the heart of the debate on evolution in the nineteenth century, but in present-day biology Lamarck is not a big star. In fact, his ideas were practically laughed out of science a hundred years ago. That physical attempts by an animal to adapt within an environment could be translated back into genetic code seemed impossible to early twentieth-century scientists. But because of recent discoveries in biology, especially the discovery of retrogenes, Lamarck's ideas are beginning to make a curious comeback, though under different names.[109] Just as basic theories in education seesaw between the relative importance of nature and nurture, and in physics between the wave and particle theories of light, so it is in biology. This "looseness" in how present-day scientists are thinking about evolution gives us philosophers a valuable opportunity to offer our insight.

The crux of the scientific debate about evolution is in the nature of the interaction between reproductive genes and the "soma" or body. Neo-Darwinists argue this interaction is a one-way street, from genes to body. For them all change or evolution derives strictly from spontaneous accidental mutations within those reproductive genes, which then provide the definitive blueprints for the organism. Lamarckians, (and actually even Darwin himself when discussing the evolution of domestic animals) claim this is only part of the story. They argue the body through adapting to its environment automatically gives feedback to those reproductive genes, putting pressure on them to change its blueprints to reflect a design that would allow it to more easily and successfully function.

Ironically, it was the rediscovery at the turn of the last century of Augustinian Brother Gregor Mendel's nineteenth-century seminal research on the inheritance of genes in bean plants that finally tilted the scientific debate between the Darwinists and Lamarckians firmly in favor of the former. Until this discovery, the Darwinists had had to pin all their arguments on the experiments leading up to "Weismann's Doctrine." August Weismann had conducted an experiment wherein he cut all the tails off succeeding generations of rats. In observing that no rats were ever born naturally tailless despite his surgical persuasions, he claimed to prove that the environment could not influence inheritance. That is considered empirical proof. But neo-Darwinists needed a theoretical paradigm. Mendel's studies illustrating the idea of genetic inheritance gave them that paradigm for promoting their idea of spontaneous genetic mutations within the genes as the causal basis of evolution to explain Weismann's lack of findings. In effect, the neo-Darwinist argument is that since genes determine the form of the living organism, spontaneous mutations in those genes are the only way to effect evolution.

Unfortunately for the fate of Lamarck's approach, genetic research began long before environmental research had even been conceived of. Even then, the effect of the environment was considered only in how it affected the physical appearance and survival strategies of living organisms. Neo-Darwinists recognize the environment only as a laboratory in which the spontaneously generated mutations of evolution were tested.

Neo-Darwinists have been slow to question their belief in one-way evolution. They insist on seeing solid irrefutable evidence for the contrary. They have limited the role of the environment to that of a quality control inspector, of a "reality check," a testing laboratory or "weeding out" force within which the chance creations of mutation compete to see which is the smartest, most skillful, fastest, strongest, most flexible, most fertile, and most successful at raising its young. Until the discovery of retroviruses, scientists had no idea of the existence of a mechanism that could reverse the process of DNA genes giving direction to body cells. They had no inkling of the existence of such a feedback mechanism that could reprogram the DNA components of reproductive cells. Recently, a group of genetic researchers have gone further in demonstrating and proving the action of such: retrogenes. They have proven that immunity to certain diseases acquired by an animal during its lifetime can be transmitted to its offspring via its reproductive cells.[110] This had already been proven for plants for the genetic transmission of resistance acquired to metal toxicity.[111] All at once, Lamarck's idea about how the giraffe got his long neck is looking more plausible.

What is interesting about the neo-Darwinists' insistence on the cold hard facts of evidence from the neo-Lamarckians is that they themselves do not have any direct empirical proof. After all it was only about fifty years ago—long after they laughed Lamarck's ideas virtually out of science—that scientists even discovered what chromosomes looked like. Within several years of the discovery of this double helical form, Howard Temin discovered the first hole in Weismann's Barrier: that made by retroviruses—viruses that actually break into the nucleus of the cell and change parts of the DNA so it will direct the cell to produce more viruses. It was only much more recently that science began reading actual genetic code and trying to make some sense of a few of those pieces and how they are associated with particular phenomena. Only in these last few years have scientists discovered we share one-third of our genes with daffodils, that round worms have two-thirds as many genes as man and that the mouse has as many. Genetic science is still in its infancy.

The neo-Darwinist has no more direct empirical proof of the exclusivity of his theory than Young had for the wave theory of light. He does not have any more than Chomsky for his proposal for genes directing our grammatical development in language or Piaget for his genetic epistemology. All three inferred a theory from mere circumstantial evidence. Their theories seem to make a lot of sense just because in the light of little contrary evidence they appear the most rational explanations. But now the neo-Lamarckian has empirical proof[112] to back his theory just like that generated by Lenard to counterbalance Young's wave claim.

Lamarck's paradigm, as incorporated into Darwin's, would allow the rehabilitation of the nurturing half of the scientific idea. Instead of viewing nature's role solely as the grim reaper—the hangman selecting and executing the unfit—we would also be able to conceive of it as the healer, or as a "guide" by improving on the basic genetic design to allow living organisms to better function and thrive within the changing environment within which they were born.

Accidental, Conditioned, Spontaneous, and Purposeful Evolution

The one-way neo-Darwinist's "accidental" explanation of evolution is being seriously questioned by many scientists in light of the post-Darwinian discoveries of the enormous complexity and seemingly infinite intricacy of biological life. Of course scientists have not thrown out the basic idea of evolution, an ascending path of development in life forms and functions over geological time from a puddle of proteins to simple cells to that of humans and all the other simpler survivors in between, whether viruses, bacteria, plants, insects, or animals. But the neo-Darwinists have neither the evidence to prove the exclusively accidental theory, nor the mathematical probability of it being correct. Scientists have discovered life is a million times more complicated than was understood during Darwin's time, and based on that complexity mathematicians have done the math and shown evolution could not possibly have progressed by pure random chance mutations alone.[113]

Some neo-Darwinists feel reduced to arguing that if it is impossible for life to have evolved on earth through genetic mutation in the timeframe available, then perhaps life immigrated to earth for instance via meteorites from another planet where it had more time and better conditions to get going, or was it imported to earth from another planet in the universe by alien space ships? These ideas were put forward by Fred Hoyle, the famous astronomer. Of course this suggestion only begs the question: how did that other planet in the universe have enough time for that virtually infinite multitude of necessary mutations? Do the laws of probability work differently there?

The present-day confusion among evolutionary biologists has also created fertile conditions for "seven-day creationists" to reassert their advocacy of biblical writings as factual accounts. They claim the whole universe was made in seven days and is only about six thousand years old. This gets them into a lot of trouble not only with biologists but also other more basic scientists like geologists who claim to show the earth is about five billion years old. It forces the creationists into dealing with questions like: If the earth really is only six thousand years old, why would God make it appear to be almost a million times older? Did Noah have dinosaurs on the ark? Why would God bother trying to make the world appear one way to all sensory evidence and then claim it was something else?

The bitter public debate on evolution is dominated by the neo-Darwinists and the one-shot creationists. Interestingly, both sides agree on the same one-way relationship between the egg and the chicken, that the egg determines the chicken. Both sides totally reject Lamarck's idea. The difference between the two is the creationists believe the chicken appeared first, through divine design, whereas the neo-Darwinists believe the egg appeared first, through totally random mutations. For the creationist, the egg is God's invention for automatically replicating his creations while he can sit back and judge their performance. For the neo-Darwinists, the chicken is the lucky recipient of the particular genes that enabled it to survive the environment's pitiless competitive testing procedure.

The confines of this public debate limit us to choosing one and rejecting the other. Both are expressed in such terms as to entirely negate the other and force us into choosing between science and religion. For the neo-Darwinists, the development of life is a crap game. For the one-shot creationists, it is the result of one week of creative work by a supernatural power. For the one it is purely accidental, and for the other, wholly purposeful.

There are religious interpretations of Genesis more congenial to the scientific approach to evolution. Whereas the seven-day creationists prefer the conception of God creating the universe in one shot, the ongoing creationists lean toward God as continually active. This idea of evolution as the manifestation of a creative spirit active in present time provides the energy and direction for both Darwin's 'perceived' mutations and Lamarck's 'conceived' adjustments, as proposed by thinkers like Henri Bergson and Pierre Teilhard de Chardin.

Gould's Punctuated Equilibria and Bergson's élan vital

Even the Darwinist's "tree of life" tracing the evolution of all life from a single cell into the millions of variations of plants, animals, and man, is in question. There are too many gaps in the fossil trail. For instance, how did the eye develop? Where are the missing transitional links between the life form without an eye and the first with one (or two)?[114] How could the first mutants survive and successfully propagate with that superfluous and still useless transitional organ? In view of how many millions of unsuccessful mutations would be needed to accidentally produce the one that "fit," why were none found? Or were those few that occurred already so appropriate to the new conditions they did not need much selection?

Instead of there being evidence of gradual genetic changes in species as they differentiated, there are only jumps from one strand to another apparently occurring at catastrophic periods in the earth's development, as claimed in Stephen Jay Gould's idea of "punctuated equilibria." Now instead of there being five billion years for evolution to progress, we are down to only particular catastrophic intervals of disequilibria, climaxes of regeneration, breaks in time for bursts of spontaneous creativity—Bergson's élan vital. Most fossil hunters have given up trying to find the transitional pieces—the "missing links."

Stones and the Living

There is a very real difficulty in coming to a conclusion on evolution. To more fully appreciate the problem, just consider the difference between inanimate matter and life-forms.

In comparison to inanimate objects, living beings have a strange relationship to the forces in their environment. Inanimate forms like rocks are totally passive. They resist change in shape and motion only as inherent in the combination of their physical properties and environmental forces. They take no initiative in the process of degradation and erode over millions of years. But life forms initiate and react in an ongoing dynamic within their environs, in a much shorter timeframe. The seed absorbs water and the seedling unfolds. It pushes the soil outward to enlarge its space and insinuates a root down to anchor itself and draw in even more water to accelerate its expansion. A shoot pushes upward fighting gravity toward the sun and unfurls its leaves to capture the sun's energy and synthesize nutrients that are then used to power itself to even greater growth, and even build up a reserve to produce within its "womb" more seeds to grow again in another place and time, to propagate itself further.

In comparison to that of a rock, there is a sly mischievousness in the plant's relationship to the physical forces of its environment. When the sun shines hard on the rock and the plant, both heat up. But the plant then uses the evaporative power of the sun's heat to accelerate water flow up through the plant, cooling and nurturing itself through transpiration. Gravity holds the rock down, but the plant wiggles its way upwards. Westerly winds bend the plant but the plant responds by thickening the leeward side of its stem to enable itself to stand upright. Whereas inanimate matter is totally passive to the onslaught of physical forces and gradually disappears as it is dissolved, the living plant reacts to protect itself, thrives as an entity, and even propagates new plants despite those forces. The rock merely dissolves into the earth's water, disintegrating into the homogeneity of entropy. But a living entity fights to establish its unique presence in contradistinction to the flow of entropy as long as it lives until the moment it dies.

The difference between the rock and the plant is rooted in sentience: "The most striking feature of our own existence is our sentience. The laws of physics and chemistry include no conception of sentience, and any system wholly determined by these laws must be insentient...The study of life must ultimately reveal some principles additional to those manifested by inanimate matter."[115]

Non-Sense vs. a Playful Mischief

Inanimate matter is a total slave to the fact of Newton's Third Law. There is no mediation between cause and effect. All natural forces can be summed up in facts of action and simultaneous equal reaction. Physicists claim there is not even the time lapse of a split second between action and reaction. It is as instantaneous as the empiricist's conception of the present as a mere dividing line between past and present. But physical forces merely "affect" not "effect" life's responses. Those forces stimulate living beings into responding, but the response is not at all predictable by Newton's Law as are the responses of inanimate matter. In living beings there is a time lapse, time to develop a response to those forces.

The general scientific view claims the plant's driving initiative arises from the blueprints of the genes controlling everything from photosynthesis to that of reproducing itself in capsule form as a seed according to an inner biological clock. But no two plants even of the same species are exactly alike. As we can see by the trees in our backyards, the older they get the more individual they become in appearance. To every apple farmer's chagrin in pruning his trees, even in a block of apple trees wherein every single tree is a dual clone of the same two parent plants, not one tree is identical to any other one.

The plant scientist has to be content to ascribe this development of individuality in the apple trees as a result of the slightly different way each tree was grafted and to differences in soil types and microclimate within the orchard, among many other factors. But is it plausible that some of that individuality is in the way a particular plant chose to react to its treatment by the environment and the farmer? Could it be each plant has some, however limited, consciousness of living? Is it only the old farmer (and Jerry Baker[116] of course) nursing a sick plant who actually believes it is recovering not only in response to the water and nutrients she is providing, but also to her caring for it?

What about the similarities between the ways in which plants grow? The fact that most plants of any one species respond similarly under similar conditions does not prove they did not exercise some element of willfulness to respond in that way. Just because a common response to a particular treatment is the norm for a population—whether of plants or people—it does not prove it was determined. In fact, every plant scientist has to use plots of thousands of plants to draw up guidelines, for example, in regard to optimum fertilizer applications. We could argue the average response just shows that response is not the rule but the norm. Within that particular combination of genetic, cultural, and climatic conditions, the usual response of their initiative or "will" is that.

The empirical scientist has no tools in her scientific method to either prove or disprove the existence of such willfulness in any life form—whether plant or animal. Though she can adjust all the environmental factors—temperature, nutrient availability, soil texture and structure, water supply, atmospheric gases, and sunlight—to characterize the plant for its normal range of maximum and minimum requirements of them, she cannot adjust the amount of "willfulness," because will has no quantity. Of course, she can eliminate "willfulness" in some plants in order to compare it with the remaining plants to check out the old farmer's belief. But, unfortunately, by the very meaning of will, the only way of separating it from a plant is to kill it.[117]

But the pragmatic agricultural extension agent focuses on the technical aspects. He strives to get a clear description of those cultivation practices that should enable the farmer to nurture a plant to its optimum production. He takes the agricultural scientist's delineation in measurable terms of the ranges between "not enough" and "too much" for all the different physical factors of growth for each particular plant. Every strain of every plant species has a unique combination of optimum conditions under which it seems most easily and fully able to achieve the ultimate form the farmer is seeking—whether the most fruitful apple tree, the plumpest grain, or the most beautiful flower. The agricultural scientist's job is to zero in on determining that just-right balance between all the physical extremes that will best seduce the plant into producing the farmer's ideal crop.

This way of conceptualizing the plant empiricist's work as identifying that optimum or center point within all the ranges of those various factors as a convenient way of transforming the given hierarchies of factors to integrate those quantifiable characteristics into one in promoting ideal growth, is similar to the way in which we integrated the facts of gravity earlier into one conception of it. Through it, we can see how too much of one factor or too little of another has a dramatic effect on the whole balancing act.

Timelines of Geology vs. Biology

Both the geologist and the biologist limit themselves to techniques of gathering evidence that can be sensibly verified to prove their various "answers." But whereas the geologist dealing with rocks and crystals can show all her findings relating directly to the laws of chemistry and physics, the biologist can interpret his findings only indirectly, as though studying beings that have to obey those in one particular way until they can come up with an even more ingenious technique of using those laws to further counter the tendency toward entropy. The existence of even the simplest form of life is witness to this mischief.

The geologist can trace the history of a rock back through various transformations and recombinations of minerals back to the beginning—the Big Bang—on a single timeline. But the biologist exploring farther and farther back to the beginning of plant and animal life has to reset his clock to a new cycle at every generational overlap. He has to deal with a multitude of births, fruitions, and deaths and puzzle over the changes that happened at the junctures and overlaps in those cycles. The study of evolution is in how to relate these two very different timelines together into one.

Biology: The Study of "a High Majestic Fooling?"[118]

Unlike physicists who have accepted the irrationality inherent in the wavey particle of light, neo-Darwinists are not ready to accept the same in the origin and evolution of life. By completely rejecting Lamarck's take on it, they end up having to base their argument in a rationality of pure accident. Is pure accident a "scientific" conclusion? What happened to science as the bastion of cause and effect?

At the least, we can all agree that scientists can demonstrate that inanimate matter interacts according to the laws of thermodynamics. But when it comes to grappling with the origin and evolution of life-forms they discover that those laws do not apply. So therefore they are forced to conclude that all happening of life must be traced back to a multitude of accidents of pure chance. But in applying the law of probability they are forced into admitting the intervention of either Lady Luck or miracles to explain it: a hot streak of exceptional fortune or a wonderful run of delightful mischief with the laws of physics and chemistry?

I'm sure that we will not all agree on the same explanation! But this exploration of how we understand evolution does clarify the differences between the neo-Darwinist and the quartet's approach to creativity. In limiting the discussion to the neo-Darwinist framework of the move forward through accidental mutation followed by an environmental check of its fitness, we are forced to rely on the creative efforts of only two members of our quartet—the theorist in originating and the empiricist in testing. The neo-Darwinist even wants to reduce the creative role of the empiricist to one of merely selecting the fit to survive while exterminating the unfit. But by revising that dual framework into a four-way one, we can accommodate our dynamic duo and broaden the nurturing part to get a more comprehensive insight into the whole. The original impulse is in the spontaneous connections between emotions and perceptions by the artist. The theorist uses those raw perceptions to give birth to the idea, and the empiricist by dwelling in it, is able to observe and experiment with the results—tweaking it here and there to get the optimum fit within the context he lives in—and finally the idealist believing in his creation guides the action to bring it back to fruition in the most cherished feelings of the artist.

We can take a fertilized embryo and divide it atomically into its constituent parts. We end up with a pinch of minerals, a drop of water and a bubble of air. How can we fathom by what alchemy they came to be combined into this mysterious amalgam of living beings, in a million stages over eons of time? The theorists and empiricists of science have conducted their post mortems on the fossilized bones buried in the garbage heaps of geological history and come up with the perception of spontaneous genetic mutations and the conception of a nurturing environment. But we need the energies of the poet and purpose of the idealist to appreciate how those bones first came to life.[119]

Religious fundamentalists want to limit their participation in the debate over evolution strictly to the neo-Darwinists, and vice-versa, by focusing solely on the issue of purpose vs. accident. But by bringing in the metaphorist's emotional apprehensions to energizes the fundamentalist's ideals, we can also incorporate

Lamarck's "causes and effects" with Darwin's "accidents" and come up with one holistic paradigm for creation as an "accidentally-on-purpose" event, or more precisely, "spontaneously-on-purpose with what we can perceive and conceive." This four-way approach gives each member of our quartet a piece of the pie to enjoy. Through sharing together, perhaps we could do some real creative work toward consciousness of the whole mystery?

17

Is There a Mediator in the House?

As human beings, we must inevitably see the universe from a centre lying within our-selves and speak about it in terms of a human language shaped by the exigencies of human intercourse. Any attempt rigorously to eliminate our human perspective from our picture of the world must lead to absurdity.
(Michael Polanyi) [120]

Richard Dawkins, a neo-Darwinist, is a pure theorist. In his book, *The Selfish Gene,* he writes "…we, and all other animals, are machines created by genes."[121] When I first encountered this idea, I merely laughed it off. But I became curious as to how anyone could confuse man with a machine. How can it be that distinguished scientists fail to discern differences apparent to the average man, woman, and even child on the street? It struck me that many scientists—especially theorists—have grossly oversimplified the role of emotions within our psyches. Like Piaget, by reducing the whole gamut of emotions to a generic energy that fuels an "engine," they have literally "boxed" themselves into considering living organisms as merely mechanical "engines.' They can only escape the box through the philosophical idea of consciousness.

Dawkins' Ghost in a Machine

The pure theorist of scientific groundings does his best to avoid more than the faintest hint or suggestion of the existence of consciousness. Of course, he cannot avoid it completely, so he reduces the conception of consciousness to that of the ghost of a watcher—an illusion floating within the confines of physically determined components that has the ability to understand them (otherwise he would not be able to write books about it) but having no real interaction with them (only an empiricist would postulate real interaction). Read what Dawkins, the

176

theoretical doyen of many scientific thinkers in academia, writes in his summing up of the nature of man:

> The individual organism…is not fundamental to life, but something that emerges when genes which at the beginning of evolution were separate, warring entities, gang together in cooperative groups, as selfish cooperators…The individual organism…is a secondary, derived phenomenon, cobbled together as a consequence of fundamentally separate, even warring agents…Perhaps the subjective "I," the person that I feel myself to be, is the same kind of semi-illusion. The mind is a collection of fundamentally, even warring agents…[The] subjective feeling of "somebody in there" may be a cobbled, emergent, semi-illusion analogous to the individual body emerging in evolution from the uneasy cooperation of genes.[122]

Do you know anybody like that? Through pure perception, by apprehending man through only the theoretical quarter of his consciousness, Dawkins can see only the vague movements of grey shadows, of a ghost haunting a machine. In a similar vein, Skinner conceived of man through only the empirical quarter of his consciousness.

Gould Ostracizes Lamarck

But even many practical scientists who accept both theoretical and empirical dimensions reject the *élan vital* or vitalism of consciousness as mystifying nonsense. They want to deal only with the fit between the facts of their experiments and the shape of their thoughts. Let's grant them that finding that "fit" is a useful, essential task. If we could not mathematically conceive of gravity, we would not be able to figure out how much gas we need to get to the moon and still have enough left over to get home. If we did not try to appreciate the workings of evolution, we would not be able to jump into a greater appreciation of the mystery and wonder of creation. If we do not see how we are trapped in B. F. Skinner's black box, how can we even imagine escaping? If we cannot learn to see ourselves as consummate participants in the "games people play," would we work to rise above them?

Stephen Jay Gould was an eminent neo-Darwinist as well. But unlike Dawkins, he was also a pragmatist. He realized that for an overall theory of everything, he had to find a place for both ends of the nature vs. nurture argument. But, like Dawkins, he accepted only the "nature" approach of Darwinian genetic mutations as the source of all evolutionary change, and had to find another place for "nurturing" aspects as in Lamarckian forces:

> Nature…works on Darwinian, not Lamarckian, principles. Acquired characters are not inherited, and desired improvement occurs by rigorous selection with elimination of the vast majority from the reproductive stream. But cultural change, on a radical other hand, is potentially Lamarckian in basic mechanism. Any cultural knowledge acquired in one generation can be directly passed to the next by what we call, in a most noble word, education.[123]

What if we accepted Gould's hypothesis? At what point in the whole range of academic subjects from poetry through psychology to physics does he draw his version of the divide between the forces of nature and nurture—that is, "culture"? Which of the school's subjects is not "natural" and thus "educational"?

Gould's theory of "everything" makes little sense. Is he suggesting that all of life can be explained, on the one hand, by the neo-Darwinist accidental theory of the origin of life as balanced by how those life-forms then learned to adapt through the stimulus-response paradigm of the behaviorists? How does the rest of academia's subject matter fit into his conception of the whole? Does he refer to the arts like Newton as "ingenious nonsense" or prefer more modern expressions like for example Steven Pinker's description of music as an addiction—"a pure pleasure technology, a cocktail of recreational drugs that we ingest through the ear to stimulate a mass of pleasure circuits"?[124] Does music merely sedate him into a dopey vegetative state? Or, if self-indulgence in the superfluous cotton candy of the arts refreshes and invigorates Gould for the return to academic battle, how did it do that? This would be a good question for him to start developing a theory of the arts and its practice.

Having no idea of the dynamics between metaphor and fact within various fields of study, Gould has cooked up a hash of biological theory and psychological empiricism to explain his facts of life and living. As we have already explored, both "natural" and "nurturing" type forces seem to be operative in all fields of inquiry in science, whether physics, biology, or psychology. They are not confined to one side of a divide between the whole range of physical sciences on one extreme to all the other subjects on the other. The real divide is rooted in the difference in approach between the theorist and the empiricist in all fields of inquiry.

Wilson's Consilience and Conscience

To the utter stupefaction of philosophers, there are some scientists—"sociobiolo-gists" like E. O. Wilson—who want to dispense with the concept of consciousness, and thus philosophers, entirely. As the ultimate reductionists, they claim that actions of all life will eventually be completely explained by the fundamental and immutable laws of physics and chemistry in one "bottom-up" explanation of what they call "consilience."

The philosopher does not question the validity of the laws of physics and chemistry. He accepts them but points out they were derived from contemplating and experimenting with inanimate matter devolving to the chaos of entropy, not living beings—evolving in the opposite direction—stimulated through the spontaneity of sensation and developing a conscience to initiate responses. In fact, the philosopher views those immutable laws of physics and chemistry as the basic condition of his freedom and responsibility. If the physical universe operated in a haphazard fashion, nothing he intended to do could have any real meaning. Without a grounding in apprehending that physical actions are accompanied by equal and opposite reactions and that mass and energy are conserved, any action he took would be so much chaotic and aimless waving of a flyswatter in the vague general direction of that pest of a mosquito.

The actions we take originate in consciousness, whether asking for a glass of water, running a marathon, writing a poem, or hammering a nail. Though we must act within their parameters, none of our actions can be forecast by any physical or chemical laws. (Remember our previous discussion of "control" in the skill of driving? Physical laws directly control inanimate matter, but self-consciously we "have control" in manipulating the implementation of those laws.)

We manipulate physical and chemical matter through our self-consciousness of them, as evident in home cooking as in industrial processing. If we practice yoga, we can even control our own heart rate and the electrical conductivity of our skin.[125] That we can learn to control them self-consciously means we already have an affect on them, albeit unself-consciously. The interaction of consciousness with matter is so pervasive that all medical treatment research has to be done "double-blind" to prevent it from invalidating the data.

Though consciousness does not make much sense in either the scientist's objective nature vs. nurture debates or in the artist's and idealist's subjective tussles between emotion and purpose, it is the idea the philosopher presents to capture the mystery of all four dimensions in one. Philosophy is ultimately a way of making common sense of everything. Consciousness is the only way the philosopher can understand he can know and accept the physical laws implicitly through his creative actions. It is only through this praxis and thus transcendence of his self-consciousness in each of the four dimensions that he can act creatively and take responsible stands.

Haunted Robot or Aspiring Quartet?

A robot simulation programmed by warring gangs of genes and mechanically animated through space by the metabolism of organic fuels while piloting through the input of environmental stimuli, cannot do the trick of emulating life. We need a being with feelings and ideals as well as ideas and awareness of facts, a being just like those very scientists who present us with a vague, barely perceptible shadow of ourselves and then argue this "cobbled semi-illusion" is the real core of our being, or that there is no core at all. In the final analysis we have to ask ourselves how we can make the fullest most common sense of our existence. Are we better described as semi-illusions haunting little machines trapped within the cogs of one huge machine, or as philosophers struggling to make common sense of all our experiences towards full consciousness within the context of a genetic inheritance and a stimulating environment?

F: <u>Literature</u>

18

The Righteous vs. the Mischievous

Apart from our passions, do we have any personalities at all?
(Robert Solomon [126] *)*

The pragmatic scientist describes us as trapped between the nature of our genetic birthright and the various stimulations and interferences from everything and everybody in our environment. But the artist prefers to strand us with someone we heartily dislike in a leaky sailboat in an open sea with a fogged up compass and a loose rudder, just to see how we fight, suffer, and maybe die through the ordeal. Whereas the scientist works to represent a reasonable explanation of life through the implacable cause-and-effect relationships between physical phenomena, the artist perversely focuses on the contrariness and stubbornness of man in all his emotional foolishness and glory. The writer delights in having the beautiful girl choose the poor struggling poet with whom she is in love over the rich man's son, or having a respected and elderly professor become totally smitten with a wily young prostitute. He glorifies the brave soldier who sacrifices his life to save his friends, and destroys the coward who chooses certain survival over risking his life for those in grave danger. He tells historical stories of the king who abandons enormous wealth and power to follow a path alone in poverty to "truth," and of the good-hearted daughter of a poor craftsman who is crowned queen.

Just as Newton crystallized his great moment suspended between the mysterious equal and opposite forces of gravity and momentum, an artist captures the audience in personal dilemmas. Novelists thrive on describing how men, women, and children end up caught in a climax of tension between all the various forces pushing and pulling them in opposite directions within the framework of a particular physical situation. They depict their characters either wriggling their way out or taking brave stands in stories of humor, inspirational epic adventure, or heart-wringing tragedy. Or more rarely, those characters descend into despair or cynicism and reduce themselves to merely manipulating others or burning themselves out in a paroxysm of wild abandon.

The Gravity of Commitment and the Moment-um of Fancy

How many times have dramatists used the same themes? Take for instance that of the man who has grown careless in his love for his wife and suddenly discovers himself enchanted by a younger woman. He is torn between his love for and commitment toward his children and the excitement and wonder of being in love again, reexperiencing that paradise of feeling he once had for his wife, a feeling now worn ragged through years of acrimony. Does he work to revive his former love, just resign himself to procrastination and being torn to pieces, or abandon his history and invent a new one with his lover?

The idealist within him argues his duty to family to fulfill the commitment he made in taking his wife as his lifelong partner and to fathering children who are dependant on him for bodily support and development as well as caring guidance through and around the many obstacles and potholes they encounter in early life. The righteous man within sees his emotional attraction to the other woman as lust and betrayal. He argues familial duty and responsibility as the roots and foundation of communal stability.

But the free spirit argues the need for emotional stimulation in recovering the vital energy of life, of keeping the self creative in an increasingly hostile world, in the cold war between partners imprisoned together in a legal bond of stale routine. The artist argues the arousal of this old energy in a new form is the revival of a dynamic essential to his psychic survival and that the kindling of this mutual flame engenders an adventure that must be seized and acted upon. He regards his old responsibilities as legal and bureaucratic red tape stifling creative energies. For him, the sharing of emotional fires is the woof to the warp of responsibility in social intercourse.

In the midst of the flurry between moral commitment and powerful emotions, does the man merely fumble his way through the path of least resistance, being pushed and pulled into bitter conclusions as in a tragedy? Or are there times in the eye of that storm when he can see clearly and act creatively through his predicament to save what he most cares about and release what he is ready to sacrifice in good humor?

Just as the great debates in science are polarized around the contradictions and complements between the empiricists and theoreticians, the great stories in literature are those revolving around the poles of idealism and emotionalism, between the moral actions of the righteous and the loving energy of the free spirits.

Othello and Falstaff: Heroic Warrior and Cowardly Dreamer

In the heat of battle fighting the rapacious marauders and invaders of our happy kingdoms, can you think of a better warrior to have on our side than Othello? In the stories told about his past, Othello was inspired by the drive to righteousness and honor, resolutely attacking the enemy at its every weak point, brilliantly coordinating and straining every fiber of every muscle toward a clear and absolute victory. The brave and loyal general did not flinch at risking his own life for his fellow soldiers for the greater glory of victory over the adversary.

"Chief Justice: 'God send the prince a better companion!'"

In *Othello,* Iago is Othello's trusted aide. In *Henry IV,* Sir John Falstaff is Prince Hal's boon companion in youth. Falstaff, the "cowardly drunken sot," argues, "Caution is the better part of valour!" After the main battle, Prince Hal laments on finding Falstaff's body. Suddenly Falstaff arises and begins crowing about how it was better to counterfeit death and survive with a real life than to die fighting and end up as only a body—the counterfeit of life. Of course, Falstaff is only "working" Hal to cover up for the fact that he himself, paralyzed by the terror and horror of a massacre in blood and guts, had fainted. All his witty bluster about caution and its sensibleness is only a cover for his cowardice and fear of physical violence.

Righteous Murderer and Merry Companion

Othello, the victorious paragon in war, finds his real troubles in the home. In the heat of military clash, the righteous warrior freezes all sensitivity to the pain, fear, kindness, agony, and aspirations of his enemy as he is chopping off limbs, smashing in faces, and cleaning up with the finesse of disembowelment. He paints his enemies as totally evil and relates to them only as he would to objects, through his senses in the groove of pure physical combat. He is "Either" and they are "Or."[127]

But on his honeymoon, when confronted by Desdemona's lace handkerchief—the counterfeited evidence of his young wife's infidelity—Othello becomes paralyzed between his "soft" emotional infatuation with her and the "hard" factual evidence of his perceptions. But in contrast to the overly sensitive Falstaff who faints at the crucial moment of reckoning, the righteous man is driven to act. Cold-bloodedly, he chokes the breath of life from his purely innocent and most loving wife. And immediately after discovering how Iago has manipulated him into murdering her, he righteously asserts, "Nought did I in hate, but all in honour."[128] As a career soldier, his honor is more important than the life of his beloved.

"Falstaff: 'God send the companion a better prince!'"[129]

But would it not be rather dull (unless we are Desdemona) to spend a whole evening with our righteous man of action, Othello, who paints the whole world black and white? Would we not rather join the mischievous Falstaff? He knows the many shades and colors of having a good time over a few pints. Who does not enjoy imagining his "marital bliss" in wining and dining the refined woman of loose repute, Doll, like a great lady? He knows idealism is as useless as a book on the joy of sex to guide the progressive engagement of lovers in the intimacy of their emotions.

If Falstaff had been a general like Othello at war, perhaps he might have cajoled and inveigled the enemy into realizing the events that led to their violent disagreement was a foolish misunderstanding. That the real struggle was within? That instead of fighting each other, the soldiers of the opposing armies should enjoin for a merry party to build up their morale and enjoyment of life to sustain them through the real hard parts?

Means or Ends, Virtue or Ideal?

Do we have any real choice in creating an ideal path through our confusions in life's trials and tribulations toward a noble and gracious state of perfection in both our intentions and our energies to achieve it?

Othello's sense of honor and integrity drives him as a courageous soldier of impeccable honor, the most loyal and faithful servant of the kingdom, as well as the murderer of his beloved. When he realizes he has been manipulated into the murder, Othello, shaken by despair to the very roots of his being, still does not waver in his integrity. He does what only the most honorable man does to bear witness to those others who loved her too. He kills himself with one thrust of a dagger into the heart.[130] Through sacrificing his own life, he begs forgiveness for taking that of Desdemona. "[I] lov'd not wisely but too well."[131] Othello could only dream of loving wisely, of having the sense of humor to muse on the paradoxes and contradictions of everyday life to "dissemble" Iago's machinations.

Falstaff knows how to enjoy life to the fullest while sharing what he has with others, as he expects them to share with him. As a consequence, he is totally deflated when, on gleefully greeting his bosom pal Prince Hal newly crowned as king, he is shunned and ostracized as disreputable company. His abhorrence of personal conflict and his sensitivity to the feelings of others is so extreme that in action he is a coward, losing his direction in equivocation and pretense. He can tell Prince Hal only what he thinks of him by telling others while pretending he does not know the prince is listening. He can only realize the ideal of being a brave victorious hero by capturing the already defeated foes of the king.

Othello the idealist or Falstaff the artist, which do you prefer? In the next chapter, we will meet a parallel pair in Don Quixote and Sancho Panza.

19

Ideal vs. Virtual Reality

Do you think that the things people make fools of themselves about are any less real and true than the things they behave sensibly about?
(George Bernard Shaw, **Candida***)*

In the Arts half of the university, the idealists and artists carry on a duel over ideals and virtues; there are those chasing their highest ideals and those striving for the purest emotions to properly energize their actions. The former construct their hierarchy of ideals like truth, honor, and justice in the fight against the anarchy of nihilism. The latter struggle between virtue and vice. Of course, the ultimate is for an artist to capture the dialogue between idealism and virtue in the same work, as Miguel de Cervantes does in *Don Quixote* in developing the relationship between the ultimate idealist Don Quixote and the virtuous Sancho Panza.

Knightly Bookworm and Naïve Farmer

Don Quixote is a gentleman, meaning he does not have to work for a living. He can do what he wants, though within a very meager income obtained from renting out his small estate to local farmers. As a bachelor, he is free to hunt wild rabbits, boars, and deer to his heart's content. But as he grows older he starts to spend more and more of his leisure hours reading books about the adventures of knights in righting wrongs, protecting the weak and helpless, winning jousting contests, battling whole armies by themselves, and saving beautiful princesses from evil phantoms. He becomes so enthralled by the knowledge in these books he ends up selling much of his land to buy more of them. His social life centers around his barber and the local priest in discussing the morality of the characters depicted in his books. In effect, the bachelor Quixote, being rather shy of women and hard work, has never been needled and cajoled through the trials and tribulations of marriage, kids, and work into growing up. But a midlife crisis does occur anyway, and Quixote, the perennial student, now decides to do something mean-ingful with his life. And since he does not feel the call to be a saint, poet, or shep-herd, he outfits himself as a knight and rides out from his village into the world of strangers to save them from the evil forces that bedevil them.

For his squire in the planned adventures, the knightly Quixote chooses San-cho Panza, a poor local peasant. The naïve and illiterate Sancho has only a vague idea of the outside world and none about knights and what they do. But he is a very good-hearted and hardworking man, faithful and loving to his wife and chil-dren. All he cares to know is he is being hired by a locally respected gentleman who will reward him enough for his services to feed and clothe his family. His hopes are raised even higher by Quixote's promises that he will become the gov-ernor of an island once they have happened into the right adventure that will allow them to rescue a kingdom from the evil forces oppressing it and return it into the hands of the good and beneficent king who will reward them with what-ever their hearts desire. Thus Quixote and Sancho set off.

But these two do not find the world of chivalrous knights, phantom sorcerers, magic potions, and sighing starry-eyed virgins Quixote insists is everywhere. In their haphazard travels on the road, Cervantes has them encounter real peo-ple—innkeepers, servant girls, muleteers, monks, merchants, farmers, shepherd-esses, policemen, prisoners, prostitutes, and even a duke and duchess—all living in the real everyday world in one great mix of greed and generosity, impatience and patience, coarseness and fineness, laziness and diligence, rudeness and polite-ness, lies and honesty.

Quixote the Real and Lone Ranger the Fakir

Don Quixote would be jealous of the Lone Ranger[132] for he is a true knight in the right situations. The Ranger, a European immigrant, rides into a different town every week with his faithful American native scout, Tonto, and quickly fig-ures out by the color of their hats, the smile or smirk on their lips, and the look in their eyes, who are the good and who are the bad. He lassoes the bad, or if he is forced to, wounds or kills them with precisely-placed silver bullets and then dis-appears from the now lawful and peaceful town into the sunset to his cave hide-out, leaving behind men, women, and children marveling at the mysterious masked stranger who risked his life to free them from their malicious oppressors and asked nothing in return. The Lone Ranger does all this not as a hired man, a policeman, soldier, or mercenary, but as an independent free man, a true vigi-lante for justice. His only authority is his conscience, and the only reward he asks is the satisfaction of seeing justice done.

On this level, the idealists, Quixote and the Lone Ranger, are alike. What differentiates them is the setting within which their respective authors place them. Author Striker and the TV screenwriters set the Lone Ranger down in a black and white world of bad and good people. Unfortunately for the Don, his author places him in the real context of ordinary people—each a mixture of good and bad—as they behave and interact spontaneously with each other in everyday life. And instead of silver bullets and the marksmanship of an Olympic medalist, the Don carries a homemade lance with a rusty spear point. Instead of Silver, the magnificent white stallion, he rides a meek old swayback named Rocinante. The Don does not even have a lean stoic Tonto riding a smart pinto to serve him obediently. Instead he gets a short, fat, sassy farmer named Sancho riding a plough mule who will not hold back his remarks and questions about "what in tarnation" the Don is trying to prove and when will he get his own island to govern.

The Lone Ranger and Tonto let their actions say almost everything for them as other heroes typical of modern action cinema. But the Don, not in the least shy of fighting, has no trouble speaking out his thoughts and debating their veracity with everyone. His closest friend is Sancho who is always ready to listen and argue about anything, even when the Don becomes impatient with his impertinence. The dynamics of Cervantes' characters grow though the back and forth between impulsive actions arising out of conscience and spontaneous actions followed by reflection and argument. This is not easy material for modern cinema to deal with. The modern film is much more successful in glamorizing the same black and white stereotypes of the chivalric genre Cervantes was parodying.

The success of the typical action film is rooted in our desire to instantly be the noble hero or the gracious heroine confidently returning home in the triumph of brave actions. We want to be in that perfect state of "nobility and grace" beyond all moral dilemmas in that quiet still place wherein we are no longer torn this way and that by conflicting forces of right and wrong, of good and evil, in which we spontaneously act rightly with all our emotional energies. But Cervantes' tale of the Don and Sancho is of both action and thought, of both the tragedy and comedy of the struggle upward in everyday life in the real complicated world of many shades and colors, where no person can be described as wholly good or wholly evil. When the Don frees prisoners being transported to be slave oarsmen on the royal galley boats where many would have been worked to death, is he acting as a criminal himself in releasing thieves, embezzlers, and murderers or rather is he a savior of loving fathers, faithful husbands, and respectful sons? When the Don battles to annihilate an "evil" opponent with his heart full of vengeful hatred, is he not contradicting the spirit of his ideals? Is any action carried out in hatred or revenge a wholesome holy act?

Some readers dismiss the Don as a foolish and mad idealist. The Lone Ranger would have come across as an idiot if the screenwriter had forced his masked hero to ride into any real town of real live people, like the one we live in, to save us and our friends from our problems with his silver bullets. But we can no more dismiss the Don than we can the appeal of any modern popular hero if we are to appreciate our own nature. Quixote's intentions as a knight are the highest and purest. He believes the role of freelance knight is the vocation that best enables him to make the most meaning of his life. And nobody is going to deflect him from his chosen path and skew his leap of faith, even if his author will not give him a world of eternally-pure sighing maidens, magic potions, horrendous monsters, and evil magicians. The Don has enough smarts to perceive them for himself.

Quixote the Warrior and Sancho the Healer

Curiously, it is the bookworm Quixote, not the farmer Sancho, who becomes the courageous man of action on their journey together. The Don knows how the world "should be." He attacks all those whom he believes to be evil with a courageous vengeance, with as much pity as an eagle feels for its terrified prey. Mounted on Rocinante, and dressed in homemade armor, he courageously takes on whatever and whomever he believes to be evil with his rusty homemade lance. Sancho is more like a pigeon. He is content to let Quixote do the fighting, while arguing the merits of parleying toward peaceful and loving coexistence, especially after every battle when he has to pick Quixote up again and care for his wounds. Panza is the faithful caretaker, Quixote's healer.

On a superficial level of interpretation, Cervantes uses the Don's adventures to make fun of the romantic chivalric novels in high fashion at the time. But Cervantes does not denigrate the moralist impulses that inspired those stories. He wants to know what they have to do with real life. He knows how important they were for his years served as a soldier in a war in which he lost an arm, for the five years as a prisoner of war in Algeria, and for the rest of his life supporting a family as a struggling playwright.

Unfortunately, we do not have the time and space here to enjoy the travels of Don Quixote and Sancho Panza. But there is no need. Though it was written about 400 years ago, the book is still in print and has been translated into English over a dozen times. Many of its readers claim it to be the greatest book of adventures ever written.[133] The reason is not for the adventures in themselves. It is just as much for Quixote's conversations with all those involved in those adventures, and especially with the illiterate farmer, Sancho, who gradually becomes his closest and wisest friend. In fact, the atmosphere between these two characters becomes so charged and intimate that at times it is as though they are but two aspects of the same personality, as though this book is but a means for the writer to explore how to make one common sense of two conflicting aspects of his personality—his idealism and his virtue, his beliefs and his loving of others.

The assignment of different aspects of his own character traits to different characters in a story or play, with an associated limitation in how they can initiate or respond in different situations, is the writer's most common literary device. At its simplest, the characters are merely stereotypes or cartoons of good and bad behavior fighting it out for victory. At its most sophisticated, the characters epitomize different dynamics of behavior. For example, in the film comedies of Stan Laurel and Oliver Hardy, neither is a bad guy. Much of the comedy arises from our embarrassment at seeing two different aspects of ourselves put into two separate persons. We like both men. They represent diverse elements of the inner fight within us in dealing with our realities. Each has a very different way of making sense of the same world, just as do Quixote and Sancho.

Whereas an ideal is an idea subsumed in overwhelming emotion, virtue concerns the nature of emotion energizing action. Quixote epitomizes idealism with his passion for ideas of justice and honor, but then pitilessly and vengefully punishes those who do not act in the right manner. In contrast, the simple Sancho is trapped between his respect and love for Quixote's honesty and bravery on the one hand, and his abhorrence of the knight's self-glorifying vengeance on the other. Indifferent to the abstraction of ideals, he values the emotion of the action itself. He appraises and values the action not by the explicit intent for which it is done, but by the emotion implicit in how it is done, whether lovingly or vengefully.

The believer Quixote, the courageous, self-glorifying, and morally vengeful knight, by himself would end up in futile tragedy. The emotion-centered Sancho, the loving but cowardly peasant, by himself would end up in farcical comedy. They are saved only by each other, as are Laurel and Hardy, in mutual friendship.

Othello and Quixote: The Empiricist and the Theorist as Lovers

Both Othello and Quixote are scrupulous and conscientious idealists holding honor, integrity, and justice as the highest ideals to guide their actions. Both believe in these ideals to such a degree that they are as real to them as laws or commandments handed down from the highest imaginable authority in all existence. For them "believing is knowing." As true believers, they act on the direction of those imperatives. Their differences must be ascribed to the influence of other members of the quartet: Othello is also an empiricist whereas Quixote is also a theorist.

When Othello is confronted with the "evidence" of his beloved's lace handkerchief from the bedroom of her alleged lover, he believes Iago's lies. He accepts this empirical evidence over that of the emotional evidence of his artistic quarter. As a hardened warrior, he has never learned to trust his "soft" side—the artist who contends "feeling is knowing." And consequently the principled idealist disciplined and hardened in warfare, and now the most highly respected soldier of the state needing to maintain the ideal of himself as a man of honor and integrity, suffocates the emotional storm of his love for Desdemona.

The theorist's dictum of "perceiving is knowing" is not as contradictory to the idealist's nature as the empiricist's "seeing is knowing." Consequently, the tensions within Quixote's character are of a very different nature. Unlike Othello, he is careful to maintain a goodly distance between himself and his "lady love." Instead of talking to her directly, he gets Sancho to be the messenger. Thus he can maintain his ideal of her as a virgin in a perpetual state of sighing in platonic desire for him while he is flying into battles to be the knight worthy of those sighs. He would never have believed her to be unfaithful on the basis of a mere handkerchief. In fact he would not have believed it even if he had discovered her with a lover *in flagrante delicto*. He would have known it was only an illusion perpetrated by evil magicians seeking to destroy his faith in her. He would have seen right through the illusory appearance of that mere empirical observation. After all, he knows she is totally dedicatedly in love with him, saving herself for him alone, forever.

In the End

What happens to our mischievous "feeling is knowing" pair? They get their women. Falstaff marries Doll and Sancho returns home to his wife and kids.

Both Othello and Quixote die separated from their beloved, surrounded only by their closest friends transfixed in a turmoil of grief and wonderment that men of such fundamentally good will and extraordinarily high ideals should meet such strange and lonely fates.

20

Belief in Metaphors and the Facts of Life

Everything can be taken from a man but one thing: the last of human freedoms—to choose one's attitude in any given set of circumstances, to choose one's own way.[134]
(Viktor Frankl, on life as a prisoner in a Nazi concentration camp)

The energies and purposes we discover in emotional experiences are just as real to us as both the ideas we perceive and the motions of the physical forms we conceive. Ever hear the anecdote of the exchange between Sigmund Freud and Miguel de Unamuno?

Freud claims, "Religions are merely projections of man's deepest aspirations for purpose, peace, and everlasting joy." Unamuno responds, "Since those projections arise out of our deepest feelings, aren't they the most real of all?"

The Love of Song and the Purpose of War

What is "real" about our experiences?

What is most "real" for the artist? When we study the subjects of our music—whether pop, rock, alternative, opera, country and western, hymnody, or jazz—we are often astounded to realize that virtually all songs are some form of emoting love. How many millions of ways are there of feeling it, as sweet, sour, bitter, tender, tough, shy, bold, facetious, joyful, superficial, suffering, ironic, deceitful, sincere, awesome, trite, blissful, fleeting, or forever, and describing what we want to do about it, as succumbing to it, fighting it, seeking it, avoiding it, remembering it, forgetting it, discovering it, losing it, yearning for it, mocking it, circumventing it, dreaming of it, doubting it, affirming it, wriggling out if it, denying it, idealizing it, trashing it, hoping for it, despairing of it, proclaiming it, hiding it, fearing it, enjoying it, suffering for it, playing with it, lying about it, being in love with it, being jealous of it, teasing it, killing for it, manipulating it, dying for it, condemning it, praying for it, complaining about it, chasing it, running away from it, wondering about it, begging for it, rejecting it, lusting for it, hiding from it, glorifying it, furious about it, curious about it? I could easily go on for a few more pages and then work out at least six billion different combinations and permutations...All these songwriters and musicians are describing their relationship to an emotional energy at the center of their being. The evidence of song all points to a fascination, if not an obsession, with a "mirage" of love as the essential energy.

What is most "real" for the purposeful idealist? Why are ideals so powerful that graying fathers and mothers can send their beloved sons and daughters so eagerly and proudly into the chaos of war and morally justify "the burning of women, kids, houses, and villages"[135] to maim and kill the "real" enemy, and in turn be maimed and killed for the glory and honor of who or what? Carl Sandburg names some of idealistic movements of recent times and puts them into a "Falstaffian" perspective in his poem "Threes":

I was a boy when I heard three red words
A thousand Frenchmen died in the streets
for: Liberty, Equality, Fraternity—I asked
why men die for words.

I was older, men with mustaches, sideburns,
lilacs, told me the high golden words are:
Mother, Home, and Heaven—other older men with
face decorations said: God, Duty, Immortality
—they sang these threes slow from deep lungs.

Years ticked off their say-so on the great clocks
of doom and damnation, soup and nuts: meteors flashed
their say-so: and out of great Russia came three
dusky syllables workmen took guns and went out to die
for: Bread, Peace, Land.

And I met a marine of the U.S.A., a leatherneck with a girl on
his knee for a memory in ports circling the earth and he said:
Tell me how to say three things and I always get by—gimme
a plate of ham and eggs—how much?—and—do you love me, kid?

Fingering the Moon

Neither the lover nor the idealist could have come to his or her peculiar focus without having interacted physically with the world. Without having been stimulated by sensations, inventing ideas about them, observing forms in motion and then purposefully initiating responses in acting outward into the world, neither would have discovered the existence of other persons. He nor she would have been able to begin crossing the frontier (or abyss?) that separates the self from that of the other without having worked out a system of communication based in the characteristics of that very frontier, to discover what is most true and real in the relationship developing with the other and choosing how to deal with it.

Whereas Zukav, as metaphysicist trapped between his perception of light as a wave and his conception of it as a particle, wonders about the one real nature of light, as "meta-emotionalists" we have to deal with the question of whether our feelings have any reality outside of our experiencing them, of whether we can make any sense of this pushing and pulling between our emotions and our ideals beyond our mediation of them.

"It is with a finger that one points to the moon, but how absurd were one to take the finger for the moon!" (A Zen Buddhist saying.)

Are the scientific theorists and empiricists, and the artistic mystics and moralists merely fingering different aspects of the same moon? Which of these fingers are real? Is there a moon?

The theorist of religion makes the argument that the soul is the only reality. But when we laypersons read those tracts of metaphysics, we have the same feeling philosophers like Henri Bergson had: "By isolating the spiritual life from all the rest, by suspending it in a space as high as possible above the earth, they are placing it beyond attack, as if they were not thereby exposing it to be taken as an effect of mirage!"[136]

What if either artist or idealist had started out believing the physical world is only an illusion and that only virtue or ideal was real? What significance can an illusion have for us anyway? What is the difference between the significance of a really traumatic life event and that of a stage drama we are watching? We can't maintain the idea of the significance of the real event if we are self-conscious of physical reality as merely a stage for actors or the setting for a mirage. How can we trust musicians to show us ourselves through how they relate to their elusive mirage of love? How can we trust our idealists who are so ready to lead us through sacrifice and bloodshed to honor and glory? How can we believe in ancient religious writings if even the physical reality of what we directly experience every day is reduced to nothing of import? We have to live and breathe in the present moment to bring our imaginations to life. We need both flesh and blood to discover our "souls."

Dreams and Experiences

When we encounter religious rituals, especially those not our own, we have the problem of learning how to relate to them. This is more difficult than relating to the creations of the dramatist, whether of highbrow theater or low-life television. Not only does the dramatist not invite us to participate in these fictions, she rarely makes any claims of either recapitulating an actual historical reality or carrying out a spontaneous event in present time. Her works are carefully and intricately scripted events with the purpose of engaging an audience vicariously in an entertaining and possibly enlightening roller coaster of thought and emotion building to a climax and ending with a resolution.

Coleridge argues the enjoyment of drama like any other art requires a "willing suspension of unbelief." The audience is supposed to forget that the actions portrayed are not real life. The problem with getting a grasp on Coleridge's argument is that it is expressed as a triple negative. He is saying the audience is asked to doubt or "not believe" what it is experiencing as "not unreal."

Let's put it into more positive language. The problem is we both believe it to be real, but not really at the same time. When we see Othello strangle Desdemona, we do not jump up from our seats and shout for the police to come. But we do experience it vicariously as though it really is happening at that moment. We can feel him choking and her being choked. We feel his raging anger and her stupefied innocence. We are horrified by what is happening. But like in that state in the middle of just awakening from a dream, we do not take it literally.

If we suddenly discovered the actor "Othello" was actually killing the actress "Desdemona" on stage in front of us, we would be "really" horrified, not at the character of Othello, but at the actor playing him in the present. We would lose the emotional thread of the drama and its plot as woven by the dramatist. We would be completely lost, because we would not have any idea what brought the actor to do it. Immediately we would insist on calling for the authorities to apprehend the actor and investigate his actions so we could get to comprehend his rationale and punish him appropriately.

The actors and actresses of the drama are even more intimately entangled in the same duality of believing and not believing in the unfolding drama than the audience. On the one hand, they have abandoned their personal identities in bringing to life their character roles. On the other, they are totally cognizant of the drama as a let's-pretend phenomenon.

There is a deep-seated complicity here between the actors and the audience. Not only do both sides know the drama is not a real event happening spontaneously in the present time, both know the drama is not in the least an attempt to replicate a particular historical event. It is only an imaginary story that all are pretending is really happening for a given period of time in the afternoon or evening in a darkened theater. All they are concerned about is that the interaction of the characters has a universal truth, in the sense that particular characters such as portrayed in the play also exist in our lives and could well act in the same way given the situation as set up in the play.

Whether this particular love triangle, made up of a renowned black general named Othello totally infatuated with a refined and beautiful white damsel from high society named Desdemona but driven into a rage to kill her because of the lies fed him by a jealous friend named Iago, ever existed is of little or no concern to us. We are interested in the universality of the personalities and how they work through their particular situations, not in whether it occurred once exactly just like that. In fact we can leave our own shoes behind to step into theirs only when we forget to be concerned whether it ever really happened or not. We focus on trying to apprehend those emotions and thoughts in that action of that situation, and later realize what we, being who we "really" are, would have felt and done.

Our experience of dreaming provides us with a much more useful template than Coleridge's expression to understand our interaction with drama. In our sleep, the brain secretes a certain chemical to keep the body from acting on anything that is happening in our dreams. We are physiologically immobilized from doing any more than tossing and turning on our mattresses, just as we limit ourselves to do no more than squirming in our seats during a theater performance. In night dreaming we are a captive audience to the illusory scenarios created from the ferment of our daytime thoughts and emotions around the "meaning" we are pursuing. In theater-going, we voluntarily make ourselves captive to how a dramatist's thoughts and emotions have coalesced in his search for meaning.

Belief in Science

It is not much different in our struggles to understand science as we squirm in our desks while contemplating the theoretical and conceptual creations of scientists. New theories are midwifed through dreams. Though both scientists and dramatists are at a loss to describe exactly how they create, some of the greatest thinkers, even eminent mathematicians like Jules Henri Poincaré and Bertrand Russell, openly admit their debt to dreaming. And we learn to believe their theories. Michael Polanyi, an eminent chemist turned philosopher, describes the role of belief in science:

> We must now recognize belief once more as the source of all knowledge. Tacit assent and intellectual passions, the sharing of an idiom and of a cultural heritage, affiliation to a like-minded community: such are the impulses that shape our vision of the nature of things on which we rely for our mastery of things. No intelligence, however critical or original, can operate outside such a fiduciary framework.[137]

Religious Ritual

Whereas the scientist is content to make connections between his perceptions and her conceptions and the arts academic between his emotions and the sense of purpose driving her into action, the religious person wants to make connections between all four.

As the audience of a play in a theater, whether dramatic or academic, we participate, but only internally. Theater is a spectator event, in contrast to religious ritual. "Historically, drama grew out of religious performance in a process wherein the play gradually separated itself from the crowd watching. The distance between watcher and watched is essential to theatrical experience."[138] Entering into a metaphor in action as we do in religious rituals is more involved than going to a theater. The difference between appreciating scientific and religious knowledge is that in pure science we attempt to see the world in abstraction from all the emotions we feel. The difference between appreciating a dramatic play and that of participating in religious ceremonies is that the directors of the latter insist they are based on factual not fictional accounts.

But ultimately, the "facts" of any particular religion are not our own personal "facts." Remember the "He scores!" fact? That fact is a real event wedded to a particular spontaneous emotion for a particular person. It happens for the hockey player's mother in real time and space. But the stories of, for example, Christ's and Buddha's lives that we hear and read, took place thousands of years ago. They are not personal facts of our particular lives. Since we cannot go into a time machine and live in those times, we can only "real-ize" our religious aspirations by establishing our own facts that give witness to our faith and belief in what "should be."

The "Blue-Skins" vs. the "Green-Skins"

Religious rituals are a preparation and commitment for our real-life battles outside that one-hour time slot on our weekly holy day and daily prayers. In everyday life, our most curious human activity is in sharing our lives with other persons, in the present moment, in realizing our ideals in action, in creating our own real life facts as witnesses to our deepest feelings and aspirations. As we will see in the encounter between the "blue-skins" and the "green-skins," that's much easier said than done.

You, a blue-skin, have been told by other blue-skins that green-skins are lazy, stupid, and dishonest, and most of them are sex maniacs. Apparently there are even statistics to prove it. Of course, when you meet one you are very cautious. You spend your time looking for evidence of all those characteristics, and no matter what that green-skin is like, you will be able to identify traces of all four. We all have traces of all four. But you figure this green-skin is actually hiding the evidence of the true depth of her deviant inclinations, because as any person does, we all put our best foot forward to try to dispose others sympathetically toward ourselves. Not trusting her to be expressing her real self, you are now firmly caught in your own trap, the mental conception of the characteristics blue-skins have invented for green-skins. There is no way to think your way out of this trap. You can see traces of evidence for your suspicions about her so you feel you cannot trust her to express her true self.

The only way out is a leap into interacting with her as though she were just a normal blue-skinned person like yourself. The problem here is she has been used to you being suspicious of her and has developed ways of dealing with that. Now you are being "nice." What's behind your new treatment of her? What do you want to weasel out of her? The shoe is now on the other foot. She has learned her prejudices about the blue-skins as well as you did about the green-skins. If she does open her mind to other possibilities, and by the time she catches on you really mean it, you might well have given up on trying this new mode and reverted to your old conceptions, which seem more "realistic" and "practical" given the way she, the green-skin, has been responding to you.

There's another problem. You only really know the culture of the blue-skins. Within its rules of behavior and set of beliefs you can feel natural and spontaneous, but the green-skin does not. And whereas she might feel somewhat pleased by your new treatment of her as your equal—as though she were a blue-skinned person too—she is still a green-skin, and thus her most comfortable and natural way of interacting is different than that of a blue-skin.

How are you going to learn to interact with the real green-skin?[139] Unless you can move totally into her culture for many years, it is impossible. You could not learn the intricate nuances of the green-skin culture without literally immersing yourself in it to discover and adopt the right reflexes and habits to feel completely comfortable within it. Besides, you already have another one. The only practical way out is to develop a third culture with her, the blue-green culture. And that requires openness and readiness from both sides at the same time. The Traveller has to be patient in watching for the moments when the Listener is ready to hear.

Whether we are interpreting blue-skin and green-skin as different races, politics, religions, ages, sexes, cultures, education levels, or careers, the problem, whether the other-skin is stranger, friend or family, is the same. Ironically, the closer we come to someone in everyday life, the further apart our differences in opinion can make us feel, because our expectations for mutual understanding are so much higher. We expect anybody else is able to understand us if only they try hard enough. So why can't or doesn't the one closest to us? The difficulty is in reversing this to admit we do not really understand the person we should know best, and meet her again as for the first and last time.

"I" as an Individual and as Everyman

How often have you sat with visitors in polite and strained conversation? The talk becomes stilted and boring. A few go on at length about their latest interests. Most say too little, whether for fear of insulting someone or starting an argument or making a fool of themselves. It is as though growing out into the world into adulthood is a moving toward stranding ourselves onto islands of separateness of my-own-color, and on which we grow ever more fearful, arrogant, or indifferent.

At the same time I have often marveled at how our own and our visitors' young children, who despite being complete strangers to each other, within a matter of minutes have struck up a spontaneous and fluid dynamic and play together happily and excitedly for hours. What is their secret? Why is it what we did so gracefully and innocently as young children, we now have to relearn as hard-earned virtues in adulthood? What is the difference between the natural unself-conscious creativity of children and our self-conscious struggle toward it as adults? "Man is like a thinking reed but his great works are done when he is not calculating and thinking. 'Childlikeness' has to be restored with long years of training in forgetfulness."[140]

Our idea of "person" encompasses our most acute and complex classifying system. We can go through categories of looks, attitudes, colors, sizes, shapes, temperaments, employment, marriage eligibility, skills, religious beliefs, eccentricities, addictions, tastes, psychological types, shopping styles, et cetera. There seems no bottom to how many different ways there are of viewing fellow humanity. Not only that, each of us have different ideas of how the criteria for each category of comparison and contrast is defined, and which category is more important than another for our estimation of any individual's overall character.

The abstract meaning of "character," as alluded to above is the structure of the idea of character. How we have developed it, in the sense of how we have structured it in our own personal ways for interpreting people's actions and behaviors through how we classify their characteristics depends on the million factors of our experiences. It is rooted in how we most prefer to interpret our reality, whether we choose to primarily focus on the physical world through the ideas of the theorist or on the imaginary forms of the empiricist or on the emotional world through the creations of the artist and actions of the idealist.

Our human classification systems are so complex that even though we know there are about six billion people in the world, it does not even occur to us that there might be even one person out there exactly like us. Can you imagine suddenly running into someone exactly like you? We just know there is not another one, even close. People are infinitely varied. And yet we expect any one of those others could understand us if only they tried hard enough, and having done that, they would accept our beliefs as the right ones for them too. We cannot understand why the green-skins do not want to become blue-skins...

We expect there is one basic common underlying truth all of us can work toward getting a grasp of and understanding in our own lives. There is this paradox between our knowledge of the infinite number and complexity of the enormous array of sensory data we accumulate every second and that of our intuition that it and all the other seconds of our lives can all be understood in one grand emotional interpretation of reality in one magnificent story.

There are many magnificent stories—historical and totally fictitious—and many created artifacts, whether poems, theories, sculptures, models, simulations, paintings, or dramatic performances. Through our dwelling in those images and the flow of their action, we feel less lonely in life. As travelers, we are not primarily interested in abstracting and delineating their essential message or meaning. Rather we get excited in our realization of what we share with their authors in how we perceive reality, in how we feel about it and how we act within its boundaries—real or imaginary—of time and space, of ideals and emotions. Through them we discover we are not alone. "No man is an island!"[141] In participating together in reenactments of the most important of those images in play as children and ritual as adults, we commit ourselves together to discovering more of each other.

Between Nothing and Everything: Discovery

> From northern Scandinavia, across the tundra and taiga of Siberia, Alaska, and Canada, to the icebound coast of East Greenland, men have lived for thousands of years. It is a hard land. The land never thaws. It is snow covered most of the year. Nothing grows. The mystery is not that men should be tossed by chance into this desolate waste; it is, rather, that within this prison of ice and wind they are able to draw from themselves images powerful enough to deny their nothingness.[142]

Losing It

We are floating in a medium of vast extent, always drifting uncertainly, blown to and fro; whenever we think we have a fixed point to which we can cling and make fast, it shifts and leaves us behind; if we follow it, it eludes our grasp, slips away, and flees eternally before us. Nothing stands still for us. This is our natural state and yet the state most contrary to our inclinations. We burn with desire to find a firm footing, an ultimate, lasting base on which to build a tower rising up to infinity, but our whole foundation cracks and the earth opens up into the depth of the abyss.[143]

> Now see that mind that searched and made
> All Nature's hidden secrets clear
> Lies prostrate prisoner of night.
> His neck bends low in shackles thrust,
> And he is forced beneath the weight
> To contemplate—the lowly dust.[144]

What to Do?

From the tortured anguish of his adult thoughts, Miguel de Unamuno declares, "If it is nothingness that awaits us, let us act as though it were an unjust act!"[145]

From the innocence of his childlike heart, G.K. Chesterton gently reminds him, "Angels fly because they take themselves lightly."

> Come then all of you, come closer, form a circle,
> Join hands and make believe that joined
> Hands will keep away the wolves of water

Who howl along our coast. And be it assumed
That no one hears them among the talk and laughter.[146]

G: <u>Two Conclusions</u>

21

Paradise Lost: The Rupture of Consciousness

I tell you solemnly, unless you change and become like little children you will never enter into the kingdom of God.
(Matthew 18.3)

In the Garden of Eden, Adam and Eve refuse to be content with the tree of life. Eve persuades Adam to eat the apple from the tree of knowledge. From having experienced the world as one timeless moment, they now find themselves in a world with a past, present, and future. Learning they have a future, they start to reflect on facts from the past and experiment with using them to control their future. Knowing they can effect what "will be," they are forced to foresee and struggle towards what "should be."

No longer are they in a paradise of only natural pleasures and spontaneous delights. Having lost their innocence, Paradise becomes only a memory of what they lost in yielding to the desire for self-consciousness. Religion is born in their creation of frameworks to reintegrate all their sensations, perceptions, and conceptions within which they can best realize their sense of purpose.

Adam and Eve with Children and the coming of Dawn

Mischievously, the male writer of Genesis names the female as the initiator of the argument between Eve and Adam that leads to the big "mistake" in Paradise. Perhaps Adam is more content enjoying the pleasures of the tree of life? But she, being less muscular and uncomfortably constrained for months and years on end with childbearing and the seemingly never-ending responsibility of caring for those children, wants stability and rules. Eve has to get him to eat from the tree of knowledge to keep him focused on the "big picture" and off Dawn. Women invent marital rules, and men counter by inventing government.

207

The war between the sexes continues unabated in modern times. In fact, it may even have accelerated if the evidence of our increasingly casual acceptance of divorce and single-parent homes is any indication. A seemingly endless war over what is right and wrong is fought between us in the privacy of "home sweet home." There is as least as much energy aroused and expended by most adults at home as in all those other battles in the workplace. There is also a public war between the sexes. Ironically, in this public war the positions of man and woman are the reversal of Eden's domestic scene.

On the one side, it is pursued most stridently by the feminists who argue there is not much real difference between the sexes, that our apparent differences are no more than that—a superficial matter of a few minor appendages, several pounds of muscle and some inches in height. They use the reality of the battle of the sexes to argue for the reshaping of laws of the land and policing a politically correct attitude that views both sexes equally and in the same way. They argue to establish their ideal of equal individual rights in the fact of law.

The other side is most vociferously represented by the chauvinists who praise the value and benefits of an apparently complementary nature. The chauvinists downplay acknowledgment of the battle, focusing their emotional persuasions in a sexual interpretation of the world of Ying intertwined with Yang in the joyful and peaceful womb of home. They highlight the idea of the complementariness of and interdependencies between male and female as a couple in raising a family.

We are not interested here in arguing the case of either of these viewpoints. They are both right and wrong. We are curious about the nature of the paradox between our ideals and our metaphors in particular situations, that it exists at all, and that there does not seem to be any way of ever finally resolving it. We are constantly inventing and reinventing rules of engagement out of the interplay between the ideals and the metaphors we share in understanding reality. It seems that we can find only temporary agreements and arrangements to carry us through to the next crisis.

Children as Mirrors to Our Past

It might be interesting to consider a third point of view, that of our children. But what do they know about it? We do know what they *care* about. They want as much lively caring attention as we can grant them in their seemingly endless series of trials and tribulations. And if we are not ready to give it, they'll dig deeper and deeper until they do get attention, whether positive or not. If they ever do give up looking to us for it, they start searching for it elsewhere.

Young children are not primarily interested in either the facts or ideals of the feminists or the metaphors of the chauvinists. Instead they are more bewildered and anxious by their parents' difficulty in caring for each other, because they themselves are totally dependent on relationships of caring for and being cared for. Caring generates the emotional punch and power that enables them in confidence and trust to enter into the images and models for action with others around them. They develop a strong foundation of the varied emotional sensibilities and skills only through live caring action in a whole gamut of situations, with their parents, siblings, and friends. Only after puberty, when their powers of abstraction begin to really develop, can they as teenagers start to take a more intellectual or dispassionate approach to life and learning.

Children and adults are tackling reality from different directions. The child wants to experience as many different aspects of seeing, hearing, tasting, speaking, feeling as he or she can in all their diversity. As young children stranded in a moment floating in a sea of infinite possibilities, we apprehend the world around the poles of our emotions and pure cognition into creating a past and future to make sense of the present. We perceive adults as the mirrored reality of our initiatives. As adults locked into self-conscious creations of time and space, we understand our world around the pole of our metaphors and facts. In losing our sensitivity to new experiences, we concentrate on organizing our past experiences and future hopes into the most complete and meaningful patterns to recapture the experience of the infant's conscious unity of all those pieces. Our children are the mirrors through which we can most vividly reexperience the innocent wholesomeness of "unself-consciousness."

From Infant to Adult and Back

The newborn, Luke, has no clue of the adult's multidimensional concept of time. Time's veil has not yet been drawn to mask the indecency and immediacy of raw emotion and direct cognition. He has just begun to perceive and conceive of individual shapes, color, sound, taste, and touch. The sensations are just an indiscriminate wonderful chaotic profusion of stimulations he can aggregate into experiences. He has no self-consciousness of himself as an entity separate from what he senses—whether perceptively or emotionally. In fact until he is well into primary school, he won't even have a glimmer of the idea that he has different senses each feeding their particular sensations which he is synthesizing into one.

The advent of the "terrible twos" dawns in the gradual realization that the world is more than him, that some of those parts with which he has been playing are not a part of himself but of others like him. This is the beginning of his self-conscious encounter with the others in his life. His life becomes focused on defining and understanding this separation and overcoming the ensuing loneliness. "…linguistic creation implies the abolition of time—of the history concentrated in language—and tends toward the recovery of the paradisaic, primordial situation of the days when one could create spontaneously, when the past did not exist because there was no consciousness of time, no memory of temporal duration."[147]

It is fascinating to watch how self-consciousness of time gradually grows in children. I remember being surprised when my youngest came home from kindergarten school and excitedly asked me if I knew the meaning of "infinite." I told her I sure did, but suspecting that she didn't really have a real clue, I asked her to explain it to me. She had no trouble doing it in three different ways. I was stunned because I knew it would be another year or two before she could even tell time, much less understand, for example, that a person older than her was born before her.

At birth, Luke lives in an eternity of the instant as one with the space he inhabits. Roused by his senses, he unself-consciously begins hypothesizing the simplest of ideas and dwelling in them to observe the most basic forms in motion and synthesizing the first ideals to direct his interaction with the world. He gradually realizes he's not alone. The world is no longer one seamless whole. In building up memories and insights of past failures and successes, and of hopes and fears in dreams of himself with others in the future, he gradually disrupts the continuity between the instant and eternity into a past and future. As an adult discovering himself living in this ruptured universe, he yearns and fights to repair it. He strives to fill in all those many awkward gaps between eternity and a point in time, to recover the original oneness with others and everything else in the world he had at his conception in the hopes of redivining his Creator.

22

Cooking Up and Digesting Metaphor and Fact

"Knowing as I do that it behooves us to obey the decisions of the authorities and to believe them, since they are guided by higher insight than any to which my humble mind can of itself attain, I consider this treatise which I send you to be merely a poetical conceit, or a dream...this fancy of mine...this chimera."
(Galileo) [148]

All the preceding chapters are an attempt at rendering tangible something that is intangible. And if the reader did not "get it," how would a conclusion serve any purpose at all? The heart of the "intangibility" problem is in dealing with emotion and metaphor. How do they fit into the whole, and how did I come up with my metaphors?

The Quartet at Loggerheads

In comparison to the Sciences, the Arts present us with a totally opposite approach to relating to who we are. When reading a poem or watching a drama, we are asked to experience the very emotions the poet/playwright felt in writing them. For the writer, the physical setting is entirely arbitrary. Whether the action takes place on a sailing ship or in a fast-food restaurant, at the Arctic Circle or in the stifling heat of the Tropics, in the Stone Age past, or in a metallic future of robots and space ships, is essentially of no importance. His primary goal is to get us to empathize with his characters whether five-star generals like the noble straight-laced Othello or mischievous drunks like Falstaff, idealistic purists like Don Quixote or simple goodhearted persons like Sancho Panza, as though we *are* them. He is focused primarily on re-creating within us the emotional dynamics of how they relate to themselves and others.

211

Whereas the Sciences strive toward assembling a picture of who we are as though we can capture it all in an idea or physical model, the Arts explores it through trying to capture our essence in the feelings we experience through various roller coasters of emotion and how we decide what to do about them. Whereas the theorists and empiricists of the Sciences fight through the resolution of ideas with facts of observation, the authors of the Arts capture their characters' struggles between what they feel as artists and what they aspire to achieve as idealists. The Sciences explore humanity through studying the "other" as object. The Arts explore it in the study of the self as subject.

The scientist is bent on penetrating the illusions of sensory perception through perceiving ideas and then dwelling in them to conceive of forms and quantifying their motions. His "arts half" is in pursuit through capturing the emotions and concretizing them into ideals for action. As students of the Sciences we pursue physical reality through constructs created by scientists and isolated from the felt emotions by focusing on the perceived patterns of change in form over time. As students of the Arts, in the act of appreciating literature or drama, we are guided to dwell in the particular emotional dynamics of the primary characters to feel the ways in which they play out through our emotions within the particular shapes of their frames of reference to decide what we would have done.

Which duality is more real—the objective or subjective pair? Are our ideas more real than the ideals that drive us into action? Are our conceptions of forms in motion more real than the emotions we feel during the action? Since our search for meaning in life is in how we relate them all together, I recognized all four approaches as merely different ways of being self-conscious of knowing ourselves. Complete consciousness is all four functioning together in the heat of creative activity. The emotional duo provides the kaleidoscope of energies and the sense of purpose for action to complement the perceptions and conceptions of the physical pair. Thus I adopted this rather quarrelsome quartet—the artist, the idealist, the theorist, and the empiricist—as the four sub characters of the same "I, the learner."

Poetic and Theoretical Metaphors

The theorist employs metaphors to perceive ideas which the empiricist then dwells within to make observations and nail down the facts, whereas the artist employs metaphors to capture the energy of emotions the idealist uses to energize the action toward her goals. It is no wonder they have such a difficult time understanding each other. The excitement in academic learning is not in the increasing accumulation of theories, hierarchies of hard facts, mysterious feelings, and inspiring goals, but in their paradoxical interplay.

We all explicitly understand what are facts and ideals, but we tend to be so immersed in the use of metaphors in everyday life that we are no more aware of them than we are of breathing. We literally wear them, leapfrogging from being in one to another in the flow of conversation. But when the average person runs head-on into one in a poem or a scientific theory he often gets all uptight, forgets common sense and treats it like a UFO.

For example, take Dylan Thomas's line, "The force that through the green fuse drives the flower." This sounds like nonsense to the average nonfan. What is he talking about anyway? First of all he's not talking "about" anything. He's created a metaphor that if we can dwell within, not think about, will evoke in us a similar emotion to what he was feeling at the time of writing. We have all seen flowers, soft, delicate, and elegant structures suspended on the end of their "green fuse" or stem. For Thomas it is as though some wonderful and powerful inner force starting deep in the roots of the plant works incredibly hard to push a scrunched-up flower through that narrow tube of stem, until suddenly it bursts forth to bewitch us with its beauty.

Of course we can only conclude this is nonsense if we stick to the biology books. But in a crude way it is a fair analogy. In this case he created a metaphor that through its physical imagery relates his feelings about the mystery and wonder of a life force working its way from deep in the recesses of the earth through a plant to culminate in a flower just as it works through us to culminate in the emotion and expression of love. Adhering to the dictionary definition of "metaphor," we say his image of the green fuse, the flower, and the force is a metaphor for our emotional experience. But a metaphor is not a riddle to solve for what a writer "really meant" by it. It is in the tension between this pairing we find his metaphorical meaning, in what is essentially identical and opposite—"a transaction between contexts."[149] The poet is into exploring emotions and how they relate persons together.

The theoretical scientist delights in metaphorical expressions, too. Thomas Young paired the results of his demonstration of light diffraction with that of the interference pattern of water waves. Now anybody would naturally be skeptical of accepting and trumpeting the significance of any such parallel between two materials as dissimilar as water and light. But it does seem reasonable that since both end up with diffraction patterns they are propagated similarly. Further if one wants to argue that light is not propagated as a wave, how else can that diffraction pattern be explained? In this way metaphorical scientists explore and elucidate the patterns of perceptual phenomena.

But unlike the artist who asks the reader, listener, feeler, viewer, or whatever integration of senses required, to provide one half of the metaphor from his or her own emotional experiences, the "objective" scientist provides both halves. The scientist studies the relationship between different parts of the physical world. The artist studies how that world relates to the emotional one.

Idealistic and Empirical Facts

What about the empirical scientist and the idealist? As purists, they frown on the metaphorical approach, even to the point of rejecting it entirely. In fiction, a classic description of a diehard empiricist is Charles Dickens's school principal, Thomas Gradgrind:

> "Now, what I want is Facts. Teach these boys and girls nothing but Facts. Plant nothing else, and root out everything else. You can only form the minds of reasoning animals upon Facts."...With a rule and a pair of scales, and the multiplication table always in his [Gradgrind's] pocket, sir, to weigh and measure any parcel of human nature, and tell you exactly what it is. It is a question of figures, a case of simple mathematics.[150]

In "real" life, we have the instructional technologists who write school textbooks, and even books, for instance *Instructional Design*,[151] on how to teach. The authors of this 450-page book mention metaphors only once, on page 173, accompanied with a warning that they are dangerous to use.[152] A related group of psychologists—pure behaviorists—reject all concepts of the theorists as "mentalist fabrications." They also feel comfortable only within hierarchies of hard facts and mathematical symbols. The empirical scientist depends on a complex array of statistical improvisations to back up her claims to a literal "objective" interpretation of reality. She plays down the wave theory of light and instead measures its energy and declares it to consist of particles that interact like billiard balls.

The purist "idealist" also eschews the subtleties of metaphor for the driving force and overwhelming power of her idealizations, for instance of justice, equality, liberty, reverence, and love, whether in national anthems or hymns to guide us in the "right" direction. Inevitably both the idealist and the empirical scientist are forced to use images, but only as signs, symbols, or analogies to illustrate, exemplify, and "explain" their evidence. In contrast, the artist and the theoretical scientist use metaphors to frame their whole outlooks to "explicate" their experience of reality.

Metaphors are essentially questions in search of universal patterns and rhythms. Facts and ideals are answers for a particular place and time. But by themselves, facts and ideals imprison body and mind. When we forget the questions we lose touch with the patterns and rhythms within which we can logically arrange and organically connect with our facts and ideals. But when we forget our facts and ideals, metaphorical questions by themselves lead us into a slippery maze of pure skepticism or cynicism, or into the triviality or debauchery of "art for art's sake." *"The idea that one can seriously cultivate his personal freedom merely by discarding inhibitions and obligations, to live in self-centered spontaneity, results in the complete decay of the true self and its capacity for freedom."*[153]

From Smoke to Glass Sculptures

Up until this point in the book, I have focused on how as philosophers we can use the ideas and images of others to understand the world. But how do we cook up our own? Frankly, this is an embarrassing and unsettling question for any creative writer of nonfiction. No writer wants to be the goose that died looking up its "sphincter."

As Moustakas writes *"The initial 'data' is within me; the challenge is to discover and explicate its nature."*[154] I focused on juxtaposing questions and experiences. But I did not try to "explain" the latter. I merely focused on getting clearer questions and more complete descriptions of how they worked within me. As these gradually became explicit in words, I could then begin to reflect on them, looking for correspondences and contradictions among them. Once started, the development of different parts of this book arose through alternating between writing, meditating, and reflecting, between pounding on the keyboard and pacing the banks of the Thames River at the back of my apple farm.

For when I was working, especially pruning, in the orchard, I developed a crude technique of meditation by repeating the same question over and over for hours in my mind to see what thoughts would arise. The heuristic researcher must be *"willing to commit endless hours of sustained immersion and focused concentration on one central question."*[155] Or as Newton said in response to the question of how he discovered his laws of celestial dynamics: *"By thinking of them without ceasing."*

Especially useful was making the particular question of the day the center of my thoughts just before going to sleep. There it simmers and bubbles all night cooking through the heat of dreams. In the morning, in the twilight moments between sleep and waking,[156] I received my most surprising images in writing through their warm remains.

One second the image is not there, and in the next there it is on paper. There does not seem to be a direct "cause and effect" relationship between wanting an image and getting it. It happens sometimes and sometimes not. When it does come, it comes on its own time as a surprise, like a gift from someone out there, or in here. Once it comes, it has to be taken for test runs to see in what contexts it can fly, where it just flops about and where it's absolutely irrelevant. Can it be "tweaked" to fit into the whole or must it be discarded in favor of another better one? Perhaps the "giver" is just being mischievous giving out only bits and pieces here and there, sharing out a limited store of ethereal celestial imagery between all the creative types each clamoring for their piece of the pie?

One thing is certain; the "giver" does not give if you already think you have the answer. If you do not have a reason to knock and ask, it will not come and answer the door. It only comes when you know you are up against a hard brick wall that seems completely incomprehensible and you are too stubborn to quit knocking to get through it. It comes in the eye of the fury and frenzy. But the voice is so soft you can only hear it if you can listen in complete stillness. Its images are so transient and ephemeral that they can only be captured if you care enough to lose yourself within its presence.

I would not recommend this as a calling to any of my friends. Living in a world of shadows and mirrors to carve out images and thoughts through individual words strung together in a line across a piece of paper is like making glass sculptures out of smoke. And then after they appear on paper, people read them and get them into their heads! Once in there, some will praise them and others will deride them as mere figments of the imagination! Have you ever heard of anything more ridiculous?

Whether they want to admit it or not, everybody participates in the creative act. But only an artist is brazen, vain, desperate, and foolish enough to publicize his artifacts for others to kick around and play with. By publishing or displaying his work, the artist asks you to eavesdrop in on conversations or doodlings with the soul. It is much more natural and normal to create in more private settings everyday spontaneously without a recorder in the intimacy of the sharing of life's promises and burdens, triumphs and defeats with a chosen one as "exercised in the still night…of their most secret heart,"[157] and treasure them as inviolate. It is a paradox that in publicly exhibiting their work, artists—the ultimate introverts so "sensitive" to the underlying rhythms of reality—can also be so thick-skinned in defying the slings and arrows of outraged extroverts as well as in bearing the stony disapproval of those who "know" better but are not going to let themselves be dragged into the open to discuss it…

The Journey

Floundering about in the darkness of wherever I went to dig up these fragments and drag them out into the light, was not a fun time. It is like having an obsession with exploring abandoned and deteriorating houses alone on moonless nights without a flashlight. The only light is this very faint one which keeps shifting perspective. What one sees one moment is gone the next. Is that faint reflection over there a part of what caused that glint of light I saw several minutes ago, or is it something new? There is never enough light to see how big the house is, or even just one room. There are holes in the floor through which a person can fall and get stuck for weeks. There is an accompanying fear of death that recurs time after time.

> "Now that my ladder's gone,
> I must lie down where all ladders start,
> In the foul rag-and-bone shop of the heart."
> (W. B. Yeats)

There is the being utterly alone intellectually, as no one has any idea of where one is going. The first thirty or forty drafts are no more than nonsense to anyone else—not even to a "friend cum mentor"—no matter how meaningful the latest draft is to the writer.

Previously, I had the idea that a mentor was some sort of intellectual sounding board who could grasp where the creative intellect was going at each step and guide it. But now I realize that would be impossible, for even I the first-hand explorer rarely had any idea where I was, much less where I was going for how long or how far. Now I realize that a true mentor is someone with infinite patience. Through empathy with the explorer he believes that the explorer is trying to get in contact, however tenuously with something meaningful. He or she as the case may be, is someone who listens more to the heart of the explorer than the words, giving encouragement at one time, a joke at another, and a snatch of wisdom at yet another. The mentor is as much an explorer as the explorer, moving as much in the dark while offering care to the heart. The mentor has already made his or her own journey into Hades, albeit to a different part.

Infinite patience? Is there a limit? How many times was I so fully charged with the adrenaline of insight that I was sure that I had "the answer." How many times did I get this all printed up into "the final draft"? How often did I go running to this friend or that and desperately plead for their approval and confirmation that this was "it"? How often was I the fool obsessed with an impossible task? Can foolishness lead to wisdom? Or is the wise man, as Merton writes about Chuang Tzu—the greatest of Chinese philosophers—one who *"knew that he had follies of his own, and had the good sense to accept the fact and enjoy it."*[158]

After ten years, the journey is not yet complete. This book is neither a perfect piece nor is it complete. But I sense it has reached a certain plateau of intelligent thought…a time to share the burden of its shortcomings and its promise.

Eureka?

Whatever words we use to describe learning, it is a most common event. We experience it most often through the use of language. But language is such an integral part of every minute of our life, it is incredibly and amazingly difficult to step out of its framework and appreciate it for what it is. It is much easier to notice it in much less frequent activities like going shopping for new clothes. We either have a strong intuition or we already know the exact characteristics of what we want that new "me" to be even though we do not have a clear picture of the new clothes for which we are looking. If we are getting them for a job interview, we want them to reflect those particular aspects of our character we want our potential employer to appreciate in us. And once we narrow our selection down to several suits, we try them on in turn. Suddenly we realize that in one in particular we look and feel just right. And in wearing it to the interview, we find out the facts of its weaknesses and effectiveness, and can adjust it for the next one.

I would advise against choosing a philosopher to help out in the fashion department. Consult an honest and experienced salesperson who has the skills to draw out your ideas and feelings on the matter to help you narrow down the choices to something manageable in the time you have allotted, and then has the good sense to leave you alone to discover which one suits you best. This is what a good teacher of philosophy does. He trots out Plato's cave, Kierkegaard's either-or, Polanyi's from-to, Unamuno's tragic sense of life, the physicist's dual understanding of light, Darwin's theory of evolution, and every other suit of ideas and paradoxes which he figures might intrigue the student enough to start reflecting on the nature of his or her presence in the world.

But deep down every teacher of philosophy believes there is one explanation of the whole—one set of clothes that will fit all. The epistemologist, who specializes in how we know anything, in an apparent disregard for the incredible diversity of learners—those who learn as easily as eating candy, others who fight with ideas like gladiators, those who methodically plod through each lesson, and others who are just confused most of the time—believes the basis of learning is identical for all of us. The problem is coming up with a model or paradigm that can also account for the differences.

To add to both the philosopher's and salesperson's challenge, neither can force the student or the customer into trying on the suit he proposes. The farmers around here say, "You can lead a horse to water, but you can't make it drink." Like the stubborn horse, you might be content to merely skim the images in this book and choose not to dwell in images of the artist burning with emotion, the theorist originating insights, the empiricist patiently grinding out the facts, and the idealist driven by purpose to act. Unfortunately, if you do not eat the food and drink the wine, you will not have anything to digest!

"When eating or drinking, become the taste of the food or drink, and **be filled**."[159]

Moments of ecstasy combined with a sense of purpose can keep a writer going for long periods of time with little support from the outside. But the final proof of the integrity of any unique synthesis of content and energy is in the reader's pleasure in eating and digesting it. Did you share in and enjoy this meal of the quarrelsome quartet? Or were you content to just think about it?

A circle in a spiral, a wheel within a wheel,
Never ending or beginning on an ever-spinning reel,
As the images unwind
Like the circles that you find
In the windmills of your mind.[160]

Notes and References

[1] Mark Van Doren, *The Happy Critic and Other Essays,* 1961, Hill and Wang, New York, pp. 71–72.

Introduction

[2] The expression "accidentally-on-purpose" is sometimes sarcastically used to describe how someone does something nasty to someone on purpose while making it appear accidental. What I mean is the way in which we have to fumble through developing a skill until we get it right, that we can only get it right "accidently," even though we have to work at it to get there.

[3] Scientists and artists define the words "conscious" and "self-conscious" differently. I use them in the sense that the experiences of feeling, thinking, observing, and decision-making separately are forms of 'self-consciousness.' "Consciousness" is the "unself-conscious" integration of all four. For a discussion, see Chapter 4.

[4] John Henry Newman, *The Idea of a University,* 1856.

Chapter 1

[5] B.F. Skinner, "Education in 1984," *New Scientist, 21,* May 1964.

[6] Interestingly, Parkinson's disease is the opposite of Alzheimer's. In Parkinson's, the sufferer loses his automatic skill but not the ability to think things through as in using a map. But in driving a car, the latter has to focus constantly on his driving habits and be thinking about them in order to keep from getting into an accident.

[7] My understanding of Michael Polanyi's theory of knowing comes primarily from his essay "Tacit Knowing," pages 1–25 in his book *The Tacit Dimension* and Chapter 2 in "Personal Knowledge," pages 22–45 in *Meaning,* coauthored with Harry Prosch. I took his "from-to" construct as applied in analyzing the act of perception of stereo photos and developed it to be able to describe a skill in action. Later, in the chapter "Rock 'n' roll of Physics", it is totally transformed into "to-fro-and-around". Ultimately, it grows into a complete cycling through the integration of the quartet.

[8] Thich Nhat Hanh, *The Miracle of Mindfulness,* 1976, Parallax Press, Berkeley, California.

[9] "Mad minutes" are single pages of sixty simple arithmetic calculations each. Typically one set has a page each of addition, subtraction, multiplication, and division. The student must stop and change to the next page at one-minute intervals.

[10] Joanna Field, (Marion Milner), *A Life of One's Own*, 1934, Chatto & Windus, later by Pelican, and later by Anchor Brendon Ltd., Essex, U.K. 1952, p. 176.

Chapter 2

[11] Maigret is the chief inspector in Georges Simenon's detective novels.

[12] In this chapter, I use the word "adrenaline" in the most general sense, that of experiencing any hormonal "rush."

[13] Boethius, *The Consolation of Philosophy*, originally written A.D. 524, Penguin Classics, trans. by Victor Watts, rev. ed. 1999, pp. 8–9

[14] Erasmus, *Praise of Folly*, 1971, Penquin Books.

[15] Thomas Merton, *Cables to the Ace*, 1968, New Directions, p. 14.

[16] Miller, G.A., and P.M. Gildea, "How Children Learn Words," *Scientific American*, 257, (3), pp. 94–99, 1987.

Chapter 4

[17] Kurt Vonnegut, *Timequake*, 1997, G. P. Putnam's Sons.

[18] W. F. Book, "The Psychology of Skill with Special Reference to its Acquisition in Typewriting," PhD Thesis, University of Montana, 1908, republished as one of the "Classics of Psychology," in *The Psychology of Skill: Three Studies*, Arno Press, New York, 1973.

[19] W. F. Book, p. 35–36.

[20] W. F. Book, p. 35.

[21] W. F. Book, p. 95.

[22] W. F. Book, p. 93.

[23] W. F. Book, p. 55.

[24] W. Timothy Gallwey, *The Inner Game of Tennis*, rev. ed. 1974, Random House, New York.

[25] Betty Edwards, *Drawing on the Right Side of the Brain*, 1989, G.P. Putnam's Sons, New York.

[26] Natalie Goldberg, *Writing Down the Bones*, 1986 Shambhala, Boston & London.

[27] W. Timothy Gallwey, *The Inner Game of Tennis*, 1974, Random House, New York, p. 20.

[28] ibid, pp. 24–42.

[29] W. F. Book, p. 17.

[30] W. F. Book, p. 109.

[31] Betty Edwards, p. 48.

[32] W. Timothy Galwey & Bob Kriegel, *Inner Skiing,* 1979, Random House, New York, p. 54.

[33] W. F. Book, p. 99.

[34] W. F. Book, p. 98.

[35] W. F. Book, p. 71.

[36] From Henri, R. *The Art Spirit,* as quoted by Edwards in *Drawing on the Right Side of the Brain,* 1989, G. P. Putnam's Sons, New York, p. 163.

[37] W. F. Book, p. 95.

[38] W. F. Book, p. 99.

[39] R. Lawrence Trask, *Language: the Basics,* 1995, Routledge, U.K. pp. 144–145.

[40] R. Lawrence. Trask, *Language: the Basics,* 1995, Routledge, U.K. p. 149.

[41] From *A Gathering of Poems* ed. by Maxwell Nurnberg, Pocket, 1979.

[42] Even in animals, most of what we used to think was 'instinctual' is actually learned behavior. See *Animals in Translation,* by Temple Grandin and Catherine Johnson, Scribner, 2005.

[43] For a comprehensive explication of why we commonly use the word "instinct" for example in the expression "gut instinct," it would be very useful to revisit Polanyi's idea of "tacit knowledge."

Chapter 5

[44] Harlan Lane, *The Wild Boy of Aveyron,* or Juli Dawson's *Wild Boy.*

[45] This idea of an "age of no return" in a child's learning capability for basic human skills is just as dramatic with the skill of visual perception, but at an earlier stage in development—at the he age of three. See the chapter "To see and not to see" in Oliver Sack's *An Anthropologist on Mars,* Vintage Books, 1995.

[46] We tend to think of puberty as purely a biological clock phenomenon. Is it the final 'push' for this psychological change in early teenhood, or is the cumulative development of self-consciousness itself an integral part of the 'release' and hormonal explosion of the 'demon-genie of sex'—this intense need and desire for 'reunion'?

[47] Closer to home, you might try the same experiment with your favourite television shows. Forget about their content. Ignore the literal meaning of the words. Just focus on isolating the particular nature of the characteristic emotional energies of each player. You'll discover that each show specializes in focusing on a limited gamut of emotions, the range of any one show creating a different overall emotional ambience from that of any other.

[48] This Greek proverb which means "to learn is to suffer," is obviously about adults learning.

Chapter 6

[49] From "Phonology" by Robert E. Callary, in *Language: introductory readings,* edited by Clark, Aschholz, and Rosa, 3rd edition, 1981, St. Martin's Press, New York, p. 290.

[50] "Sounding Your Os and Rs" by William J. Cromie in *Harvard University Gazette,* 2/17/2000.

[51] Michael Polanyi, *The Tacit Dimension,* 1983, Doubleday & Co, pp. 35–36.

Chapter 7

[52] Carl Sandburg, *Harvest Poems,* 1960, Harcourt Brace & Co, p. 16.

[53] William Shakespeare, *As You Like It.*

[54] Monty Roberts, *The Man Who Listens to Horses,* 1998, Vintage Canada, Toronto.

[55] Be careful not to confuse the concept of these "signaling systems" with the sign language of the deaf. Sign language is structured with the same universal grammar as we employ in spoken language.

[56] R. L. Trask, *Language: the Basics,* 1995, Routledge, U.K. p. 6.

[57] Steven Pinker, *The Language Instinct: how the mind creates language,* 1995, Harper Collins, pp. 233–234.

[58] Albert Einstein, *Ideas and Opinions* (1956, London: Alvin Redman), p. 25.

[59] You can make your own rocket from a plastic two-liter pop bottle, a truck tire valve stem, a bicycle pump, and some water in a few minutes. Fill the bottle one-third full of water, push the valve stem about one or two centimeters into the neck, angle the bottle upwards, and start pumping. Be careful. It can easily travel thirty meters.

[60] Mircea Eliade, *Myths, Dreams, and Mysteries,* p. 36.

[61] The "middle way" of Buddhism, the *medan agan* or "golden mean" of Aristotle, or Carl Jung's "midpoint."

Chapter 8

[62] Stephen Jay Gould, *Questioning the Millennium,* Harmony Books, New York 1997, p. 33.

[63] Clifford Stoll, *High-Tech Heretic: why computers don't belong in the classroom and other reflections by a computer contrarian,* Doubleday, New York, 1999, p. 122.

[64] Merleau-Ponty, *Phenomenology of Perception.*

[65] Stanley I. Greenspan, *The Growth of the Mind: and the endangered origins of intelligence,* Perseus Books, Cambridge, Massachusetts, 1997, p. 21.

[66] Hakan Olausson (Sahlgrenska U. Hospital, Sweden) & Dr. Catherine Bushnell (McGill U.) in July or August 2002, Nature Neuroscience. (Nature Neuroscience 2002; 10.1038/nn896).

[67] Tangible feelings of for example pleasure, pain, bitterness or sweetness are not by themselves emotions. They are merely elements from the spectrum of the affective dimension of sensation that we transmute into emotions. For example we feel pain when the impact of that sensation is so strong as to literally overwhelm all the other elements of affective sensation in that moment.

[68] For Dr. Stanley Greenspan, a preeminent child psychologist, it is the failure of dual coding that results in autism.

[69] This version sounds better than the politically correct, "the child is parent of the adult," to modernize Wordsworth's expression "the boy is father of the man."

[70] In textbooks on sensory perception, a dual-purpose sensory system is only acknowledged to exist in the olfactory nerves of the nose—believed to be the first sensory organ to have appeared in the evolution of our senses. (p. 142, David R. Soderquist, *Sensory Processes,* Sage Publications, California, 2002.) You have to go to textbooks on purely medical physiology for the dual evidence on the other senses. (Private communication with Prof. J. Sequin, Dept. of Physiology and Pharmacology, School of Medicine, U.W.O., Canada)

Chapter 9

[71] The colloquial use of "ego" implies an imbalance, as though one member of our quartet is dominating the other three.

[72] Carl Jung, *Memories, Dreams and Reflections,* Harper Colophon, 1959. The closest parallel to this quartet in academic psychology is the Meyers-Briggs Type Indicator. But the MBTI is a descriptive approach, whereas my quartet captures the dynamics of my quartet in action. To use an analogy to biology, the MBTI quartet of pairs of contrasting characteristics is sort of a "botany" of Carl Jung's "mandala" or quaternary of personality. Whereas Jung was focused primarily on psychoanalysis to elucidate and delineate the cornerstones of personality, that is, to "square-the-round," I am focused primarily in psychosynthesis in construing how the corners function together in one cycle, to "round-the-square." Having

rounded the square into a cycle in the last chapter, we can now go backwards from it to get more insight into each of its four corners.

[73] For Greenspan, it is the failure of this bonding or 'dual-coding' that results in autism. I like to think of autism as the failure of the natural cycling through our quartet. Note how it seems the autistic child is stuck in repetitive actions as though he can't make it to the next stage. He can get so stuck, he may become an "idiot savant" who can for example memorize phone books or make astounding mental calculations. Furthermore, the child's language is very mechanical, lacking the proper integration and dynamics necessary between the four modes of knowing to spontaneously generate language.

[74] Antonio R. Damasio, *Descartes Error: emotion, reason, and the human brain,* Harper Collins, 1994.

[75] Michael Polanyi, "The Body and Mind," in *The New Scholasticism 43:2* (Spring 1969) 195–204. The essay (available on the Internet) was adapted from a recording of an address to psychiatrists at Duke University on April 16, 1964. In this article, Polanyi discusses "indwelling."

Chapter 10

[76] M. Polanyi tried to explicate the roles of the theorist and empiricist by themselves as if this pair could be wholly comprehended without explicating the role of their complements—the dynamic duo of artist and idealist. He was very aware of the existence and influence of the latter pair. He never rejected or disparaged their "presence." In fact, this latter pair are profoundly implicit in all his seminal writings, underpinning his very meaning.

[77] I like to think of "shall" as the contraction of "should" and "will", as in "what should be because of what I will it to become." But I suspect that the words "should" and "will" were initially derived from the self-consciousness of the imperative "shall."

[78] From a letter by Einstein to the recently widowed wife of his close friend, Michele Besso.

[79] from the Gloria Patri: "Glory be to the Father and the Son and Holy Spirit, as it was in the beginning, is now, and ever shall be, world without end, Amen."

[80] Joseph Conrad quoted in *The Portable Conrad,* edited by M. D. Zabel, originally pub. 1896, 14th printing by Viking Press, 1947, p. 707.

[81] Miquel de Cervantes, *Don Quixote,* translated by Ron Rutherford, Penguin edition, pub. 2000, p. 46.

Chapter 11

[82] Brewster Ghiselin, *The Creative Process: a symposium,* The New American Library of Canada Ltd., 1965, p. 106.

[83] All de la Mare poems used are from: *Walter de la Mare: Selected Poems,* edited by R.N. Green-Armytage, Faber and Faber, London, 1954.

[84] "A Private Universe" video produced by Harvard-Smithsonian Center for Astrophysics" 1987, ISBN 1-57680-404-6.

[85] from *Anerca,* Ed. Edmund Carpenter, 1959, J.M. Dent & Sons, Toronto.

Chapter 12

[86] Of course, this is true only for those doing this in the Northern Hemisphere.

[87] Mircea Eliade, *Myths, Dreams, and Mysteries,* Harper & Row, 1959.

[88] This description of gravity is too short to give Galileo his due in working out the basics for Newton to expand upon later.

[89] Gary Zukav, *The Dancing Wu Li Masters,* William Morrow and Company, Inc., New York, 1979, p. 49.

[90] Tying a bag of sand on the end of a rope is a safer way of carrying out this experiment. Gradually increase the weight of sand in the bag.

[91] After Newton, scientists should have adopted the term "gravicentric" to integrate and supercede the old distinction between geocentric and heliocentric.

[92] If you prefer Einstein's physics of the noun instead of Newton's of the verb, you will substitute a visualization of distortions in space, caused by the interference of gravitational waves, guiding the motions of the planetary masses through planes of least resistance. We'll come back to this in a later chapter.

[93] Pierre Teilhard de Chardin, *The Phenomenon of Man,* originally pub. in French 1955, English translation pub. by Harper Colophon 1975, p. 264–5.

Chapter 14

[94] To refine this further, note that the angle of earth's orbit to the trajectory of the sun's is about fifty degrees.

[95] Kepler's Law is not valid for the actual distance traveled. It is valid only for the relative area swept out between any two bodies. To be even more exact, it is valid only for the area swept out between a planet and the center of gravity between it and the body it is orbiting, and vice versa.

[96] Isaac Asimov, *Understanding Physics, Volume II, Light, Magnetism and electricity,* p. 139, Barnes and Noble, 1966.

[97] Gary Zukav, *The Dancing Wu Li Masters: an overview of the new physics*, William Morrow and Company, Inc., New York, 1979, p. 116.

Chapter 15

[98] John Dewey, *Experience and Education*, 1938, MacMillan Publishing Co., New York, p. 17.

[99] Sharan B. Merriam & Rosemary S. Caffarella, *Learning in Adulthood: a comprehensive guide*, Jossey-Bass Publishers, San Francisco, 1991, p. 160.

[100] as quoted in *Psychology Today: An Introduction*, 3rd ed., New York, CRM/ Random House, 1975, p. 68 in Robert D. Nye's book, *What is B. F. Skinner Really Saying?*, 1979, Prentice-Hall, New Jersey, p. 32.

[101] Dorothy Singer and Tracey Revenson, *A Piaget Primer: how a child thinks*, Plume/Penquin, Rev. ed. 1996, p. 18.

[102] Jean Piaget, *Intelligence and Affectivity: their relationship during child development*, (trans. into English by T. A. Brown and C. E. Kaegi), 1981, Annual Reviews Inc., Palo Alto, California.

[103] My interpretation of the development—increasing differentiation—of the mental structures is correlated with greater self-consciousness from the most general to the most particular in all four modes. In effect, it becomes more and more difficult to return to the original less-differentiated state which allowed the infant to initiate language—our most comprehensive and integrative feat of learning.

[104] Though Piaget was very aware and appreciative of the lively and curious intelligence at the center of the learner, conceptually he was trapped within a dualistic framework to explain it. I like to think that he would have preferred my four-way model that allows intelligence to emerge naturally through interaction with the world, instead of being genetically directed.

[105] Of course as an adult, she is making her choices with lots of assistance from her cultural heritage, peers, guardians, mass media, etc., just as the rest of the quartet does. The older we get, the more experiences and knowledge we have to take into account to draw our conclusions. But as an infant—psychologically within the "seamless whole," innocent of the big picture—reality was much more immediate, simpler, and direct.

[106] Will Durant, *The Story of Philosophy*, 1926, Simon and Shuster, New York, p. 487.

[107] 'Occam's Razor,' attributed to William of Occam (1285–1350) is also called the "Law of Parsimony." It holds that the simplest explanation is usually the best.

Chapter 16

[108] My response to Einstein's remark on a completely different subject in the Born letter "I am convinced that He does not play dice."

[109] Interestingly, Arther Koestler states that "contrary to popular belief, Darwin had no objection [to] the 'inheritance of acquired characteristics'—decried as moral heresy by neo-Darwinians. On the contrary, in his *Variations of Animals and Plants under Domestication,* and in the later editions of the *Origin,* he gave a series of examples of what he believed to be inherited characteristics in the off-spring, due to adapative changes in their ancestors. But he refused to accept adaptations as the only, or even the main cause of evolution." (*Acts of Creation,* Arkana/Penguin, 1964, p. 137—8.)

[110] Edward J. Steele, Lindley, R.A. & Blanden, R.V., *Lamarck's Signature: how retrogenes are changing Darwin's natural selection paradigm,* Perseus Books, Reading, Massachusetts, 1998.

[111] Ibid. p. 196.

[112] There have been others before Steele's work. The best-known controversy is centered around the suicide of biologist Paul Kammerer who was accused of scientific fraud for his experiments with the inheritance of acquired sexual characteristics in the midwife toad. For an account of his tragic story, see Arthur Koestler's *The Case of the Midwife Toad,* Hutchinson London, 1971.

[113] Francis Hitching, *The Neck of the Giraffe: Darwin, evolution and the new biology,* A Mentor Book, pub. by The New American Library, 1983, p.65.

[114] Richard Milton, *Shattering the Myths of Darwinism,* 1997, Park Street Press, Rochester, Vermont.

[115] Polanyi, Michael, *The Tacit Dimension,* Doubleday & Company, 1983, pp. 37–38.

[116] Jerry Baker is the author of popular books on the emotions of plants.

[117] Or to implement the double-blind experimental technique to eliminate its influence, as used in medical science to test new drugs. Health researchers knowing the powerful influence of consciousness—whether as caring or belief—attempt to eliminate it as a factor by using the double-blind placebo methodology in testing their new drugs. Both the real medicine and the placebo are made physically identical. The dispenser of the placebo to the control group and the real medicine to the guinea pig group is not allowed to know which bottle has the real stuff, nor who belongs to which group.

[118] From Carl Sandburg's poem "Laughing Corn" in *Harvest Poems.*

[119] At the present, though there is no widely accepted theory of evolution, it is an exciting field with many intriguing approaches like Hans Driesch's "vitalism" and Rupert Sheldrake's "morphic resonance." A more encompassing view is described in *The Universe Story* by Brian Swimme and Thomas Berry, Harper Collins, 1992.

Chapter 17

[120] Polanyi, Michael, *Personal Knowledge: towards a postcritical philosophy*, 1958, The University of Chicago Press, Chicago, p. 3.

[121] Richard Dawkins, *The Selfish Gene*, Oxford Univ. Press, 1976, p.2.

[122] Richard Dawkins, *The Selfish Gene*, Oxford Univ. Press, 1976.

[123] S. Jay. Gould, *Life's Grandeur*, Vintage Books, London, 1997, pp. 221–222.

[124] Steven Pinker, *How the Mind Works*, Penguin Books 1999, p. 528.

[125] Check out the video game "The Wild Divine." It works through biofeedback mechanisms.

Chapter 18

[126] Robert C. Solomon, 1983. *The Passions.* Notre Dame, Ind.: University of Notre Dame Press.

[127] Kierkegaard's "Either—Or".

[128] William Shakespeare, *Othello*, v. ii, li. 345.

[129] William Shakespeare, *King Henry IV, Part II*, I, ii, li. 227.

[130] If you get yourself into a similar situation, please don't do this. Go to prison and become a literacy teacher or go to a big city and work in the slums. I'm sure Shakespeare would approve. He had only a few hours to present the whole story of Othello, so he had to make a quick end to the thing before the audience got tired and decided to go home. He therefore had to figure out how to show Othello atoning for his heinous sin in only a few minutes. That's theater. We have the rest of our lives.

[131] ditto, li. 399.

[132] The character of the Lone Ranger, originated by Fran Striker, first played on radio in 1933 and transitioned to television in 1949.

[133] For example, William Faulkner reread it annually.

Chapter 20

[134] Victor Frankl, *Man's Search for Meaning: an introduction to logotherapy*, 1959, rev. 1986 (3rd edition) a Touchstone Book, pub. By Simon & Shuster, p. 75.

[135] Paraphrased from the ballad "Alice's Restaurant Massacree" on the album "The Best of Arlo Guthrie."

[136] Henri Bergson, *Creative Evolution,* trans. by Arthur Mitchell, 1920, Mac-Millan Co., p. 283.

[137] Michael Polanyi, *Personal Knowledge: towards a postcritical philosophy,* 1958, The University of Chicago Press, Chicago p. 266.

[138] Margaret Visser, *The Geometry of Love: space, time and meaning in an ordinary church,* 2000, HarperCollins, Toronto, Canada.

[139] Establishing a 50–50 basis of reciprocity between blue- and green-skin is impossible if the blue-skin is the only representative of his culture within the green's culture, e.g., the blue-skin working in a foreign land. The green-skin, not being able to study him in interaction with other blue-skins, can't grasp the dynamics of how the visiting blue-skin is acting. If the blue-skin doesn't realize this, he feels anger by the green-skin's inability in accepting him for what he 'really' is, and being treated warily, as we do any stranger.

[140] Daisetz T. Suzuki, in the Introduction to *Zen in the Art of Archery* by Eugen Herrigel, Vintage Books, 1989.

[141] John Donne, "Meditation XVII: No man is an island."

[142] Edited by Edmund Carpenter, *Anerca,* 1959, J.M. Dent & Sons, Toronto.

[143] Blaise Pascal, *Pensees,* translated by A.J. Krailsheimer, 1966, Penguin Books, p. 92.

[144] Boethius, *The Consolation of Philosophy,* written in A.D. 524, translated by Victor Watts, revised edition, Penguin Books, 1999, p. 6.

[145] Miguel de Unamuno, *The Tragic Sense of Life,* 1921, translated by J.E. Crawford Flitch, 1954, Dover Publications, New York, p. 262.

[146] from "Wolves", a poem by Louis MacNiece.

Chapter 21

[147] Mircea Eliade, *Myths, Dreams, and Mysteries,* Harper & Row, 1956, p. 36.

Chapter 22

[148] Galileo, p.83 in *Galileo's Daughter* by Dava Sobel, Penguin Books, 1999.

[149] Ivor Armstrong Richards, *The Philosophy of Rhetoric,* 1936.

[150] Charles Dickens, *Hard Times.*

[151] Patricia L. Smith and Tillman J. Ragan, *Instructional Design* (Maxwell Mac-Millan, 1993, p. 173).

[152] To make sure that new generations are 'protected' from this dangerous tendency, note how little poetry students are exposed to in the modern school cur-

riculum as compared to previous times. The memorization of poetry does not fit into task 'objective' outlines. Poetry's spontaneous 'combustible' nature is the antithesis of useful fact and directed programming. I suspect it is this very nature that explains why so many of our elders value the poetry that they were induced to learn as children. When depressed, confused and world-weary, they can recall those poems, prayers and songs, and feel up-lifted and revived, without digging into a bottle of Prozac pills.

[153] Thomas Merton, *The Way of Chuang Tzu*, New Directions, 1969, p. 17.

[154] Clark E. Moustakas, 1990, *Heuristic Research: Design, Methodology, and Applications.* Sage Productions, Newbury Park, CA. p.13.

[155] Moustakas, p.14.

[156] Hans Seyle, *From Dream to Discovery, On being a scientist,* New York, McGraw-Hill, 1964.

[157] From Dylan Thomas's poem "In My Craft or Sullen Art."

[158] Thomas Merton p. 29.

[159] from *Zen Flesh, Zen Bones: a collection of Zen and pre-Zen writings,* compiled by Paul Reps, Doubleday Anchor.

[160] From the song "The Windmills of Our Minds" by Berger and LeGrand.

Outline of Subtitles

Introduction: An obsession with a question: rooting for memories of the phoenix…the child's secret…a roundabout step-by-step process…a workbook of intuitions

A: Doing

Chapter 1 An anatomy of skill: the effortless skill of driving…idea fused with emotion…a warning to experimenters…mad minutes of math…typing without crutches…learning to sing…teachers forgetting the questions

Chapter 2 Danger and delight in insight : the study of vacuum cleaners…the goose of learning…the sock problem…Archimedes' bath study…the art and rush of bingo…the drama of organized play…fool's gold…emotions for sale…adrenalin and frameworks

Chapter 3 The art of dune buggy racing: learning to fly…opposite frames of reference…the dune buggy racer and the video game player…working to "zone" in reading…becoming the song

Chapter 4 Learning to type and talk: a progression of purposive accidents…remember the goose?…intuitions and the right questions…conscious, self-conscious, unconscious or un-self-conscious?…the progressive emergence of skill…gene-actualization or creativity?…instincts or emotions?

B: Language

Chapter 5 Reflections on learning a foreign language: re-learning to play…emotional rhythms and punctuation…parrot or genius?…"mathein pathein"

Chapter 6 The syllable: marriage of consonant and vowel the alphabet and phonetics…from cooing to babbling…language as tool or archetype?

E: Science

Chapter 13 **The pigeonholing of knowledge:** the quartet in Thailand...four pigeonholes of knowledge...spice and salt: mystics and bean counters

Chapter 14 **The theorist and empiricist of astronomy and light:** observing the solar system from the stars...steady state or pulsating orbits?...from equal and opposite forces to gravitational waves...'seeing' and 'feeling' the light...from wave and particle to photon...the meta-physics of duality

Chapter 15 **Nature and nurture meet the emotional duo:** Self-actualization or external discipline?...the theorist's thoughtful robot...the behaviourist's wild cards...puppet of nature and nurture, or freedom fighter...the theorist vs. the artist...the empiricist vs. the idealist...two styles of science and the pragmatist...from pragmatist to philosopher

Chapter 16 **War over the bones of creation:** an awkward discrepancy...anger and confusion over the bones of creation...Darwinian genes vs. Lamarckian retrogenes...accidental, conditioned, spontaneous and purposeful evolution...Gould's *"punctuated equilibria"* and Bergson's *'élan vital'*...stones and the living...non-sense vs. a playful mischief...timelines of geology vs. biology...biology: the study of *"a high majestic fooling?"*

Chapter 17 **Is there a mediator in the house?** Dawkins' ghost in a machine...Gould ostracizes Lamarck...Wilson's consilience and conscience...haunted robot or aspiring quartet?

F: Literature

Chapter 18 **The Righteous vs. the Mischievous:** the gravity of commitment and the moment-um of fancy...Othello and Falstaff: heroic warrior and cowardly dreamer...righteous murderer and merry companion...means or ends, virtue or ideal?

Chapter 19 **Ideal vs. virtual reality:** a knightly bookworm and a naïve farmer...Quixote the real and Lone Ranger the fakir...Quixote the warrior and Sancho the healer...Othello and Quixote: the empiricist and the theorist as lovers...in the end

Chapter 20 **Belief in metaphors and the facts of life:** the love of song and the purpose of war...fingering the moon...dreams and experiences...belief in science...religious ritual...our own facts: the "blue-skins" vs. the "green-skins"..."I" as an individual and as everyman...between nothing and everything: discovery, losing it and what to do?

G: Two conclusions

Chapter 21 **Paradise lost: the rupture of time:** Adam and Eve with children and the coming of Dawn...children as mirrors to our past...from infant to adult and back

Chapter 22 **Cooking up and digesting metaphor and fact:** the quartet at loggerheads...poetic and scientific metaphors...idealistic and empirical facts...from smoke to glass sculptures...the journey...eureka?

978-0-595-34615-8
0-595-34615-4

Printed in the United States
33309LVS00004B/94-108